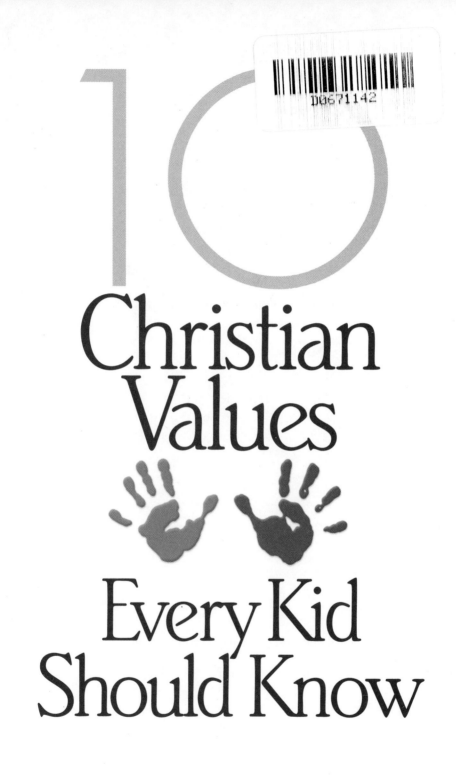

10

Christian Values

Every Kid Should Know

ALSO BY
DONNA J. HABENICHT
How to Help Your Child Really Love Jesus

To order, call
1-800-765-6955.

Visit our website at
www.rhpa.org
for information on other Review and Herald products.

10 Christian Values

Every Kid Should Know

A HOW-TO GUIDE FOR FAMILIES

BY
DONNA J. HABENICHT, ED.D.

REVIEW AND HERALD® PUBLISHING ASSOCIATION
HAGERSTOWN, MD 21740

The author assumes full responsibility for the accuracy of all facts
and quotations as cited in this book.

This book was
Edited by Penny Estes Wheeler
Copyedited by Delma Miller and James Cavil
Designed by Trent Truman
Electronic makeup by Shirley M. Bolivar
Cover design by GenesisDesign/Bryan Gray
Typeset: Berkeley Book 11/14

PRINTED IN U.S.A.

04 03 02 01 00   5 4 3 2 1

R&H Cataloging Service
Habenecht, Donna J
    10 Christian values every kid should know: a how-to guide for families

    1. Values.   2. Moral education.   3. Religious education.   4. Christian education.
I. Title

                         303.3

ISBN 0-8280-1506-6

This book is
lovingly dedicated to

Herald, Larry, Nancy,
Debbie, Bruce, Liza, Jeffery,
Jonathan, and David

Acknowledgments

When I was a graduate student at Andrews University I took a class about character development from Ruth Murdoch, my adviser and mentor. She inspired me to delve deeply into this subject. For 17 years I have taught this same class to graduate students. We have a lot of fun exploring how children and adolescents develop values and a strong moral character and how the process continues during adulthood. Our discussions have challenged and inspired me.

My students from the winter 1999 class contributed a great deal to this book. They wrote many of the scenarios from real life and contributed to some of the general guidelines for specific values. I want to thank each one personally for their contribution: Marcia Azevedo, Brett Carnduff, Pablo Huerfano, Israel Jean-Leone, Hillman St. Brice, Fred Toaloa, and Cynthia White. I especially want to thank Israel for the additional scenarios and guidelines he wrote during his spring break.

Many other people contributed to this book. I could not have written it without the support of the School of Education at Andrews University. My special thanks go to Karen Graham, the dean, and to Elsie Jackson and my other colleagues in the Department of Educational and Counseling Psychology. Their support was essential. Ralph Schroder, my graduate assistant, provided invaluable help at the computer and in the library.

Tim Crosby encouraged me to sign a contract for this book. Without that contract I fear the book might never have been written. Jeannette Johnson kept me writing when I wanted to give up. She put up with too many deadline delays. Penny Estes Wheeler edited and encouraged and served as liaison with the Review and Herald. Thank you for your patience.

I want to thank the parents who have attended my workshops, the families I have counseled, the students in my classes, and my close friends. They have challenged my thinking and shared their experiences. The stories in this book are about real people, but I have changed names and identifying details to protect their privacy. A few of the stories originally appeared in columns I have written for *Our Little Friend* and *Parent Talk*.

My family made this book possible. When I was a child, my parents provided me with an environment in which I could develop strong Christian values. My husband has been my greatest supporter and cheerleader. Our children and grandchildren taught me a great deal about how values and character develop in the crucible of daily family life. Larry and Debbie graciously provided me with a room overlooking the Caribbean, where I began this book. Nancy and Bruce gave encouragement and friendship along the way and shared family experiences. Our grandchildren are the heroes of some of the stories.

To everyone, thank you!

Contents

A Word to the Reader

Values and character have been "hot" topics during the last decade. We have been bombarded with the immoral actions of government officials, high school kids, securities traders, and sometimes even our friends. Books on how to teach values to children have hit the top of the New York *Times* best-seller list. Everyone talks about the "character" of elected officials and teenagers.

God, in His Word, has plenty to say about values and character. I think it's time we listened. As we begin a new millennium nothing could be more important than helping our children learn basic Christian values to guide their lives.

This book is divided into two main parts. The first part, "The Values Tree," focuses on general guidelines for teaching values to children. They are the foundation from which the specific values emerge. The second part, "The Fruits of the Values Tree," looks at 10 important Christian values I believe every kid should live by, a chapter for each value. These chapters are like a sourcebook where you can go for information about a specific value.

Each chapter describes a value, looks at God's view of the value, and provides general guidelines for helping children develop this value. Most chapters also have focused guidelines for teaching different aspects of the value. Each chapter has a section on how to help children who have trouble with this value. The "Trouble?" sections cover many areas of concern to families—disrespect, hyperactivity, laziness, irresponsibility, temper tantrums, drugs, dating, divorce, and others. The chapters end with ideas for family activities, quotable wisdom, nature trails, and everyday trails for helping children latch on to this value as their own and embrace it for living.

God wants to bless us and our children with His wisdom. May His Spirit be with you as you read.

—Donna J. Habenicht

PART 1:

THE VALUES TREE:

How to Help Children Learn Values

CHAPTER 1

The Values Tree

Blessed is the man who does not walk in the counsel of the wicked. . . . But his delight is in the law of the Lord. . . . He is like a tree planted by streams of water. . . . Whatever he does prospers. Ps. 1:1-3.

I love pussy willows. Rubbing my fingers across their soft fuzziness makes me feel good, and they add a special touch to bouquets. When we moved to southern Michigan, I saw my chance to have all the pussy willows I wanted, for the plants loved our soil and climate. Almost overnight I saw new growth, and by the third or fourth year, my pussy willow bushes looked like trees. They were as tall as our two-story house. Of course, in the springtime, all the pussy willow branches I wanted to cut were out of reach at the top of the "trees."

The gardening consultant I spoke with advised me to chop the "trees" off about one foot above the ground. I shuddered. How ruthless! I couldn't chop down my lovely pussy willow trees. Would they grow again? But I couldn't reach the blossoms, and the lower part of the "trees" did look rather sparse. Finally I decided to follow the consultant's advice, and one afternoon we chopped them off a foot from the ground. To my surprise, the following year they grew into round, full, beautiful pussy willow bushes, much more attractive than before. What seemed so harsh was the best thing for them.

Growing a child is a lot like growing a tree. What does it take to grow a healthy tree? Good genetic stock, the best soil for that tree, water, fertilizer, occasional pruning, sunshine, and protection from storms.

What does it take to grow a child? **Good genetic stock.** Just as some children are tall and others short, research has shown some are naturally more compassionate than others. It comes with their genetic makeup, just as it is easier for some children to resist peer pressure and to be responsible workers. It comes with their inborn personality.

Does that mean others cannot learn these basic values? Of course not! But most likely more teaching and practice will be needed, more leaning on God. We take what we get in children, remembering that each one is a special child of God with unlimited potential.

The match between parents and child is the **"soil"** in which our children grow. Alexander Thomas and Stella Chess, lifetime researchers on child temperament, call this match "goodness of fit." As we look at our children's temperaments, we quickly see that some are easier to teach than others. As for those with difficult temperaments, we must make many adjustments in our home environment for them to prosper and grow.

Children also need the **sunshine** of our love and warmth, daily **watering** with gentle teaching from God's Word and life's experiences, the boost of the **fertilizer** of special teaching experiences, the **pruning** of discipline, and **protection** from strong winds and storms that are more than they can bear.

Some children need more protection than others. Some need more teaching or more discipline or more watering. But they all have the potential to grow sturdily in God's garden. Some children are like palm trees, others like oak or maple trees. They will grow at different rates and in different ways, but each has the potential to be strong and beautiful in God's time.

Growing a child with strong Christian values—a tree growing by a stream of water, a tree that will prosper as described in Psalm 1—is not easy in a decidedly secular world. As Robert Coles, who has decades of research experience with American children, said in *Family Weekly* 15 years ago, "children need more than good food, a nice physical environment and psychological understanding; they need to learn ethical principles—a firm notion of what they ought to do, and what they ought not to do, and why." He went on to say that children "need to believe in something beyond themselves, in principles and purposes that transcend their personal lives."

In the end each person must know "what she lives for, what she believes in, what she will stand by through thick and thin." Values are important because they provide a basis for all decisions and actions during life. Values play a central role in life. Values are who I am. They become my character, the real inner person. They are expressed in what I do and how I act.

A strong Christian value system will be of immeasurable worth to your children throughout their lives. It will light the dark moments of decision, point the way to the path of integrity, and keep their souls in tune with God. Values provide a sense of purpose for life. They direct the means and ends of actions. They are standards of conduct. They are qualities of the soul. They matter in every aspect of life.

Without sound values and beliefs children do not know what they believe or who they are, and their self-image suffers. When children have solid Christian values they feel loved, accepted, and secure; they make responsible choices and feel approved by their family and community. Their self-respect blossoms.

Values are not just personal preferences. Whether I like blue or red, suits or business casual, short or long hair, Shaker or modern furniture, Escorts or Geos, draperies or miniblinds or both, is simply a matter of personal likes and dislikes. My core values might be expressed in how much I pay for any of these items or how important they are to me. If maintaining a "perfect" home is a more important value to me than nurturing my children's spiritual growth, I will act out my core value by spending more time on cleaning and decorating than on teaching my children. If my career is more important to me than nurturing a relationship with my husband, I will act out this value by spending more of my time on my career. How I spend my money loudly announces my core values.

Whether I prefer a campfire or a fire in a fireplace, as one of the items in a popular values clarification activity asks, is a matter of personal preference. It is not a moral value. Another values clarification activity asks whether I prefer to be Virginal Virginia or Mattress Millie. *That* choice is based on moral values—purity, self-control, and respect—not just personal preference. My values are expressed in whether I choose to have sex with my boyfriend, even though we're both only 16 and nowhere near to making a marital commitment, or whether I choose to be a virgin when I marry. The hormones pull me toward sex, but my strong values of purity, self-control, and respect help me make that decision. The strength of my values will determine whether it is an easy or difficult decision.

Strong moral values are in short supply today. We see immorality proclaimed in newspapers, TV programs, news magazines, and advertisements. The lives of people around us—and maybe sometimes our own living— make us wonder, "What happened to moral and ethical values centered in God?" People just don't seem to be aware that their decision involves a moral or ethical value with important consequences for themselves and others.

Kayla was the proud possessor of a new D.D.S. degree and eager to establish her own dental practice. After a long search for a location, she found two established dentists who were willing to share their facilities. All indicators seemed favorable—the area was not saturated with dentists, the office was conveniently located with adequate parking, and the financial arrangements satisfactory.

So Kayla went about the process of marketing her services. She announced her new practice location through the newspapers. Friends distributed cards at their places of business and told their friends. She posted convenient late-afternoon and evening hours to lure prospective patients and hired a chair-side assistant.

But no patients came. A practice is primarily built by word of mouth from satisfied patients, so Kayla worried as the weeks went by. She needed a few patients to get that word-of-mouth recommendation started. Each week the office receptionist shook her head and said no one had called requesting an appointment.

After many weeks of diligent marketing efforts with no results, Kayla began to get suspicious. So she asked one of her friends to phone for an appointment. A honey-voiced receptionist cooed, "I'm so sorry. Dr. Kayla has no openings for months. But Dr. B and Dr. S have openings. Would you like to see one of them?"

End of mystery. What happened to honesty and integrity? In business, is anything OK? What has happened to kindness and compassion, responsibility, loyalty, and commitment, and other moral values? Where have they gone?

Teaching your children to live by Christian values is your most important responsibility as parents. How can you be most successful in teaching Christian values to your children? Turn to the Values Tree. First, we will examine how to teach values in general, and then we will focus on how to teach specific core values for Christian families.

FAMILY ACTIVITIES

The following activities will help you learn about family members' favorite things: colors, shapes, animals, books, stories, games, vacation places, friends, foods, Bible stories, Bible verses, helping story, and anything else you can think of.

My Favorite Color: One person tells their favorite color and then everyone else can name as many things as they can think of that are that color. Make a poster for that person about her favorite color by pasting magazine pictures of things that are that color on a large poster board. Write the person's name at the top of the poster.

My Favorite Things: Make a poster for each family member, pasting a picture of the person at the top of the poster. Each person can work on his or her own poster by finding pictures of their favorite things to paste on the poster. This activity could be part of Family Night each week for a month or it could be part of the first week of each month. Talk about each person's favorite things. Stress that each person is different and so we may like different things. God made us that way. There are no right or wrong favorite things.

My Favorite Bible Verse: Copy each person's favorite Bible verse on a card with their name. Post the cards in conspicuous places about the house. You may add a pretty sticker or sketch stars or flowers around the edge of the card.

Growing a Plant: Help your child plant some seeds, either outdoors or in a pot indoors. Then teach the child how to care for the seeds and later the plants. Talk about what is needed to grow a healthy plant.

Growing a Child: God has a very special garden. He doesn't grow plants—He grows children in His garden. How does God help each child grow a strong character? (Explain to young children that character is what you are and how you act.) For 6- to 12-year-olds explain the analogy between growing a tree and growing a child as described in this chapter. Your family could illustrate each thing (soil, rain, sunshine, etc.) with pictures, or the children could make up a little skit about each one—the funnier the better.

The responsibility of parents is not toward their children's happiness, but toward their character.

—Haim Ginott

GOD

LIVE the values

TEACH the values

PROTECT your child's mind

MAKE right and wrong very clear

DEVELOP self-respect and confidence

GIVE lots of practice in making decisions

SHOW your child how to deal with peer pressure

MAKE

GOD

REAL

CHAPTER 2

Values Begin With God

The things that are important to people are worth nothing to God. Luke 16:15, ICB.

Notice that the Values Tree begins and ends with God. From the root system, through the trunk, to the growing tip of each branch God is the life of the tree. Without the life-giving sap flowing through the tree's structure carrying nutrients, the tree dies.

Without God, values die. This is evident all around us in our local communities and the world. The world in general has rejected God and His values. Thousands are massacred in Rwanda and other countries. An African-American high school honor student is killed by classmates who resented the standard of achievement she was setting. Two high school students enter their school and kill 12 students and a teacher. The AIDS epidemic escalates.

According to the Barna Research Group, who have conducted extensive surveys of young people published in their *Generation Next,* three quarters of adults and youth believe that truth is relative to the situation and people. They believe that there are no absolute moral truths. More than half of the youth say that lying is sometimes necessary. Many believe that suicide is simply one of the many choices available to a thinking young person. Eighty-two percent have had sex with the opposite sex by age 19. Before graduating from high school, one fifth of all students will have had at least four sex partners. More than 1 million teenagers are expected to contract a sexually transmitted disease each year.

A large number of marriages end in divorce. Millions of babies are born to single mothers. Football games are more important than family devotions. Careers are more important than family relationships.

We live in a post-Christian, or postmodern, society without a central core of values. We are pressured every day to accept anything, anyone, any actions, any deviancy, as OK. Otherwise we are labeled "prejudiced."

A post-Christian society has no anchor for values, beliefs, and actions. The individual is autonomous and the ultimate source of authority, since pluralism believes that all truth is relative. This attitude has resulted in downgrading the Christian moral values that have held society together.

God is no longer the source of values for most people. Values begin with *me,* not God. As Christians we can easily be seduced by the *me* values without realizing what is happening to us. They are pervasive, everywhere and in everything. *My needs* are most important—my career, my sexual desires, my appearance, my status, what I want to do. Take care of yourself first. Don't help other people too much or put their needs before your own or you will be codependent, and the list goes on.

Society emphasizes values that are false in God's sight: athletics, materialism, physical appearance, and status. Even though some of them have good aspects, all of these values emphasize *me*—what *I* can do, what *I* own, how *I* look, how important *I* am. They are self-centered. Such values are a big reason our children suffer from poor self-esteem, for they emphasize externals and result in a constant negative comparison of self to others.

In December 1994 *Parent Magazine* published the results of a survey they conducted, "What Are Your Family Values?" Seven thousand people responded. The top 10 values chosen by respondents were: basic ideas of right and wrong, importance of education, standards of sexual behavior, tolerance, marriage and family, friendship, good manners and social behavior, achieving individual potential, religious beliefs, and need for hard work and delayed gratification.

These parents stated that they would feel most distressed if their child was convicted of a violent crime, regarded people of other racial and ethnic groups as inferior, used illegal drugs, was convicted of white-collar crime, and never finished high school.

On the other hand, they would be less alarmed if their child became an atheist, lived in a homosexual relationship, had a child outside of marriage, lived with someone of the opposite sex without getting married, got divorced, never had any children, and never got married. These respondents clearly reflected the emphasis in our society on tolerance for ethnic, racial, and sexual differences, and the sexual behaviors emphasized by the sexual revolution.

Values that begin with God are sometimes drastically different from the secular values that surround us. Are we willing to pay the price to follow God's values? What if that price means being less popular? Or less successful in our job? What if it means being peaceful and humble instead of aggressive? being self-controlled instead of acting out all our impulses and desires? being kind and compassionate even though it inconveniences us? being honest when it hurts? remembering our marital commitment when we want out?

In June 1994 *Good Housekeeping* magazine published the results of their Happy Marriage Contest. The winning words of Mr. and Mrs. Dillon Bayes were:

"We gave . . . when we WANTED to receive.
We served . . . when we WANTED to feast.
We shared . . . when we WANTED to keep.
We listened . . . when we WANTED to talk.
We submitted . . . when we WANTED to reign.
We forgave . . . when we WANTED to remember.
We stayed . . . when we WANTED to leave."

What are God's values? God is not hesitant to let us know. In Scripture He gives us a condensed version of principles to guide our living: Galatians 5:22, 23; 2 Peter 1:5-7; 1 Corinthians 13; Exodus 20; Matthew 5:3-11; Romans 12, to name a few.

When I was preparing to write this book, I searched many different places for lists of core values—the most important ones. I discovered a multitude of values from which one might choose. I also asked participants in some of my workshops to decide which are the most important values to teach our children. Their lists were helpful.

I struggled with the biblical values, trying to translate them into words we use today, without losing their biblical meaning. It would have been easy if I could have made an endless list of important values. But I wanted to limit the list of core values for Christian families to 10. I believe these 10 values are essential for living God's way in a secular, postmodern society.

God's values are qualities of the soul, not just outward actions. When your values begin with God, they begin inside of you. God doesn't want you to just act honest. He wants you to *be* honest. Being honest means you abhor dishonesty and live transparently honest. Honesty flies in the face of common business practices or little white lies. If your values are truly qualities of your soul, you will continue to be who you are regardless of how others act.

We cannot generate qualities of the soul—they come from God. He puts them inside us. They come as a natural result of our close friendship with Him. The more we talk with Him, read His words, think about their meaning for us, and listen to His Spirit speaking to our minds, the more we will resemble Him. The better we know Him, the more like Him we become. Our character will reflect our friendship with Him. This is the most important thing to communicate to your children—values come from God. He puts them inside us because we are His friends.

Sometimes the process of planting values in our character hurts. God allows trials and difficulties to come our way because He knows we need to toughen up. The road to learning God's values isn't a straight, smooth, six-lane interstate highway. It is more like a narrow, curvy, rutted, cliff-hanging mountain road. Many people give up. They'd rather travel on the interstate. They forget that the view is at the top of the mountain and God is the driver. They think they have to drive alone, when all they really have to do is trust His driving. He will take them safely to the mountaintop.

Carefully choose the values you want to teach your children. Without value goals for your family, you run the serious risk of meandering all over the values landscape without really teaching anything worthwhile. If you know what values you want to teach your children, you can focus on those and make their teaching meaningful. Your children will come to understand that your family believes in these values, that they come from God's Word and are very important for everyday decisions and actions.

Our values list for Christian families includes: faith in God, respect, responsibility, self-control and moderation, honesty and integrity, kindness and compassion, contentment and thankfulness, patience and perseverance, peace and humility, loyalty and commitment. All of these values are rooted in love—God's love and the love He gives us. Without love in the center of your being, these values cannot be expressed. All of these values are part of the definition of love. That is why it is not on the list. Do they sound like what you want for your children? As you read the chapters about specific values, you will discover that some of your favorites you thought were missing from the list may actually be included, but under a different heading.

FAMILY ACTIVITIES

Select some of these activities to help your children learn more about God and His values:

God's Values: Pick one of the Bible passages that describe God's values (see page 23). Read it with your children, using your favorite version. (Note the reading level of some of the best-known Bible versions: International Children's Version, grade 5; Good News, grade 7.3; New International, grade 7.8; New King James, grade 9; New Revised Standard, grade 10; King James, grade 12.) Make a list of the values mentioned in the passage. Talk about what each one means. Draw a picture or act out the meaning of each one.

A Picture of God: Find Bible verses that describe God or Jesus. Make a list of words that describe God, according to these verses. After you have explained the words, ask younger children to act out what they mean.

Bulletin Board Idea: Make a family bulletin board display about God and Jesus. (Use the verses you found in the above activity, "A Picture of God.") Place a beautiful picture of Jesus in the center and surround it with words and pictures that describe what He is like.

Word Search: Find words that compare God to something else. For example, Jesus said, "I am the bread of life." What does that mean? Why does Jesus say He is like bread? Find out how bread is made. Find out why bread is good to eat. How can we "eat" Jesus, the bread of life? Find a different comparison each time you do the Word Search. You could do a different word each week for a year and not exhaust the possibilities.

Values Search: Read one of the Bible passages suggested on page 23. As a family, watch the evening news or read the news stories in the paper with a focus on values. Analyze the news using the values from the Bible passage. How many did you find? How many opposites did you find? For example, 2 Peter 1:5-7 mentions brotherly kindness. While fighting is the opposite of brotherly kindness, distributing blankets to the homeless clearly shows kindness.

Values Tree: Start making a Values Tree for your family bulletin board. Your children could draw a large tree on butcher paper or make it from construction paper. Help them write some of God's values on the trunk and at the tip of each branch.

Values in My Heart: Cut a large heart from red construction paper. Paste a picture of Jesus in the middle. Talk about the values your family wants Jesus to put in your hearts. Write the values on the heart, or draw pictures of them. You could do one each night for family worship time.

Storms make a strong tree; testings make a strong Christian.

—*Uncle Ben's Quotebook*

KEYS TO CHOOSING GOD'S VALUES

1. Choose core values for your family from God's Word. Be sure your values come from God.

2. Reject values that do not come from God. Be sure your children understand the difference.

3. Teach children that sometimes they will be different from other children because they choose to live God's values.

4. Focus on values as qualities of the soul. Ask God to plant His values in your family.

5. Study divine character. Cultivate a close friendship with Jesus.

6. Provide many opportunities for children to focus on God's values.

GOD

LIVE the values

TEACH the values

PROTECT your child's mind

MAKE right and wrong very clear

DEVELOP self-respect and confidence

GIVE lots of practice in making decisions

SHOW your child how to deal with peer pressure

MAKE

GOD

REAL

CHAPTER 3

Live the Values

Each tree is recognized by its own fruit. . . . The good man brings good things out of the good stored up in his heart. . . . For out of the overflow of his heart his mouth speaks. Luke 6:44, 45.

One of my favorite cartoons shows a boy answering the doorbell. It's the newspaper kid, come to collect. The boy turns to his mother, standing just out of sight, and asks, "Do you want me to tell him you're not here again?" It's today's lesson in honesty, and junior is a quick learner.

Living the values you want to teach your children is the most effective and important way to get your point across. As a parent you are always teaching values, whether you want to or not. It happens every day, many times a day, and in many different ways.

Who you are is more important than what you teach. Someone has wisely said, "Children are natural mimics—they act like their parents in spite of every attempt to teach them otherwise!" Are you having trouble teaching your kids to be kind and courteous? Stop and listen to yourself. Run a tape recorder during late afternoon and evening to see how you sound. Do you say "please" and "thank you" to your spouse and children? Is your "home person" as courteous as your "business person"? If not, well, your children will become what you are, not what you say they should be.

The real person is who you are at home. If you came to family life with any hidden personality weaknesses, the pressures of parenting will surely uncover each and every one. You hear yourself saying and doing things you swore you'd never do to your kids! Wow, who's that angry person who just lost control? Surely not *me!*

Maybe you and your spouse don't agree on values issues. He thinks a little white lie doesn't matter and she believes in strict truthfulness. He believes children must learn to be aggressive and competitive if they are going to succeed in business, and laughs at her stress on peace and humility. She wants entertainment and he wants quiet times at home. If you and your spouse disagree on very many of the core values, you have a difficult job ahead just to keep the marriage together. I believe that a shared core of values is vital to the success of a marital relationship. Your children will also be getting mixed messages about values. You live it one way and your spouse another. A tough situation, but not totally impossible.

The values message *is* much stronger when both Mom and Dad live it. But God is equal to any difficult situation. Pray a lot and build your friendship with Jesus. Make your values attractive. Stress the happiness that comes from living God's values. Have a lot of fun times with your children. Agree with your spouse, if you possibly can. Save the battles for the really important values. Provide opportunities for your children to get acquainted with other adults who model Christian values.

So shall we give up teaching values because it's so hard to live them? Of course not! We'll take steps to change.

First, go to the Lord with this problem. He knows how to change your personality weakness into a strength. He can change you from the inside out. That's the only kind of change that really sticks. Every personality trait is two-sided when it comes to parenting. If Mom or Dad has strong impetuous feelings, they may have trouble controlling their on-the-spot anger, which is difficult for kids to handle. But they may also hug and kiss, laugh, and fill life with instant joy, which kids love. God will help you use your strength more often and soften your weakness.

When you're wrong, admit to your spouse and children that you aren't perfect yet. "I goofed. I'm sorry. Please forgive me. I'll try to do better next time." Admitting your mistakes makes you a real person trying to deal with real problems in everyday life. Your kids will respect you more for being transparent and humble than if you pretend to be perfect when they know you aren't. Children are very forgiving. They forgive and forget quicker than adults do.

If the problem is within your marriage, then get serious about communicating with your spouse and working on the issue. If the marital problem is deep-seated, get professional help—your children are worth it! As far as child rearing is concerned, a strong marriage is more important than superior parenting skills. Children bask in the warm glow and security of a couple who truly love each other. Their loving relationship surrounds the children with an attractive example of God's love and creates an atmosphere of trust that nurtures the best in a child.

Children also absorb the model of other important people in their lives—older siblings, grandparents, teachers, baby-sitters. Younger children look up to their older brothers and sisters and try desperately to copy their behavior. It pays off to spend a lot of time teaching your oldest child. Does your baby-sitter or day-care center worker live the values you want your child to learn? What about your child's schoolteachers? You don't have a choice about grandparents and extended family, but you do have a choice about day care, school, and church. Choose with values in mind.

Make it clear how you live by explaining and pointing out the value. Just living your values is not enough to be absolutely sure children catch on. The research on modeling clearly points out that a model is more effective if she explains what she is doing and why.

For example, it's a blustery winter day and Mom is driving her daughter to school. They're going down a quiet street near their home when Mom almost runs into a large trash barrel that has blown into the middle of the street. Instantly she has a choice: swerve around the obstacle or stop by the side of the road and return the trash can to the neighbor's yard. The neighbor won't know if she returns the container or ignores it, and Alisha is almost late to school. But the weather is getting worse, and the road is slightly slippery. Someone else might come along, and there might be oncoming traffic.

Mom makes a quick decision and turns to park on the side of the road. "I think we'd better get that trash can out of the road," she tells Alisha. "It might cause an accident, or it might get smashed if someone runs into it." They both jump out and quickly haul the trash can to the neighbor's yard and leave it where the wind cannot carry it away again. As they pull out on the road, Mom says, "It's our responsibility to do what we can to make the road safer for someone else and to help our neighbor."

Good deed for the day. But it was more than that. Mom made a values decision—responsibility and kindness are important—and she acted on those values. She also made the values message clear to Alisha by her actions and her explanation of why she acted as she did. Her model was more effective in teaching Alisha because she also took the time to explain what she was doing and why. Alisha was also part of the action.

If your value decision is a tough one, let your children hear you think it through. Talk about the values decision you had to make at work that day and the possible consequences of that decision. Sometimes living your values is difficult. It would be easier to fudge once in a while. But each time you do what you know is right, your values get a little stronger. Living the values becomes a little easier, and your children begin to understand that values are really important. They are worth the effort because they are important to Mom and Dad.

What a family does with their time gives powerful value messages to their children. Take a look at your calendar for the past six months. Work and sleep occupy most of your time. What about the rest? What does your family do with any free time? Your choices give a strong value message.

Adult-child time is the core of teaching values. Today parents spend 40 percent less time communicating with their children than their parents did. Most children are learning their values from other children because their parents don't have time to teach them. Insufficient time and overly scheduled lives keep families on a constant racetrack.

You really have only one chance to teach your child—make it good! Maybe it's time for your family to have a conference and look at your schedules. What are the activities you truly enjoy? Which ones are ho-hum? How many church offices do you hold? How many nights a week are you at committees for school, church, or community activities? How many activities are your children involved in?

As a family decide on some general guidelines for taking control of your lives. Two extracurricular activities are probably enough for most children. If your children are involved in two music lessons a week, swimming lessons, basketball, band, and choir they have too much on their plate. It's enough to cause time indigestion.

For parents who work full-time at demanding jobs or are home-schooling their children, one major community activity is probably enough. Pick the one you find most rewarding and enjoyable and gradually extricate yourself from the rest. You'll have many years for community activities after your children are grown. Right now your most important contribution to the community is rearing children with strong Christian values.

Since the activities of each family member affect the rest of the family, it's a good idea to bring proposed major new activities to a family council. Everyone can examine their calendars and discuss the importance of the proposed new activity. Should something else be deleted? Or can the activity safely be added to your family's activity load? Never say yes on the spot to a new demand. Check it out with your spouse and your family. They are often much more objective about what you can really handle than you are. It will take a while to get your lives under control, but it will be worth the effort.

Today we talk a lot about having "quality time" with our children. Quality time only emerges from fairly large quantities of time together. You can't schedule 10 minutes of "quality time." It simply doesn't happen that way. You must invest heavily in time with your child before you will be rewarded with quality time—the special moments you will always remember, the times you teach values at a deep level.

Because today's children know about time pressures, they also know that time together is very special. You are giving them a gift that no one else can give, a gift that tells them how much you love them in a way that nothing else can.

FAMILY ACTIVITIES

Try some of these activities for insight into the values your children see modeled in your family.

Childhood Memories: Tell your children about a situation you remember from childhood that shows the values your parents lived. Ask your children for a childhood memory story.

Mom's or Dad's Sayings: Write or record on an audiocassette as many of your parents' instructions as you can remember—the things they said repeatedly to guide you. For example, "Birds of a feather flock together." Do you use any of these with your children?

Core Values: Arrange a quiet time with your spouse when you can talk about your values. Begin by each making a list of your 10 most important values. Compare lists. Talk about your differences. Talk about your shared values. Try to come up with a joint list of 10 important values to teach your children. If 10 seems intimidating, start with four or five.

Values at the Workplace: Share an experience with your children about a values decision you had to make on the job, preferably while it is in process so they can really feel you thinking it through. Talk about the consequences of the decision.

KEYS TO LIVING THE VALUES

1. Model the values you want your child to learn.

2. Explain and point out the values you are living.

3. Discuss value decisions family members must make.

4. Be a real person. Admit you aren't always right.

5. Strengthen your marriage. Your marital relationship is a key factor in living the values.

6. Teach your oldest child with great care. He or she will model for younger children.

7. Choose day care, school, and church with values in mind.

8. Unclutter your life and make time for your children.

9. Limit child and adult activities to reasonable amounts.

10. Give your child large amounts of time. Quality time springs from quantity time together.

Values Journal: Begin writing or recording a values journal, recording any experience you have that impacts on your values and how you live them.

When we live what we teach, we are able to teach others to live.
—Andrew Murray

GOD

LIVE the values

TEACH the values

PROTECT your child's mind

MAKE right and wrong very clear

DEVELOP self-respect and confidence

GIVE lots of practice in making decisions

SHOW your child how to deal with peer pressure

MAKE

GOD

REAL

CHAPTER 4

Teach the Values

You shall teach them diligently to your children, and shall talk of them when you sit in your house, when you walk by the way, when you lie down, and when you rise up. . . . You shall write them on the doorposts of your house and on your gates. Deut. 6:7-9, NKJV.

Many years ago I read a story in *Guideposts* about a family who decided to take the instruction in Deuteronomy 6 very seriously. They were constructing a new house that had open-beamed ceilings in all the rooms, so they decided to wood-burn a favorite Bible verse on a supporting beam in each room. The children chose Bible verses for their bedrooms, and the whole family decided on the verses for the common living areas of the home. They also chose a family verse for above the front door.

What a marvelous teaching tool for the entire family. Every day those Bible verses were being etched into the subconscious memory of each family member to become permanent guideposts for their lives.

While living your values is the most powerful way of influencing children, you must also deliberately teach these values. **Teaching reinforces your living model.** Make your teaching forceful, positive, and passionate. Your strong family leadership is crucial for teaching values. It provides a model that your children cannot ignore.

Make your propaganda early! Prepare your child for the future. Teach in anticipation of the decisions and dilemmas you know your children will have. Teach about dating and choosing friends, for example, long before your child is a teenager. Once the hormones start flowing, it is much harder to get your message across. To make the river crossing into adulthood, you must teach your child to be a strong swimmer before he plunges into the raging current of teenage values decisions. It's too late to give swimming lessons then. If your teen is not a strong swimmer, he or she will drown. Many teens do. And you can't hold her on the bank waiting for swimming lessons. The push toward adulthood is inexorable.

In order to pull this off, you need to think ahead. Ask yourself, What is my child likely to confront during the next year? the next two years? Gather ideas from your own growing up years. Read a book about child development. Talk with your friends who have older children. Soon you will have a very good sense of what lies ahead for you and your child. Then you can focus your teaching on the future as well as the present.

There are many ways to teach values. The more different ways you use, the greater you'll reinforcement the value.

1. Focus on the value. Make a systematic plan for teaching values. Focus specifically on one value at a time. You might select a value related to a holiday and focus on one a month. To get you started thinking, on the following page is a list of the values in this book, with a suggested month for each one. Naturally, you could rearrange the values to fit with your local holidays.

Or instead of focusing on a different value each month, focus on values as they come up in the everyday experiences of your family. Victor is faced with a heavy-duty choice—his girlfriend keeps pushing him for sex—"if he loved her he'd show her" sort of thing. He really likes the girl, but seems unable to get her to understand why he doesn't want to have sex with her now. She's threatening to drop him for someone who will "do it." This is perfect timing for focusing on self-control, or loyalty and commitment, or even faith in God, whichever will help Victor the most. If your family is like most families, you probably will not know that Victor is facing this heavy-duty choice. However, you can assume that any teenager will face this decision sometime.

You should be aware, however, that there is a danger in focusing too heavily on the value that your child is struggling with, especially with teens. You run the risk of alienating your adolescent. Some teens are struggling so much with making their own identity and separating from their families that they will do the opposite of what you teach just to assert their

VALUE	MONTH	HOLIDAY
Peace	January	New Year's Day
Kindness and Compassion	February	Valentine's Day
Patience	March	Arrival of Spring
Humility	April	Easter
Respect	May	Mother's Day
Responsibility	June	Father's Day
Perseverance	July	Independence Day
Loyalty and Commitment	August	Family vacation
Honesty and Integrity	September	School begins Labor Day
Self-control	October	Halloween
Contentment and Thankfulness	November	Thanksgiving
Faith in God	December	Christmas

independence. So walk this pathway with care, caution, and much prayer. Hopefully, you "made your propaganda early," and now you only have to gently remind, dialogue, and encourage what your teen already knows and really believes.

Joyanna comes home from the first day of third grade telling of a new girl who has a huge scar that almost covers the right side of her face. Her arm is covered with scars also. "Mom, she's really ugly—almost like a scarecrow. All the kids stared at her and teased her, and nobody would even talk to her. I didn't say anything, but I'd be scared to touch her!" Perfect timing for focusing on kindness and compassion. Read about burns and skin grafts and scars. Dialogue about the situation during mealtime. Share experiences with persons with disabilities. Encourage Joyanna to invite the new girl home to play after school sometime soon.

You could also choose to focus on a value in anticipation of special issues in a child's life. Carlos is thinking about running for a student association office for next semester. The outcome of the election, naturally, is uncertain. A focus on perseverance might be helpful as he anticipates what a campaign might be like.

2. Use teaching strategies. Teaching values is not like teaching math or geography. Rote learning will not do the trick. Teaching values combines thinking and feeling. Some strategies emphasize one more than the other. Others combine the two powerfully. Pick what you feel most comfortable using first, then try out some new ideas. You will soon learn what reaches your children best.

Stories are one of the best strategies for teaching values. All ages love them. They have a powerful emotional pull as well as the effect of nudging listeners to think. Children can try out different roles by identifying with any character in the story with a lot less risk than trying out those same roles in real life. Stories come back to impress the heart in moments of decision.

Read or tell stories with feeling and drama. Make the story live. As children get older, read-round robin as a family activity. Get older children to prepare a story for the family. Children and adults like to hear favorites many times.

If you engage children in dialogue about the story, you will increase its teaching power. Examine how each character felt, what they did, and how they made the tough decisions. Find out what the children think. Don't tell—ask. Dialogue means talking back and forth about what each person thinks or feels. You don't have to moralize. Saying "and now the lesson we should learn" turns kids off. The story will speak for itself, especially with dialogue.

I have found stories with wonderful teaching potential almost any-where—the local library, Christian bookstores, general bookstores, schoolbooks, current and old copies of children's magazines. An early childhood favorite at our house was a little Golden Book bought at the food market. Even your parents' or grandparents' attic might be worth investigating. Collections of children's stories are available with values indexes to make it easy to find just the right story. Check your Christian bookstore or ask your librarian.

The best stories of all are from your own childhood—the tough decisions you faced growing up, your feelings, your temptations. Your stories are more meaningful because they are yours. No one else can tell these stories. Use their power to inspire your children.

Everyday situations can make ideal teachable moments. Grab the moment and run with it. It might be a two-minute "moment" or a month-long "moment." Either way it will be the perfect time to teach values because your kids are involved in the situation. Because it's real life, it really means something to them.

All morning long 3-year-old Jonathan eagerly watched the activity next door as men shoveled and carted away loads of dirt, hammered the forms for the new cement driveway, and leveled the foundation. Later in the day, when he came into the house he had a small stick dangling from his mouth.

"What's that in your mouth?" his mother asked.

"My mouth candle," replied Jonathan. "You know, like the men who are making the driveway."

Suddenly Mommy understood. "You mean a cigarette, don't you?"

"My mouth candle," the child insisted.

Mommy quickly decided it was time for a lesson on the dangers of smoking. Carefully she explained how cigarettes make people sick, emphasizing that God wants us to keep our bodies healthy and strong.

The next morning Jonathan was eager to watch the men pouring cement. But this time he had something important on his mind. At the first opportunity he spoke to one of the men.

"Mister, why don't you stop smoking? It's not good for you! You'll get sick!" Mommy's lesson had lodged in his little mind and he wanted to pass on the information. It had been the perfect moment for teaching, and

Mom had seized it. (Adapted from *How to Help Your Child Really Love Jesus* [Review and Herald Pub. Assn.].)

Questions often teach better than lectures or scolding. It works this way. You hear screams coming from somewhere near your house—children's screams of laughter mixed with cat yowls. You rush out to investigate and discover the neighborhood bully swinging your cat by the tail, with a circle of kids—your own included—screeching with laughter at the cat's misery and the cat swinger's antics. While you are annoyed at the cat swinger, you're also upset at all the other children whose laughter egged him on.

What should you do? You could scream above their noise, "Stop that this instant!" And they would probably stop. Indeed, you may have to do that to get their attention, if they don't stop as soon as you appear on the scene. You could then lecture them about kindness to animals. If you deliver a very strong lecture, your own kids might get the message and the neighborhood kids would quickly disappear.

There is a more effective way. These kids—your own included—need to learn to think about their actions. Questioning is more likely to get them to think than lecturing. Often children aren't doing any thinking about the situation—just tolerating your reasoning. They need to learn to reason about life.

There are many questions you could ask: To the cat swinger, What are you doing? What will happen if you keep swinging the cat? To your children, What is our rule about how we treat animals? What should you do to follow the rule? To all the kids, What are you doing? What should you have done? How do you suppose the cat feels?

In order for questions to be effective you must follow these guidelines:

Ask only one question. Wait for the response. If the child does not respond, ask again. If she comments but does not respond to the question, acknowledge the comment, but repeat the question. Eventually she will answer.

Keep your voice normal, or lower than normal, and keep your whole demeanor respectful of the child. You cannot get respect unless you first give respect.

Do not give up. Questions take more time than commands, but they build the moral understanding and reasoning your children need to internalize values.

The dialogue about the cat might go something like this, assuming the cat swinging stopped when you showed up, meaning that these children have some conscience and felt a little guilt:

You: "What were you doing?"

(Children remain silent.)

You: "What were you doing with the cat?"

Children: "Aw, we're just havin' fun."

You: "What were you doing with the cat?"

Children: "Swinging it by the tail. [sigh] But the cat didn't mind— cats like that."

You: "How do you think that felt to the cat?"

Children: "Dunno."

You: "What was the cat doing?"

Children: "Yelling."

You: "How do you think the cat felt?"

Children: "How should I know—I'm not a cat [from the bully]."

(Some kids laugh.)

You: "How would you feel if a giant came along, grabbed you by the finger, and dangled you over a deep precipice while he laughed and laughed and said he was going to drop you?"

Children: "Scared silly. I'd probably scream. [Pause] Do you really think that's the way the cat felt?"

You: "What do you think?"

Children: "We didn't think about the cat's feelings. Maybe it hurt, and the cat was scared."

You: "How do you think we should treat animals?"

Children: "Not hurt them. They have feelings too."

You: "What are you going to do next time somebody suggests hurting an animal?"

Children: "Tell 'em, 'No way!' Take the animal away."

You: "You've got the idea."

By using questions instead of commands, you led the children to an understanding of what their actions felt like to the animal. They then decided on the proper actions for the future. The likelihood of treating animals kindly in the future is greater than if you had come out screaming and lecturing.

If your children are already older than 8 or 9 and you have never used the questioning method, they may not be used to thinking about the other person. Use very simple lines of questioning to help them mature in empathy.

Stay with it, and you will be rewarded with increased understanding. Remember, ask only one question and calmly wait for an answer. Persist until you get the answer. Then help the child move along in reasoning by using additional questions.

Questioning is most appropriate when you want to teach your child moral reasoning. It is also effective in getting children to acknowledge their behavior and make a commitment for the future.

Act-it-out or role playing is another effective way to teach values. This method is especially useful for teaching children how to deal with peer pressure. The strategy is simple. You and your child act out an imaginary situation similar to one that is tough for your child to deal with. First, you play-act the part of your child, and your child can be the other person—the child teasing him, for example. Then you reverse roles. Your child play-acts himself and you act the part of the other child.

Act-it-out provides opportunity to actually practice what to say and do in advance of a situation. It is a very useful strategy for practicing new behaviors. If you start doing this strategy when your child is 4 or 5, by the time she is 10 or 12 she will be adept at act-it-out, and you can work through many situations before the fact. She will also be adept at understanding how others feel, because she has practiced putting herself in their place.

Making a drawing is a powerful way to get children to express their feelings. Some children have a hard time talking about feelings, but they can draw or paint how they feel about the situation or person. Follow these simple guidelines: *Never tell the child what to draw.* Just suggest he make a drawing about how he feels. *Don't hover over the child while he is drawing.* Go do something else and come back in a bit. *Don't comment about the drawing.* Instead say, "Tell me about your drawing." Don't say it is good, or beautiful, or ugly. Just listen to what your child says, with an occasional supportive comment. When he is finished telling about the drawing, make a comment that reflects what you think he feels about this situation. "You felt frightened by that bully." After that you may be able to talk more about the situation he confronted and help him think of ways to deal with it in the future.

Use key guiding phrases to reinforce your teaching. Use them frequently. Post them about the house where everyone can see the message many times a day (such as above the kitchen sink or on the bathroom mirror).

Selected punchy Bible verses carry the weight of God's wisdom:

"Even a child is known by his actions" (Prov. 20:11).

"Do you see a man skilled in his work? He will serve before kings" (Prov. 22:29).

"Every fool is quick to quarrel" (Prov. 20:3).

"Commit to the Lord whatever you do, and your plans will succeed" (Prov. 16:3).

"A gentle answer turns away wrath, but a harsh word stirs up anger" (Prov. 15:1).

"Envy rots the bones" (Prov. 14:30).

"There is a way that seems right to a man, but in the end it leads to death" (Prov. 14:12).

Remember those things your mother used to say? "Birds of a feather flock together" was one of my mother's favorites. Another one has proven its wisdom over the years: "Don't believe anything you hear and only half of what you see." It has kept me from jumping to conclusions on many occasions. I'm sure you have a storehouse of values wisdom passed on from your family. Use the ones you especially like with your own children. If you don't have a built-in selection, get a book of sayings from the library and select a few that seem especially appropriate or use some of the ones I suggest in the chapters on specific values.

Posters and pictures are valuable teaching aids also. Look in your Christian bookstore for posters that give the value messages you want to teach. Change them periodically. Make your own small posters with graphics from the computer. Of if you are artistically talented, draw or paint some. Have a contest and let your children design some posters on a specific value.

Every home with children should have a good-sized bulletin board in a prominent place. Children can display their work; parents can post sayings about values, lists of jobs to be done, charts to check off jobs done, the family's calendar of events, school notices, etc. Each month post a prominent poster about the value you're focusing on that month. Use the bulletin board to congratulate children and adults on wise decisions.

Older children and teenagers can keep a **values journal** in which they write about values decisions, or copy anything that appeals to them about values. The family could have a values journal in which they record special times when a family member made a tough values decision and how it turned out. Favorite Bible verses or sayings could be recorded in the family journal. The journal could be organized chronologically, as most journals are, or you could have a section for each of the values you want to teach, and record the event, Bible verse, or saying under the specific value. This has the advantage that whenever a family member finds something especially appropriate, it can be recorded under that value for future reference.

3. Help children think about values. Raising values to a conscious thinking level goes a long way toward helping children make the right decisions. How is the value important? What are the consequences of ignoring it? What are the consequences of following it? Even 3- and 4-year-olds can be guided to think about their actions. No complicated reasoning for them. Just simple ideas that they can grasp. Allow them to do as much of the thinking as possible, with only a few suggestions from you to guide them in the right direction. You'll find more about how to teach children to think and make wise judgments in chapter 8.

4. Adapt your teaching to your child's age, understanding, and learning style. During early childhood children are learning what is right and what is wrong. They need very specific teaching with clear consequences for doing what is wrong and lots of practice doing the right. Their thinking is not mature yet, so reasoning should be very simple and clear. They can begin to learn values, but by a simpler name. If you can put in a strong foundation of what is right and wrong in the situations they confront, teaching during late childhood will be much easier.

During late childhood (ages 6 to 12) children in school confront many different sets of values. This can be very confusing. For this reason many families today are home-schooling their children during the first few years of grade school so they can have stronger input into values before their youngsters confront the multiplicity of values in schools. Many parents choose a Christian school for this same reason. However, if neither of these options is available to your children, they will need your help to sort out the values in their school.

Late childhood is the time to really focus on teaching values in a serious way. Children can better understand what it is all about. They can learn the values vocabulary. They need help living out their values. Every day they will have to make decisions that involve values. They need lots of practice in decision-making and learning how to deal with peer pressure. If your children enter adolescence with a strong set of principles based on solid values that can guide their decisions, you and they are fortunate. Their teen years will be much easier.

Adolescence is the time for loosening emotional family ties. Teens work hard to develop their own identity and be separate from Mom and Dad. For some teens this process may be very threatening, and so they bend over backward to develop their own identity—including their own set of values. However, most teens respect the values they have learned in the family. Parents are still their most trusted adult counselors, according to many surveys of teenagers.

Your job during the teen years is to help your adolescent rework the values she has learned earlier so she can truly claim them as her own—not just hand-me-downs from Mom and Dad. She will have to work through all the whys and wherefores and what those mean in real life. Hopefully, she will emerge into young adulthood with a strong set of Christian values to guide her life.

Timing is very important in teaching values. Methods that work for a 4-year-old will definitely not work for a 14-year-old. Adjust your teaching to your child's stage of development.

Children also have different learning styles. Your values teaching will be more effective if you can cue into these styles. Some children learn best through hearing (auditory learners), others through seeing (visual learners), and others through bodily movement (kinesthetic learners). Some children want to see the big picture first and then fill in the details (global), while others must have all the details before they will even consider the big picture (analytic). Each of these learning styles suggests a different way of helping your child learn.

This book includes many ideas for family activities that teach values. Pick and choose the ideas that appeal to you and might interest your children. Select ideas that suit your child's development, understanding, and learning style. Some could be used for family worship time, while others make great family night activities. Some even make interesting mealtime conversation. Most important of all, have fun teaching values!

FAMILY ACTIVITIES

Review this chapter and select activities that your family enjoys. Consider your child's stage of development, level of understanding, and learning style.

Building children is better than repairing adults.

KEYS TO TEACHING VALUES

1. Focus on the value you want to teach. Grab important moments.

2. Use many different teaching strategies: stories, real-life situations, questions, act-it-out scenes, key guiding phrases, drawings, posters and pictures, values journal.

3. Make your propaganda early. Prepare your child for the future.

4. Help children learn to think about values.

5. Adapt your teaching to your child's age, understanding level, and learning style.

GOD

LIVE the values

TEACH the values

PROTECT your child's mind

MAKE right and wrong very clear

DEVELOP self-respect and confidence

GIVE lots of practice in making decisions

SHOW your child how to deal with peer pressure

MAKE

GOD

REAL

CHAPTER 5

Protect Your Child's Mind

I want you to be wise about what is good, and innocent about what is evil. Rom. 16:19.

Computers make me think of a child's mind—the "garbage in, garbage out," programming, viruses, and data entry. The results in kids' minds are almost as predictable as computers. Except for the delete key. Except that kids' minds are much more complex. Computers have to be told what to do, programmed by somebody's mind—maybe your kid's mind.

"Garbage in, garbage out" might be a good slogan to write on your child's forehead. Input good data and protect from garbage. Both are crucial for learning Christian values in a world mostly filled with garbage values. No wonder our kids are selfish, disagreeable, unkind, grabby, ungrateful. "Garbage in, garbage out."

INPUTTING GOOD VALUES

Even before a baby is born, his brain is busy inputting data from his surroundings. Recent research has shown that newborns prefer hearing the kind of music or TV programs that were played a lot while they were growing inside the mother's body. Thus your baby is born with some music or TV preferences already built into his brain. Awesome, when you think about it! Frightening, too.

Imagine how sensitive that new little brain is to input from the world around him. Think about that when you put on a CD or turn on the TV.

What kind of music do you want him to like when he is 16? Play it now! Naturally, there may be other things that will influence what kind of music your child likes when he is 16, but you might as well get a head start on this music business. We all know it's one of the difficult value areas.

Your child is constantly inputting data about his world, data that will influence his choice of values. While your child is young, you can control a lot of that input. Later on it will be more difficult to control. Since the mind is the most sensitive to new information while a child is young, the early years are most important for inputting good values. Children learn more during their first three years than all the rest of life. You are in a race with Satan to fill your child's mind. You can't afford to let him get the head start.

Input into the mind comes from the senses—seeing, hearing, touch-

---

IDEAS FOR INPUTTING CHRISTIAN VALUES

Decorate child's room with spiritual influences—picture of Jesus and children, praying children, nature objects.

Read or tell Bible stories every day.

Talk about Jesus, connect your love with Jesus' love in your child's mind by hugging your child whenever you talk about Jesus' love.

Read storybooks with Christian values every day.

Play CDs or tapes with character-building songs.

Buy toys that teach Christian values.

Teach Bible verses using many senses—pantomime the verse, draw a picture, learn a song, color a picture about the verse, write it in sand, make a mobile, act it out.

CHART CONTINUES

CHART CONTINUED

Pray with your children every day.

Fill God's holy day with family activities that teach Christian values so your children will look forward to a special day together.

Post Bible verses or sayings at strategic places in the home.

Learn about nature—God's other book—and the values God wants to teach us from His creation.

ing, tasting. So watch what your child hears, sees, tastes, and feels. She is not just passively being held in your arms—she is *learning* whatever she sees or hears. Fill her senses with positive input. The chart above gives you a start on ideas for filling your little one's mind with good values.

When you are selecting activities for positive input, be guided by Philippians 4:8. God asks us to think about things that are noble, just, pure, lovely, of good report, virtuous, and praiseworthy. If we really followed God's guidelines for input, I think we would have to reject most TV programs, videos, and popular music, as well as many computer games and toys. They simply don't come up to God's standard for brain input. Can we trust Him enough to follow His way? God made us. He knows how our brains work.

PROTECTING YOUR CHILD'S MIND

You've heard the old story of the camel and the traveling Bedouin. The sand was blowing fiercely on the desert. The camel, braving the storm outside his owner's tent, begged for mercy. "Please let me put just my nose inside the tent!" After many pleadings the master finally agreed. But soon the camel wanted to get his eyes into the tent, then his ears, his head, his front feet. You know the story. After a while the whole camel was inside the tent and there was no room for the Bedouin master.

Satan works the same way. In subtle ways he works to input evil into the minds of our children. Most of the time we are not aware of what he is doing.

Desensitization is a powerful way of letting the whole camel in without realizing what has happened. In reality, it is a simple tool used often by psychologists to help individuals with extreme fears and phobias. Desensitization works on the principle that a person cannot be relaxed and tense at the same time and, when relaxed, a person is more open to changes in attitudes and feelings.

Television is a perfect medium for using desensitization. The hundreds of rapid linear movements flickering across the screen create an overload for the brain. The brain, to protect itself, changes its way of thinking to a more relaxed state (alpha waves). For children, this usually happens in 30 seconds or less; for adults in two to 10 minutes. Of course, that's why we watch TV—to relax after a long hard day at work. It works very well.

However, in this more relaxed state the brain takes in information uncritically, without thinking as it would if it were functioning using beta waves (alert, thinking state). It's the perfect setup for desensitization. Relaxed state, uncritical flow of input to the brain. Easy way to change a person's attitudes.

At least two thirds of television programming appeals to the right side of our brains. The right brain specializes in feelings, attitudes, music, visual images, the global view, and nonverbal communication. The left brain specializes in language and logical thinking, and analyzing the parts.

Television's messages are primarily visual. In our relaxed state, we take them in uncritically in our right brains. Soon our attitudes have changed and we are not aware of the changes. Gradually our values change to conform to what we see day after day.

Children younger than 7 or 8 years of age also tend to think that TV is real life. They will judge what happens in real life by what they saw on TV. In church children will correct a Bible story by saying, "That's not the way it is. I saw it on a video." They form their ideas about life from what they see on TV or videos.

Older children and teenagers don't do this quite as much, but they are influenced by television images far more than we realize. When television portrays adolescence as one long sexual orgy, teenagers come to think that is the way it should be. Somehow they're abnormal if it isn't that way for them. They want the clothes, food, and drink seen on the screen. Their values are heavily influenced by what they see.

VALUE MESSAGES CHECKUP

Media Messages	God's Messages
Do what you want—getting caught is bad.	Do what is right, even if no one knows.
Happiness is having lots of money, beautiful clothes, houses, cars, and other things. All you want. You deserve it.	Happiness is trusting God. God is our source of happiness. Our treasure is in heaven.
Consumerism is an accepted way of life.	Discipleship requires giving up and living humbly. Our money is entrusted to us to use to help others.
Any problem can be solved in 30 minutes, often with violence or sex.	Problems require time, patience, and endurance to solve God's way. Peacefulness and respect for others are important.
People are sex objects used to satisfy my personal desires.	Sexuality is a gift of God, which comes with responsibilities. People are never "things." They are God's creation, made in His image, to be respected and loved.
Children are smarter than adults. They tell adults what to do and are better problem solvers.	God has provided parents to guide children. They have more experience. Children are to respect their parents.

CONTINUES NEXT PAGE
▼

Media Messages	God's Messages
Winning is the most important thing. Win at all costs.	Playing the game of life well is the most important thing. In God's sight everyone can be a winner.
Power and control over other people will get me what I want. Some people are more important than others.	In God's view, all people are equally important and are to be treated with respect and dignity.
I deserve to have what I want right away. Waiting is too hard.	Patience and endurance are key to the Christian life. Denying self is God's way.
Alcohol and drugs solve my problems and make me feel better. Smart people drink and smoke.	Your body is the temple of the Holy Spirit. Alcohol and drugs destroy your communication lines with God.
Religion is a detriment to living the good life. Only the simple-minded believe in God.	God created human beings to be in relationship with Him. We are complete only in Him.
Honesty is only for fools. Can't run a business on strict honesty. Better to cover up what you don't want others to know.	Honesty is the only way. My entire life is open to God's eyes. Honesty and openness are the foundations for trust.

CONTINUES NEXT PAGE
▼

CHART CONTINUED

Media Messages	God's Messages
The occult spirit world is intriguing and helpful to humans.	The occult is the devil's deception for humans. God sends His Holy Spirit to guide His followers in the right way.

In general, the value messages of the media contradict God's Word. We and our children take in the messages uncritically until we believe they are OK. Check up on how much the media messages have influenced your family with the Value Messages chart on the previous pages.

Since television is the popular culture of our time, we must constantly be monitoring what we see. We must compare the values we see on TV with our Christian faith, sorting out the positive and the negative. We must intentionally keep checking our family's values. Pray that God will enlighten your mind and ring an inner bell, if you please, to alert you.

The media value messages are not limited to television. Keep asking yourself, *What values is my child learning from this activity?* Are they Christian values or are they the world's secular values? Ask yourself these questions about every toy, computer game, book, magazine, video, TV program, game, movie, picture, CD, or audiotape you are considering bringing into your home. Evaluate everything.

Recently we were providing care for about 50 children 2 to 4 years of age at our church during evening adult meetings. Usually we provided an active program for them with songs and learning activities. One evening we had them for three hours, so we occupied some of the time by showing a simple Bible video. Some of the children were absolutely mesmerized by the video and others preferred playing with the toys in the room and barely glanced at the TV. The teachers noticed that the children who were glued to the TV were the same ones who couldn't really play with the toys. They just ran around the room, but didn't really play with the toys. They also had difficulty doing imaginative activities such as pretending they

TAMING THE MEDIA MONSTER

Decide how much of your life you want to give to the monster. (Include TV, popular music, computer games, the Web, the newspaper, books, magazines, etc.)

Evaluate the TV programs you watch, the music you listen to, the computer games or Internet surfing you do. Compare the values in each area to God's values. Ask yourself, What values are my children learning from this activity?

Develop your family's criteria for viewing, listening, and reading. Do this with your children. Let everyone contribute. Take your time, maybe several weeks, to work through the criteria.

Post your family's viewing, listening, and reading criteria prominently on the TV set, computer, CD player, and bookshelves.

Post a list of alternative ideas. Add new ideas each week. Help your children contribute to this list of ideas. Try out at least one new activity each week, more often if possible.

Devise a system to decrease TV watching time. Rate programs and assign points. Give each child coupons for the week. Assign more points to less desirable programs. At the end of the week exchange unused coupons for money, prizes, or privileges.

Increase family activity time. Plan times to do things together. No media activities during family times.

Have at least one "no TV day" each week—adults and children.

CHART CONTINUES

CHART CONTINUED

If all else fails and your family is still addicted to the media monster, **throw out the TV** (put it in the attic) until you conquer your addiction. **Cancel your subscription to cable and to the Web.** See what happens. Give your family time to discover life without the media. You might like it!

---

were washing the dishes or driving a car. The children who weren't interested in the video (it's reasonable to think that they probably did not watch much TV at home) could easily play pretend activities and loved playing with the toys.

TV robs children of their creativity and imagination. No wonder our kids act bored with life. We have robbed them of their inner resources.

A couple times each year I take a stroll through the aisles of a major toy store to see what toy makers are selling. I am always impressed with the large number of toys that teach values contrary to God's Word. Many aisles are stacked almost to the ceiling with toys that focus on violence, the occult, monsters, and extraterrestrial beings. Other aisles contain toys that promote a self-centered, pleasure-seeking lifestyle. Personal beauty and clothes are everything. Are these the values we want our children to learn?

Does the media monster have your family in its grip? What can you do to tame it?

Without your family's addiction to the media, you will discover a whole new world out there. A world that might include playing catch, reading a good book together, skateboarding, building with blocks or Legos, learning to make music together, helping your neighbor, playing marbles, writing a letter, doing arts and crafts, riding bikes, hiking, doing puzzles, playing anagrams, taking photographs, riding horses, finger painting, making a piñata, shooting hoops, collecting stamps or baseball cards, roller blading, growing plants, getting together with a friend, writing and putting on a play, memorizing the names of the states and their capitals, learning about Russia and Mongolia, making and flying a kite, making a model airplane, starting a neighborhood newspaper, jumping rope, making creative scrapbooks with your photos, camping, observing the stars at night . . . the list is endless.

Protect your child's mind. "Garbage in, garbage out." A mind is too valuable to fill with trash!

FAMILY ACTIVITIES

God's Word: Read Philippians 4:7 and 8 together. Then look at each word for further thought. Find pictures or examples of each word. Talk about its meaning. Use the word during the week until everyone uses it. Next week think about the next word.

Media Criteria: Develop your family's criteria for the media: television viewing, the Internet, reading, and music. Tackle only one area at a time. Take it slowly. Listen to your kids' ideas. Offer yours. Consult God's Word for guiding principles. Decide together. Print the criteria neatly (or make a sign on the computer) and post them prominently.

TV Select: Once a week look at the list of upcoming TV programs. Decide as a family which ones you want to watch. Post the list.

Dialogue: Watch a preselected program with your children. Talk about what you are seeing. Focus on values. Gradually your children will begin to think and evaluate. Rarely let your children watch TV by themselves. You need to see what they are watching so the dialogue can occur.

KEYS TO PROTECTING YOUR CHILD'S MIND

1. Use every possible opportunity to fill your child's mind with good values.

2. Limit exposure to secular values, especially to the media.

3. Decide on your family's criteria for TV viewing. Post them prominently on the TV set.

4. Develop criteria for other areas of the media: music, reading, computer games, surfing the Internet, videos, movies, etc. Post them prominently.

CHART CONTINUES

CHART CONTINUED

5. Decrease time with the media. Increase family activity time.

6. View TV programs together as a family. Dialogue about what you are seeing, with a focus on values.

7. Post a list of alternative family and individual activities.

8. Keep asking, What values is my child learning from this activity? Act to eliminate negative value activities.

9. Select toys and games that teach Christian values.

Family Activity: At least once a week do a family activity together instead of watching TV or playing video games. Plan ahead to have supplies ready. Encourage the kids to choose from the list or offer other suggestions. See the list above.

Activities Brainstorm: As a family develop a list of activities you would like to do together. Post it on your bulletin board. Make up a list of activities that your children can do by themselves. Post that list on the TV set and computer. When children watch large amounts of TV their creativity is often stunted. It will take time for them to learn how to be creative. Don't give up. Keep enticing them to try one more thing.

The eyes and the ears are the teachers of the soul.
Your mind is your most valuable asset. Invest it carefully.

GOD

LIVE the values

TEACH the values

PROTECT your child's mind

MAKE right and wrong very clear

DEVELOP self-respect and confidence

GIVE lots of practice in making decisions

SHOW your child how to deal with peer pressure

MAKE

GOD

REAL

CHAPTER 6

Make Right and Wrong Very Clear

There is a way that seems right to a man, but in the end it leads to death. Prov. 14:12.

Especially today children need very clear right and wrong values messages because the world at their doorstep believes any behavior is all right. Sometimes it's difficult to determine what is right. The line between right and wrong can become very blurry, especially if the input to a person's brain has included an overdose of secular values.

How do we know what is right or wrong? We need to get it clear in our own heads before we can teach our children. It's time for serious thinking.

1. What is the source of your values? Who says it is right or wrong?

2. *Why* is it right or wrong? Is it an issue of taste or preference, or is it a moral/religious issue?

Go to the most reliable source for the Christian—God's Word. For many issues God has given very clear guidelines. Check out Exodus 20:3-17. Do this, don't do that. Pretty clear. Then Jesus reduced the whole thing to only two rules: Love God and love people (Matt. 22:34-40). First Corinthians 13 describes how to love. Matthew 5-7, Romans 12, and the book of Proverbs expand on how God wants us to live and provide more details about what is right or wrong.

Even with all this guidance from the Scriptures, there are times when we really wonder what is right. Today's world throws value decisions in our laps that the ancient writers never imagined. When our kids are teenagers the issues seem to get especially confusing.

Go back to the Bible, search for a principle that applies today, and pray for a discerning mind. I believe God always answers that prayer. But be prepared for answers that might be a bit uncomfortable, out of step with the world around you. God's values can seem drastically different. They can throw you into a tizzy, make you struggle with obedience. But if you are really willing to live by God's answer, He will make it clear. Willingness is the key that unlocks God's wisdom for today's problems.

HOW CHILDREN DEVELOP MORALLY

Children understand what is right or wrong quite differently, depending on their age and stage of moral thinking. Babies, toddlers, and 2-year-olds are learning some things are "no-no's" based on their parents' reactions. They are making a mental storehouse of dos and don'ts. By the time most youngsters are 3 they have become moral beings. They know some things are right and some are wrong. The beginnings of conscience are in place, and they feel guilty when they do something they have learned is wrong.

At this point children are moving into the first stage of moral thinking. The following descriptions of the stages come from research by Lawrence Kohlberg, William Damon, Thomas Lickona, Robert Selman, and many others. I have also included some ideas gleaned from my own research on how children from Christian families develop their understanding of salvation. The chart summarizes how children think about right and wrong and what you can do to help your child mature in moral thinking.

Mr. Three and Miss Four show very self-centered thinking about right and wrong. Getting their own way is the right thing to do. The real reason to be good is to get rewards and to avoid punishment. They tend to think of God in these same terms—He'll punish them for doing something wrong or reward them for doing right. They are at stage 0 of moral thinking.

Miss Five and Mr. Six have usually moved on to stage 1. They generally do what they're told. They want to stay out of trouble because they still respect adult authority. Their conscience, based on the rewards and punishments they have experienced, is still in its formative stages. Right now they are learning many do's and don'ts based on very simple rules for behavior.

During the early elementary grades children are generally in stage 2 of moral thinking. Self-interest reigns supreme. "What's in it for me?" is the

HOW CHILDREN THINK ABOUT RIGHT AND WRONG

Age and Stage	Child's Thinking	How to Help Child Grow
• Birth to 3 years. • Premoral stage	• Learning do's and don'ts. • By age 2 acts guilty when does "bad" action. • Thinks of acts, not reasons. • Beginning conscience. • Becoming a moral person.	• Bond strongly with child. Give child much love. Pair your love with Jesus' love. • Teach specific do's and don'ts. • Use consequences to teach don'ts. • Be very consistent. • Give very simple choices.
• 3 to 4 years • Stage 0 • Me first	• I want my own way. • What I want is good. • Be good to avoid punishment. • Be good to get rewards. • Beginning conscience.	• Use rewards and punishments to teach right actions. • Build foundation of do's and don'ts. • Increase number of choices. • Be very consistent. • Give simple reasons for right actions. • Focus on Jesus' love. • Don't make your love dependent on "good" actions—always show your love.

CONTINUES NEXT PAGE ▼

Age and Stage	Child's Thinking	How to Help Child Grow
• 5 to 6 years • Stage 1 • Avoid trouble	• Do what I am told. Stay out of trouble. • Respect adults. • Conscience based on rewards and punishments.	• Teach simple rules for behavior. • Be consistent with rewards and punishment. • Teach simple reasons for rules • Emphasize how others feel. • Help child think about others' feelings. • Focus on God's love and help for daily living.
• Early to middle or late elementary years • Stage 2 • Be fair	• What's in it for me? I have to look out for myself—be fair to people who are fair to me. • It's OK to be sneaky. • I have to pay everything back. • Adults shouldn't boss kids. • It doesn't matter to me how other people feel. They got what they deserved.	• To gain cooperation use their reasoning: I did this for you, so you should do this for me. • Teach religious values that appeal to love. • Pair God's love with your love. • Model kind and caring actions.

CHART CONTINUES

Age and Stage	Child's Thinking	How to Help Child Grow
	• Thinks God isn't always fair. • Conscience based on rules from outside.	• Nurture a loving relationship with child so they will care about your expectations.
• Middle/ late elementary to junior high years • Stage 3 • Be nice	• I want to be good so other people will think well of me and I will feel good about myself. • I will live up to the expectations of important people and God. • I can think about how others feel, be forgiving, and consider their motives. • True conscience, but is both inner- and outer-directed.	• Encourage strong family life and identity. • Strengthen relationship with child. • Encourage child's sense of self-respect. • Emphasize learning about Christian values. • Promote independent thinking. • Together discover God's principles behind the rules. • Balance love and control.
• Senior high to college years	• I feel responsible to my friends, team, family, church, school, and community.	• Encourage responsible actions that demonstrate a Christian creed and philosophy of life.

CONTINUES NEXT PAGE
▼

CHART CONTINUED		
Age and Stage	**Child's Thinking**	**How to Help Child Grow**
• Stage 4 • Be responsible	• I want to be loyal and fulfill my obligations. • Developing a personal creed, a philosophy of life, and an independent conscience based on self-respect and God's will for me and others.	• Be available to discuss issues. • Respect child's growing independent conscience based on God's will. • Move toward an adult-adult relationship based on mutual respect and love. • Encourage independent thinking about issues.

first question. I have to look out for myself, but I need to be fair to those who are fair to me—a sort of tit-for-tat reasoning. They get into a lot of fights because they think everything has to be "paid back." "It isn't fair!" is their battle cry. They can resort to being sneaky if they don't get what they consider fair.

During this stage children can be quite mean to other people. They have lost their fear of adult authority and think adults shouldn't boss kids around. They are often insensitive to the feelings of others.

Growth to the next stage of moral thinking is not automatic. Some adults still use stage 2 in thinking about right and wrong. They have never moved beyond the self-centered approach to morality. You can help your children grow by challenging their thinking and modeling the next stage.

By middle to upper elementary grades children should be moving into stage 3 of moral thinking. This stage is a big step forward. All the previous stages were very self-centered. Now children are beginning to look outward and think more of what others think of them. They usually think they should be nice people and live up to the expectations of people they know and care about (parents, friends, teachers). They want to be good so others will think well of them, and they will feel better about themselves.

Their version of the golden rule guides their behavior: Treat others well so they will treat you well. They are beginning to think of what others need and are quite capable of good deeds when they put themselves in the other person's shoes. They are more forgiving and flexible. (Sigh of relief! You thought they'd never get to this point!)

Children now have a true conscience, but it is both inner and outer directed. It has internal standards, but it depends on others to decide what those standards should be. A true internalized conscience guided by principles is still in their future.

Most children are in stage 3 of moral thinking for a number of years, probably until early to mid teens. Many never get beyond this stage and are always dependent on what other people think for their decisions about right and wrong. You can help them move toward more independent thinking by following the suggestions in the chart.

These are extremely important years for learning the difference between right and wrong. They will set the tone for adolescence and beyond; they build on what was accomplished before. They are the bridge between childhood and adolescence. You cannot give too much time and thought to your child's sense of right and wrong during these years.

As your teenager moves into senior high school and the late teenage years, she should also be maturing into stage 4 thinking. Peer pressure will lessen because she is not so dependent on what others think. She will begin to think much more about her responsibilities. She wants to be somebody who fulfills her obligations to the system. She needs to do this to maintain her personal sense of self-respect. If she lacks this needed sense of belonging to a social or value system, she will be vulnerable to the pull of cults or other fringe groups that offer a powerful feeling of belonging.

He is ready to think seriously about values and how his personal values affect others. He can understand questions such as "What if everyone did it?" He needs help in developing an independent conscience based on self-respect and an understanding of God's will for his life and the lives of others around him. He needs to develop a personal life philosophy to live by, a creed that will guide him in the future, with values firmly rooted and grounded in God's Word.

Stage 4 adults are generally viewed as "good" citizens and "good" church members. They do their part to keep things going and feel a sense of responsibility to the group. They are loyal. They don't question the status quo very much and are not known for their "far-out," independent thinking. They believe in God's Word and willingly follow the direction of their spiritual leader.

There is one more generally accepted stage of moral thinking, stage 5, which comes into focus during the college or young adult years. Most people never reach this stage of independent thinking. According to the research, individuals at stage 5 have a truly internalized conscience built on the principle of respect and care for every human being. They are very independent thinkers who question the status quo and strive to make careful, well-thought-out judgments about every moral issue they confront. Education at the graduate level tends to encourage this type of thinking.

In the Christian context, these people carefully evaluate each issue by the principles from God's Word and are not afraid to make an independent, unpopular decision. They are less concerned about the group than about "truth" or the "right decision." This does not mean that they're not cooperative, contributing members of a church group, but they are not unquestioning followers of a religious leader. They need to think things out for themselves.

RULES AND PRINCIPLES

"Kathi, don't hit your brother! It hurts him."

"Jon, don't throw your food on the floor!"

"Briana, pet the kitty gently."

Children begin to learn about right and wrong from the specific do's and don't their parents enforce during early childhood. During these years they appear to be little legalists—concerned only about the rules. There aren't any extenuating circumstances that would change the rule or the consequence. Grace is an abstract idea that is somewhat beyond them. They are focused on what they can see and handle.

However, this focus on rules has a good side. This is the time to teach very specific kinds of behaviors so children will learn to live Christian values, even though they cannot articulate those values or their source yet. They are learning to live the "right" way. Later they will learn the reasons.

Rules also provide a foundation for understanding grace. Without God's law, there would be no need for grace. When we disobey, the power of grace comes in to save us from our sins. Jesus says, "I love you. I died to save you from your disobedience. I died to renew your relationship with God the Father." Our children need to understand God's grace as soon as they can grasp these ideas.

One of your rules might be, Don't hurt people. Rules that say what *not* to do are understood better by younger children. There is a principle (reason) behind that rule. God wants us to treat people with respect and love because each person is important to Him. God loves everyone. Jesus died to save each person in the world. You can begin to teach that rule—minus the explanation—when children are 2 or 3. Insist on obedience to the rule and provide some consequences that your child dislikes when he disobeys the rule.

By age 3 or 4 children can understand simple reasons for the rule: "It hurts Lizette when you hit her. Jesus wants you to be nice to your sister." "Lizette feels good when you hug her." "Let's give the baby her bottle. We love Baby and Jesus loves Baby."

Maria will probably be 10 or 12 before she begins to understand the more abstract reasons for the rule, Don't hurt people. Even then her understanding is not complete. Respecting people, as God does, means loving them as He does. It takes a lifetime to learn that. This is an all-of-your-life rule, yet it is simple enough that young children can understand and practice it.

Think carefully about the rules you teach your children. Have only a few, well-thought-out rules that express the values you want them to learn. If you consistently enforce those rules, you will be helping your children learn the Christian values you believe in.

TEACHING LIMITS

"Reesa, remember our rule: Study first, then play." "Josh, you may ride your bike to the corner and back. Stay on the sidewalk." Limits form boundaries within which children feel safe and loved. Limits can also feel stiffling and oppressive. The difference is how you set the limits.

Set appropriate limits. When setting limits ask yourself:

- Is it necessary?
- Is it reasonable?
- Is it OK for my child's age?
- Is it enforceable?

If all answers are *yes,* go ahead. The limit will contribute to your child's personal growth. If even one answer is *no,* STOP.

Enforce the limit set.

When enforcing limits:

Be clear. Your child needs to understand the limit and its reasons.

Be predictable. Don't pass one day and punish the next. Your child needs to be able to depend on your limits. Otherwise he is confused.

Be confident and firm. Your child needs to know who is in charge.

Be loving. Love is the key to your child's heart. Yes, you can be loving and firm. They are not contradictory.

Be reasonable. An exception might be appropriate.

TEMPERAMENT AND LIMITS

Your goal is internalized values, values that your child believes are her own—not values imposed by you. This is a little tricky, but definitely possible.

An important key to internalization of values is something called "emotional arousal." Your child needs to experience just the right amount of arousal for your message to be internalized so she thinks it is her own value. Too much arousal breeds resentment, and the message is lost. Too little arousal, and the message is ignored.

You must give your values message enough importance that your child feels a little uncomfortable with the way she was acting and thinks, *Whoa! Dad thinks this is really important. Maybe I better pay attention.*

This is where your child's temperament comes in. Some children are very sensitive to your messages. You can probably look that child in the eyes, say your message clearly with a little emphasis, and he will remember and internalize the message. He will feel it is important to you and, therefore, important to him. If you yell and punish severely, it will probably be overkill for his sensitive nature. He will wallow in the mud of his resentful feelings and never learn the message you were trying to teach.

Instead, he will remember the incident with anger.

Other children need a much stronger message. They are not sensitive. They're kind of "tough." They don't pay attention unless you are very firm and impose consequences that really hurt. Then they will pay attention and begin to internalize your message.

Any time your message is unfair or delivered at the wrong time, feelings of resentment sprout. Your message is lost. All your child remembers is his hurt feelings.

Now you know why I said this is tricky. You need to know children very well, understand their temperaments and how much arousal is necessary to get your values message across. If the arousal is just right with your values message, your child will think the message is his own. He will accept it and internalize it as his. Study each child's temperament carefully and use that knowledge to teach values.

HOW TO TEACH RIGHT AND WRONG

Children need a very clear right and wrong values message. Whether they internalize that message or not will depend on *how* you teach.

Teach with love. Be loving and caring. Show your love many times a day. Smiles, hugs, kisses, loving messages, compliments for effort and accomplishment, compliments for just being themselves. Use a loving tone of voice. Especially show love when something has gone wrong. Your child shouldn't have to earn your love. He is your child; he is God's child. Of course you love him, no matter what, just as God does. Be sure he knows that.

Teach with accountability. Hold your child accountable for her actions. When little, she is accountable to you, her parent. As she grows older, she will learn to be accountable to God. Along the way she will be accountable to her teachers, maybe her extended family, and church leaders. Some families emphasize being accountable to each other. Important decisions or difficulties come to family council to be discussed. Children think twice about their actions because they know they will have to explain what they did to the entire family. Siblings can be quite pointed in their comments. No excuses accepted. Accountability helps all of us grow.

Teach with support. Children need to feel supported, that their parents are on their side. You can communicate support in many ways.

Listen carefully and respond to your child's feelings. Pitch in to help with a difficult job. Practice catch or throw baskets or help make a costume. Be understanding when your child needs some time alone. Respect his likes and dislikes—spinach is probably not essential to life! Neither is yogurt, mayonnaise, or avocados, for that matter. Plan parties for her friends. Be there for basketball games and music recitals. Show your pride in fair play and "hanging in there" when things are tough. Make your home a warm and welcoming place where the hurts of life can be healed.

Teach with grace. Grace is unmerited favor. Be sure your kids don't have to earn your love. Give it freely, even when they are ornery and "impossible," especially then. Pray for God's love in your heart so you can pass it on. Do something special to help your child over a rough spot. Hang up her clothes the morning her alarm didn't go off and leave a note, "I hung up your clothes because I love you." Walk beside her to hold her up when she can barely put one foot in front of the other. Forgive and forgive and forgive some more. Bury the past and never dig it up, and don't put up a gravestone. Focus on the future. Every day is a new start. One of my favorite sayings is "Today is the first day of the rest of your life."

If you teach with love, accountability, support, and grace your children will want to follow God's way. They will have experienced God's love through you.

FAMILY ACTIVITIES

Love: Give five minutes for each family member to find something he or she could use to show love to someone else. Each person demonstrates how to show love with their object. (Example: dishcloth to dry the dishes when it isn't his turn as a way to show love to sister, who needs more time to practice her recital piece.)

Love: Ask an older child to pretend he or she cannot speak your family's language. The child could dress up in a costume or in some way act as though he cannot understand. Then ask family members to show love to the "foreigner" without talking. Each person has to think of a way no one else has used, so start with the youngest child and end with the adults.

Accountability: Play "Who's Responsible?" Make up little skits or scenes that show situations in which someone should be responsible. After the skit or scene, ask, "Who's responsible?" For example: Pretend to be a child who just drops his skates in the driveway. Daddy comes in after dark and runs over the skates. Who's responsible?

Support: Write family members' names on slips of paper and place them in a small paper sack. Ask the youngest child to draw a name. Use a paper crown or a ribbon with a medal to designate the special person. Each family member then tells something special about that person, something he or she really likes about the person, or something the person did that was especially nice. Continue drawing names until each family member has had a turn as the "winner."

Support: Blindfold a family member. Ask another person to lead the person around the house. Then reverse roles so everyone has a turn to lead and to follow. Talk about what it felt like to trust the other person to lead you. For little children, play "Catch Me" with Dad. Place the child on a high spot, such as the top bunk of a bed, and then hold out your arms to

---

KEYS TO TEACHING RIGHT AND WRONG

1. Know your own values.

2. Base decisions about right and wrong on God's Word.

3. Give children a clear message about right and wrong.

4. Understand your child's moral development. Teach according to his or her stage of development.

5. Help your child develop internalized values and a conscience based on God's Word.

6. Begin by teaching do's and don'ts, continue with simple rules, then develop principles.

7. Help your child understand the reasons for rules and principles.

CONTINUES NEXT PAGE
▼

CHART CONTINUED

8. Set appropriate limits that teach Christian values.

9. Enforce limits clearly, predictably, confidently, firmly, lovingly, and reasonably.

10. Understand your child's temperament and adjust your values message to fit your child.

11. Teach right and wrong with love, accountability, support, and grace.

catch her when she jumps. Remind her that you will always catch her. You will never, never let her fall. Jesus is like that too. He will always help us.

Grace: When someone in your family has been offended and needs to forgive, do the following visual activity to help children understand forgiveness. After talking about being sorry and the need to ask for forgiveness and give forgiveness, have the children draw a picture or write about the experience. Then explain that forgiveness means we throw the wrong thing away and never find it again. You can dig a hole and bury the paper or light it with a match and watch it burn. We don't talk about it again. It's gone. Explain that is what Jesus does when we do something wrong—He throws it in the deepest ocean and never brings it back (Micah 7:19). Pray with your children asking for Jesus' forgiveness. Learning to forgive takes practice.

There is no right way to do a wrong thing.

GOD

LIVE the values

TEACH the values

PROTECT your child's mind

MAKE right and wrong very clear

DEVELOP self-respect and confidence

GIVE lots of practice in making decisions

SHOW your child how to deal with peer pressure

MAKE

GOD

REAL

CHAPTER 7

Develop Self-respect and Confidence

*I can do everything God asks me to do
with the help of Christ who gives me the strength
and power. Philippians 4:13, TLB.*

One of the best gifts you can give your child is a sense of self-respect and confidence. If your child respects herself, she will be less likely to be swayed by peer pressure. If she feels confident, it will be much easier to say no when faced with the temptation to go against her values. She will have the courage to speak up and maybe suggest an alternative activity, or just plain stand up for what she believes is right.

We hear a lot these days about self-concept and self-esteem, but not so much about self-respect. Each of these terms has a slightly different meaning. Self-concept is who we think we are, and self-esteem refers to how we feel about who we are and our judgments about our own worth. A person can have different self-concepts as well as a global self-concept. For example, Jon might think he is a very good soccer player but a poor baseball player. His overall sports self-concept might be mixed, depending on how important baseball is to his family and friends. Jon might also think of himself as poor in most academic subjects, but he might think he is taller and better-looking than most of the kids in his class. Thus his academic self-concept might be low, but his physical appearance self-concept might be high. His global self-concept and his self-esteem might be quite different from the specific ones. Jon might have a relatively strong self-esteem—he generally likes the way he is.

I think the term *self-respect* comes closest to what our children really need to help them live by their values. The *Random House Dictionary* defines *self-respect* as "proper esteem or regard for the dignity of one's own character." I like the inclusion of both dignity and character in this definition. I believe that self-respect implies, from a Christian viewpoint, that you think too much of who you are in Jesus to do anything degrading to yourself. A strong sense of self-respect provides a barrier against downgrading actions. You simply think too much of the dignity and character God has given you as His child to trample on it.

How can you help your children develop this strong sense of self-respect and the confidence that accompanies it? It definitely is not a gimmick, and your children will not develop it by doing workbook exercises or wearing buttons that say "I'm OK." It is a fundamental part of your child's personality, along with self-concept and self-esteem, and develops gradually over time. Self-respect is a quality of the soul.

The building blocks of self-esteem and self-respect are much more central to personality development than merely wearing a button or doing an exercise. I believe that Christian self-esteem and self-respect begin with teaching children that **God is an essential part of who they are.** Without Him they will always feel incomplete, because God made us to be united with Him. Norman Wright has said it well in his formula for self-esteem: **God + Me = A Whole Person.**

God loves each child. He made each one special with unique characteristics. He loves them even when they do wrong. He died to save them, and plans for them to live with Him eternally. God is the Christian's foundation for positive self-esteem. You cannot emphasize this too much.

Stanley Coopersmith, well-known authority on the development of self-esteem in children, believes there are four essential components: significance, competence, power, and virtue. All are important for self-respect as well.

SIGNIFICANCE

A child needs to feel loved and approved by people who are important to her. Parents are usually the most important people in a child's life, followed by other family members and teachers. What can you do to help your children feel loved and approved of? Show your affection through words and actions. Give sincere compliments for a child's efforts. Be specific in your compliments. "I like the bright colors in your picture. It looks like a happy picture" is much more effective than "Great picture." Be tuned in to your child's feelings and respect them. Listen to her opinions. Recognize your child's accomplishments.

Have a special Cool Crown that the child who has mastered something special gets to wear at the evening meal while he receives everyone's congratulations. Have a Congratulations Corner on your family bulletin board: Use it for encouraging effort as well as accomplishment: Congratulations to Maria for working hard on her essay for English class, to Victor for practicing his free throw, to Elena for helping Mom when she was tired.

COMPETENCE

All children need to perform well on tasks that are important to them. They get discouraged when their performance is poor. You can help build self-esteem by coaching your child to improve skills—batting a ball, in-line skating, addition, spelling, or reading a map. Helping your child develop specific skills will have a real impact on confidence. Sometimes grandparents or older brothers and sisters have more time for coaching than busy parents. Enlist their help. Coach by helping the child learn one step at a time until the full skill is accomplished.

Provide ways for children to recognize their accomplishments, to know how much they have learned and progressed. Young children need immediate feedback, but older children can look back on the past year to recognize their accomplishments. Keep a list of skills your children have learned so you can remind them that "now you can in-line skate." Older children can keep their own list of skills learned.

Help children set realistic goals for themselves. For example, if a child has never gotten more than 50 percent on a spelling test, it is unrealistic to say to the child, "I know you can get them all right this week!" This sets the child up for yet another failure. Instead, say, "I know you can get two more words right than you did last week." Then help her study to get the extra words right. This is a realistic goal and helps build self-esteem and confidence. Unrealistic goals tear down self-esteem. Eventually she may get so she gets them all right, little by little increasing her skill. Or spelling may always be hard for her. Teach her how to compensate (such as using a dictionary or spell check on the computer). It's not the end of the world.

Some children—and parents—have goals that are unrealistically high. Nothing but **perfection** will satisfy them. No one can be perfect all the time, and this expectation sets most children up for low self-esteem. Many little perfectionists are afraid to try because they might not do it perfectly.

If your child is a budding "perfectionist," help him try something just for fun. Don't emphasize performance. Just trying something new is enough. You yourself can model how to have fun, even though you make mistakes. Laugh at yourself and go on. The old adage "If it's worth doing, it's worth doing well" assumes that everything must be done perfectly. Some things aren't worth the time and effort perfection requires. Some things are. Help your child discover the difference. Encourage her to keep trying when perfection matters.

When my friend Janice told me she used to play the piano before she married, I was surprised because I'd never seen her play. "Oh, I quit because my husband criticized everything I played because it wasn't perfect. He couldn't stand any mistakes, so I stopped playing the piano." What a pity! Janice has been robbed of a lifetime of musical enjoyment because her husband is such a perfectionist.

Help your children learn how to deal with **mistakes** and **setbacks**. Demonstrate in your own life how to laugh at yourself, pick yourself up, and go on. Mistakes are stepping-stones to better things. What can you learn from that mistake? Talk about what your child can do differently next time and encourage him to try again. Children who are terribly afraid of making a mistake seldom try anything new. This attitude reinforces a negative self-esteem. These children lack confidence.

Help children **compensate** for their weaknesses. Encourage them to focus on their positive strengths, while at the same time learning specific strategies for dealing with weak areas. They need to develop a **realistic appraisal** of themselves—neither an overinflated feeling that they are "better than everyone else" nor a self-deprecating feeling of being "worse than everyone else." Neither extreme goes with a healthy self-respect.

Misguided but well-meaning parents sometimes insist that their children must **finish everything** they start. Granted, learning to be persistent is important, but there are times when finishing what you started is not the best idea. My college friend Polly is a good example. She started college with a math major, but decided that she really wanted to do something else. Her parents would not let her change majors. "You started math; you have to finish what you start!" Brilliant woman that she is, she finished the math major, but has never done anything with it. Instead, she has been a successful elementary teacher all her life, which certainly did not demand the high-level math skills she once possessed, and required that she go back to school for education certification classes.

Help your children develop their natural **talents and abilities.** Try to be realistic about your child's abilities. You may want your child to be a professional musician or tennis player because that's what you wanted to do. Back off and look realistically at your child's natural talents and abilities. Capitalize on these to build self-respect and confidence.

When our daughter was in high school, the band teacher expressed great surprise that we had let her quit flute lessons after one semester. He thought we should have insisted she continue. But when she wanted to join the band, our agreement had been that she could try flute for one semester. If she didn't like it, she could quit. She never did learn to play an instrument in the band, but she sang in many choirs. There was plenty of music in her life. We thought she deserved a chance to try something without making a lifetime commitment. She has never regretted not learning to play the flute, but she has been singing in ensembles ever since. Singing is her natural gift.

POWER

A sense of power and control over their life is an essential building block for self-esteem and self-respect. Many children feel they have no control over their own lives or anyone else's. All decisions are made for them. Children need to develop a sense of power and control over their own lives—the belief that they can make decisions. This builds real self-esteem and confidence. Begin by allowing very young children to make small decisions. Gradually move on to more difficult decisions. I won't say much here about how to teach children to make decisions, because the next chapter is on this topic. As children mature, they can feel a sense of satisfaction from earning some money and learning to spend it wisely. Support children in taking risks (e.g., running for a class or student association office). Help them to recognize and accept that sometimes a person doesn't succeed in the way he or she anticipated, but there is always another time and another way. The old saying applies in developing self-esteem and self-respect: "Nothing ventured, nothing gained."

VIRTUE

Children respect themselves more when they do what is right. Self-respect suffers under the onslaught of a guilty conscience. But first they must be taught the difference between right and wrong. Again, parents and grandparents can take action here. Virtue and a strong sense of morality are real builders of self-esteem. When a child does what is right he feels good about himself. A solid sense of competence and self-esteem cannot develop without a commitment to live morally and to follow the pathway laid out for us by our Saviour and Lord. When Enrique rejected his friend's appeal to steal the exam questions ahead of time, he felt good about his decision. His self-respect grew. He knew he had done the right thing, even though his friend called him a scaredy-cat.

Remember, self-esteem and self-respect can always be changed! Begin today to help your children build a positive self-respect.

FAMILY SYSTEM

Teaching values always occurs within the family system. A healthy family system is much more effective in teaching values and building self-esteem and self-respect than a dysfunctional one.

In their efforts to teach values, many conservative Christian families use authoritarian methods. They mistakenly think these are God's ways. They command and demand rather than teach and guide. They demand "perfection," do not allow their children to question or evaluate what the parents or the church says, load them up with guilt, use God and the Bible to control, deny feelings and any family problems, and rigidly enforce rules and regulations.

The results of this type of dysfunctional family system are predictable and disastrous. The children have self-concepts that drag in the mud—their self-respect and confidence are almost zero. They reject their parents' values and their religion, or else they become spineless conformists who never really understand God's grace. They live their lives trying to please a God who cannot be pleased. They really do not trust anyone. How sad!

In a healthy family system the family members trust each other, affirm and support each other, communicate and listen supportively, respect each family member and his or her privacy. Healthy families also make sure that each member is heard; they share responsibility for the family, play together, laugh, and have interesting family mealtimes and conversation. They also have strong family rituals and traditions. Healthy families share a deep religious core, they teach a sense of right and wrong, they help others through service, and they admit problems and get help when needed.

The results of growing up in a healthy family system are also predictable. The children and parents have a warm relationship. The children have a strong sense of self-respect and confidence, their self-esteem is positive, and they appreciate the values they have learned in their home. They have positive views of God and a growing religious experience. They know they are accepted by a gracious God who offers love, compassion, and mercy to human beings who are not perfect. They trust God and other people. And they go on to develop these same healthy attitudes in their own families. What a wonderful heritage!

SUPPORTIVE COMMUNICATION

Supportive communication is an essential part of a healthy family system in which children learn positive values. The Bible has a great deal to say about communicating with love and support. The wise one admonishes that "reckless words pierce like a sword, but the tongue of the wise brings healing" (Prov. 12:18). Isn't that what we want to bring to our families—healing from the daily affronts of life, encouragement, and love?

Study the Bible verses and guidelines in the following outline (next page). They will make a very big difference in your family.

Authorities on communication believe that only 7 percent of the message is the actual words said. The remaining 93 percent of the message comes from the nonverbal language. This includes the tone of voice, facial expression, eye contact, posture, gestures, touching, and the distance between the people. If you want to communicate love and support to your child, use a soft tone of voice, smile and look interested, lean toward the child, get down on his level so you can look him in the eye, touch the child gently, keep the distance between you close, and use open gestures instead of folding your arms over your chest and shutting everyone else out.

COMMUNICATING WITH LOVE AND SUPPORT

Communication Actions	Scripture
1. Listen. Stop what you are doing. Listen to the words. Listen to the language of behavior. Listen to feelings "between the lines."	Prov. 18:13
2. Think before speaking. Answer questions. Respond to feelings. Allow for differences of opinion.	Prov. 21:23 Prov. 15:28 Prov. 10:19
3. Watch the timing.	Eccl. 3:1, 7 Prov. 15:23 Prov. 25:11
4. Use a calm, soft answer. Express your feelings, rather than accuse. Off limits: labeling, sarcasm, ridicule, nagging. Anger breeds resentment. Soft answers come from God.	Prov. 15:1, 4 Eph. 6:4
5. Be encouraging. Forgive and forget. Focus on future potential	Prov. 12:18, 25 Isa. 50:4 Prov. 10:12

It will take some practice to communicate with love and support, especially if you are used to the command and demand mode. The effort to change will be worth it. A healthy family system is the most effective way of building your child's self-respect and communicating your values to your children.

FAMILY ACTIVITIES

Launch Out: Try something new, something silly, something crazy, or something daring. Have fun trying. Laugh and be a little crazy. Laugh together.

I Can Do That: Help each family member make a personal "I Can Do That" list. Little kids can draw pictures of things they can do. They can act them out, too. Older children and teenagers can focus on one specific area of competence, since there are so many things they can do. Kids tend to focus on what they can't do. A can do list builds confidence.

Who Thinks You Are Important? Start with the youngest member of the family. Ask each family member to suggest one person this child is important to and why. Then ask the child for additional suggestions of people she thinks she is important to. For each suggestion, give the child a paper doll with the person's name written on it. (Older children can easily make strings of paper dolls for this activity. Fold a sheet of paper several times horizontally. Cut half of a person's outline, with the

---

KEYS TO SELF-RESPECT AND CONFIDENCE

1. Begin with God + Me = A Whole Person. Without God we are incomplete persons.

2. Help your child feel significant to God and to important people in his life.

3. Help your child develop competence in many areas of life.

4. Recognize your child's accomplishments.

5. Concentrate on developing realistic goals.

6. Help your child develop power and control over her life.

CONTINUES NEXT PAGE ▼

CHART CONTINUED

7. Do everything possible to create a healthy family system.

8. Communicate with love and support.

---

arms outstretched. Unfold, and you will have a string of paper people.) At the end, talk about each person's string of people. Reinforce how significant we all are to others.

What you are is God's gift to you.
What you make of yourself is your gift to God.

GOD

LIVE the values

TEACH the values

PROTECT your child's mind

MAKE right and wrong very clear

DEVELOP self-respect and confidence

GIVE lots of practice in making decisions

SHOW your child how to deal with peer pressure

MAKE

GOD

REAL

CHAPTER 8

Give Lots of Practice in Making Decisions

How long will you waver between two opinions?
If the Lord is God, follow him; but if Baal is God,
follow him (1 Kings 18:21).

Learning to make decisions takes a lot of practice and patience.

As we arrived at Deer Park, I gave Sherise and Allen $2 each to spend during our visit. Their options were fairly limited—food for the animals, or rides on a donkey or a camel, or in the amusement area. Obviously they couldn't do everything. At 7 and 9 years, they were quite capable of keeping track of their money.

We started out with a walk down Storybook Lane, with plenty of opportunities to feed the animals—ducks, hamsters, sheep, geese. They both looked at their money and decided not to spend it to feed the animals—at least not the ones here and so early in the day. Shortly Allen noticed that plenty of feed had been dropped by other visitors along the path. Soon both kids were busily gathering food pellets and feeding them to the animals. When we came to the end of Storybook Lane, they'd had a good time feeding the animals and still had $2 each.

We enjoyed the deer and llamas the same way—feeding them food that others had dropped. The kids quickly found discarded food containers to hold their gleanings and seemed to have almost as much fun scrounging for food as they did feeding and petting the animals.

They decided the donkeys were too little for them to ride and a five-minute camel ride wasn't worth $2. I had to agree. I had always thought the camel ride a bit overpriced at this park.

We rode the free train around the park several times, admired more animals, took pictures, ate our lunch, played on the play castle, and then headed for the amusement rides. Sherise and Allen still had their $2. After riding the helicopters and the race cars, Sherise wanted to ride the mini Ferris wheel, but Allen didn't want to. She wouldn't go without him, so we sat on a bench for almost 20 minutes trying to decide. She really wanted to go, but not by herself. I get too dizzy to ride Ferris wheels, and there was no one else nearby that she knew. What to do? Decisions, decisions.

Finally Sherise decided she would go by herself, but by now the Ferris wheel wasn't running. It was a slow day at the park and the operator turned it on only when there were kids who wanted to ride. Somehow going over to the operator and asking him to ride seemed to be too much on top of going by herself. So we sat another 10 minutes mulling over the problem of talking to strangers, especially Ferris wheel operators, and the kids lamented they weren't like their cousin who isn't afraid to talk to anybody. Clearly we were stalemated, so I motioned to the operator, and he immediately came to the gate. Sherise jumped up and was just positioning herself in the seat when Allen made a sudden dash for the Ferris wheel. He had decided to go after all. Grinning, they went round and round together, the only kids on the ride.

We had "done" the park with money left over, so they decided to go back and buy food for some of their favorite animals. Everyone declared it a "fun day." No one had whined or begged for more money or rides. Sherise and Allen were happy with their choices, and I had enjoyed the day with them.

The day was a learning experience, as well as fun. They had made their choices carefully. They got to do everything they thought was interesting and had a feeling of control over their day. I had avoided all the whining, begging, and teasing for rides or money.

And I had the opportunity to practice patience. They couldn't be rushed into decisions, so we weighed pros and cons and took all the time they wanted. I had to be careful not to interfere by suggesting what I thought they might want to do or by expressing annoyance at their pace. There were no "right" or "wrong" decisions at Deer Park. Their choices for spending their money were strictly their own preferences. The decisions had to be theirs, and theirs alone, in their time. However, when shyness threatened to overwhelm Sherise, a little encouragement smoothed the way.

Deer Park gave us lots of value lessons. The kids' day included opportunity to practice responsibility, loyalty, self-control, contentment, and kindness. I brought responsibility, respect, self-control, and patience to our day.

Teaching children how to make decisions and giving them lots of practice are crucial for learning values. Many Christian parents are afraid to let their children make decisions for fear they will make the wrong ones. They are so afraid their children will reject their values that they never allow the kids to have choices.

During the past 50 years many research studies have shown that children who grow up in tightly controlling, authoritarian homes are the most likely to reject the values of their family. God allowed Adam and Eve to choose their own way. He has been working with His human family ever since to deal with the effects of their choice. But notice, God did not reject humans because they made a wrong choice. He allows each of us to freely choose or reject His way. We must allow our children the same freedom of choice.

How can we help our children learn to make wise decisions? Eventually everyone makes decisions of some sort, but many people make unwise, foolish decisions with serious consequences that affect the rest of their lives. We want our children to learn how to make wise decisions. Here are some simple steps for helping your children learn how to make wise decisions.

1. MAKE A FENCE WITHIN WHICH DECISIONS CAN BE MADE.

A fence defines the boundaries for the choice. What defined the fence at Deer Park? I gave the children $2 each. They didn't have an unlimited amount of money, and there were a limited number of ways to spend it. Anything they chose was OK with me. There were enough alternatives within the fence to make it interesting and challenging, but not overwhelming.

That same fence would have been too big for Miss 3-year-old who cannot keep track of money yet. A fence for her might have been "Which animals would you like to feed with the three dimes I just gave you? You can buy food three times. Each time the food will cost one dime."

If Mr. Twelve had been along on our day at Deer Park, I might have given him all the money I intended to spend for the day and let him pay the entrance fees, figure out how much each person got for spending money, and help the younger children figure out what they could buy with their money. He would have had his own spending money for the day as well.

Suzanne and Joe were committed to teaching Sherene to make choices. When she wanted a snack, Suzanne would take the 2-year-old into the pantry and show her the shelf with 10 to 12 boxes of different snacks. Inevitably, Sherene screamed and fussed and was unhappy with any choice she made, and wanted a different one. When they asked me what was wrong, I told them that young children are overwhelmed by too many choices. "Sherene can handle a choice between two things, but not a whole row of different snacks," I said. "She feels frustrated and inadequate. She needs lots of practice at this simple level of a choice between two things. When she is a little older, add one more item to the choices menu."

They tried it, limiting her choices of snacks to two items, and the fussing and tantrums over snack choices disappeared.

The fence protects children from choices that are overwhelming for them. For Sherene, trying to choose a snack from a menu of 15 choices was like roaming around alone in a 40-acre, unfenced pasture. Any 2-year-old would be frightened.

As children grow in skill, make the fence bigger by giving them more alternatives. But be sure that everything inside the fence is OK with you. Which toy would you like to share with your friend—the truck or the ambulance or the fire engine? Which of your play shirts do you want to wear today? What kind of fruit would you like for supper?

If your children have had practice in making increasingly more difficult choices, by the time they are teenagers they will be ready for the almost overwhelming decisions confronting them. Sometimes they will still need your guidance, but they will be ready for the challenge.

Even teenagers need a fence within which they can make their choices.

Your family might have a "fence" that says that your teens can be involved in up to four or five activities a week in addition to school and work. You could have a family council to decide which kinds of activities fit the description of wise choices, so that the guidelines are clear. Helping to formulate the guidelines for activities is part of learning to make wise decisions. Within those guidelines, your teens can choose their activities.

Your high school senior might be capable of handling an even larger fence. He is used to making wise time choices and he has learned the skills of making wise decisions. The only fence he might need is an agreed-upon time to be home every night, a time when he helps the family with household chores, and an agreement that he will show up for certain family meals. He can be counted on to meet his school and work commitments. He is almost ready for life on his own. Another 17-year-old might still need the guidance of a secure fence in order to make wise time decisions. Make the fence fit your child's experience and decision-making skills.

2. PROVIDE MANY OPPORTUNITIES TO PRACTICE MAKING DECISIONS.

Children need many opportunities to practice wise decisions until they become automatic—the child wouldn't think of doing otherwise. Then the values are really a part of who the person is, deep down inside. Many life situations are lots easier if there are some automatic responses.

One Friday afternoon I approached the drive-in teller at our local bank with a deposit and request for cash. When counting my money before leaving, I discovered the teller had given me $100 too much. I immediately spoke to her about the overpayment. It never occurred to me to do differently. I didn't go through a long decision-making process in my head. It was a totally automatic response. That automatic response has kicked in many times when I've been given excess change at the cashier or something else that did not belong to me.

Resist the impulse to make all decisions for your child. Many times it is easier to make the decision yourself, rather than to go through the decision-making process with your children. They are inexperienced and slow sometimes. They have a hard time making up their minds. Time is pressing and you would like to get on with your day, and so, in exasperation, you make the decision for the child. That conveys the message that she is inadequate and you do not trust her to make the decision. And so she does not acquire the experience she needs in learning to make decisions.

What can you do when you simply must get on with the day? You can't wait forever for Deniece to decide which outfit she wants to wear. You have to get to work on time, and she has to get to school. You could have a standing agreement with Deniece that if the decision isn't made by a certain time, you will make it for her or she will wear a standby outfit that is always ready. Remind her once of the time limit for the decision. Don't berate her or sigh with exasperation. At the agreed-upon time simply hand her an outfit. Your agreement with her includes no backtalk and no whining about your decision. She had her chance and did not use it. That is a useful lesson to learn, too. Give Miss Indecisive other opportunities to make decisions when time is not a factor.

3. TEACH YOUR CHILD DECISION-MAKING SKILLS.

I have noticed that many college freshman don't have the faintest idea how to make decisions. They never learned the skills of critical thinking and decision-making. I have seen this lack even in graduate students. Many people come to counseling because of poor decision-making skills. But decision-making skills can be learned, and you can teach them to your child. Even though your child may be learning critical thinking skills at school, home is the best place to practice these skills in real-life decisions.

Step 1: Collect facts. Find out everything you can about the subject. Mr. 9-year-old can look for facts about a drug (a decision he may have to make soon). Encyclopedias and a Bible concordance on CD-ROM and the Internet make this job easy and fun. Miss Sixteen can gather facts about a potential career or AIDS or abortion, all of which demand future decisions in her life. You can help Mr. Five gather facts about bicycles for children his age. Once a month have a fact-finding night at your house focusing on areas in which your children will need to make critical decisions.

Step 2: Test the facts. All sources are not equal. Discuss the sources. Evaluate the facts. Which ones are most likely to be accurate? Which sources are the most reliable? What is the difference between a fact from an encyclopedia and an instruction from God's Word? What kind of facts are on propaganda and advertising? Discard facts from questionable sources. This process helps your child learn critical thinking skills. They won't be taken in nearly so easily by false advertising or smooth-talking friends or strangers if they have learned to evaluate the source of the facts.

Step 3: Weigh the facts. All facts are not created equal. Some are much more important than others in making a decision. Make a plus and minus list for the decision being considered. Place the most important facts at the top of the list. One fact might be so overwhelming it will override everything else on the opposite side. Consider future consequences of this decision. What is likely to happen? What or who else might be affected? Children have to learn to anticipate consequences. They aren't born with this ability, although some children will learn it more easily than others. They learn bit by bit as you point out the consequences of a decision or ask them to think about the future consequences.

When weighing the facts, teach children to ask these questions:

Is there a clear right or wrong, according to God's Word? Teach children to go to God's Word for help in decision-making. A word Bible concordance helps find the right passage. Copy all the verses that seem to apply to this decision. Discuss the meaning of the verses. Let your children see you searching God's Word for guidance. Make it a family practice to go to God's Word for help in weighing the facts.

If there is no clear right or wrong, is this just personal preference? Or is there an undercover values issue that needs to be sorted out? Many decisions are simply personal preference: "What color shall I paint my bedroom?" "Shall I take tennis or swimming lessons? I don't have time for both." Although many decisions of modern life are not specifically mentioned in the Bible, they may have implications for living our values. Sometimes it isn't easy to figure out the undercover values issues and to find a biblical principle that applies. The Bible doesn't specifically say "You should not wear tight, very short skirts" or "You should not dye your hair purple," yet many people believe these involve moral values issues. How tight is tight? How short is short? Is it right because everyone else is doing it? What does modesty mean? Help your children think through these issues by asking probing questions.

When I first came to the university campus where I now teach, the dress code stated clearly that women students could not wear pants except to work at the furniture factory or for sports or similar activities. In a couple years the dress code allowed women to wear "pantsuits" during winter quarter (presumably for warmth in our cold climate), but tops had to cover the hips, and no jeans were allowed. A few years down the line women on campus were wearing pants all year. In another five years they were wearing jeans and T-shirts to classes. Eventually walking shorts were allowed during spring and summer quarters (presumably because it is warm). Now I see women wearing them during the winter with tights.

But back then no one was discussing how much jewelry a student could wear, as we are today. When I was in college the big dress issues were low necklines and bright makeup. When our daughter was in high school it was short skirts.

I usually tell this story to my graduate students in a class on character development and end with the question "Where is the principle here?" Is there an undercover issue? Sorting out guidelines for choosing clothes is a toughie, but it is an important area in which you and your children must make decisions. Your decisions need to be guided by carefully thought-out principles. The process of developing these principles is crucial for developing the skills of making wise decisions.

Are there other people who will be affected by my decision? Who and how? Even seemingly small personal preference decisions sometimes involve other people. The family is repainting the bedrooms this summer. Ebenezer wants his room painted bright orange, his current favorite color. The family budget won't cover a new bedspread and curtains to go with orange. Other people are affected by his decision. What compromise can be worked out? Can he earn the money to buy a new bedspread and curtains? Can he make them? Maybe the Goodwill store might have some at bargain prices. Maybe he can use orange as an accent color. Will he like orange next year? The family won't be repainting for at least three years. Some of these things could be added to his plus and minus list and might swing his final decision.

Step 4: Pray about the decision. Writing all the facts on a plus and minus list doesn't always settle matters of the heart, for decisions include both thinking and feeling. Some children are naturally thinkers. That's how they make their decisions. They will take easily to collecting facts and weighing them. Others are naturally feelers. They want to make decisions based on feelings, not facts. They can be taught to include facts in their decision-making process, but they will always want to turn to feelings first.

All decisions really involve both thinking and feeling. Sometimes a child says, "It just didn't feel right. I don't know why, but I knew it wasn't right." That seems like feelings, but her intuition about the situation was probably built on past experience and facts that were not conscious at the moment of decision. Her decision was probably based on feelings and thinking that merged to make intuition, a right brain activity. The right brain specializes in going for the big picture—intuition—everything merging in one strong sense of direction. I also think the Holy Spirit sometimes plays a role in what we call intuition, by nudging us in the right direction. Children should be taught to follow those hunches that come from intuition—they are usually right.

Your teenager may have collected all the facts, tested and weighed them, but his feelings still pull toward the opposite side from the carefully weighed facts. How can you help him control those feelings? Maybe the facts don't seem clear and the decision is difficult. Outside insight is needed.

The Holy Spirit has a way with hearts. Prayer can help align his feelings with what he knows is right. The Holy Spirit specializes in clear directions: "This is the way. Walk in it." The Holy Spirit also specializes in undercover work—finding the principles. Every significant life decision needs the input of the Holy Spirit as our partner in decision-making.

Wisdom comes from God. He eagerly responds to our requests for wisdom. Help your children claim Bible promises for wisdom (see James 1:5; Prov. 9:10; and Prov. 2:6-8). Post these promises in prominent places in your home. Refer to them when tough decisions pop up. Children need to know on a mental and a feeling level that God is deeply interested in every aspect of their lives and will guide in every decision. He will carry them through the difficult times. He will help them make wise decisions.

ENCOURAGEMENT AND SUPPORT

As children are learning to make wise decisions, they need humongous amounts of parental support and encouragement. Your encouragement will make the difference between an unwise or a wise decision and will let your children know you care about their decisions.

Let your child know you love him and are proud of him. "Honey, I'm proud of you!" "I love you lots and lots [hugs]!"

Affirm your child when she makes a wise decision. "You handled that decision well. You carefully weighed the pluses and minuses and came up with a wise decision. Great going!"

"Good choice!"

Respond sensitively to your child's difficult choices. "It's tough to decide to do something different from what your friends are doing. You want to be liked, and yet you knew what they were doing was wrong. You made a wise choice, even though it was hard."

Notice progress toward a decision. "This is a toughie, but you are making good progress toward a decision."

Express confidence and positive expectations. "I know you can do it, even though it isn't easy."

Guide toward a decision without being autocratic. "I wonder if you could help the other kids make a wise decision by suggesting something different to do for Halloween."

HANDLING MISTAKES

Children will make mistakes along the road to wise decisions. Expect them. Don't berate your child for a misstep in judgment, and don't be too quick to rescue her. Allow natural consequences to take over. They are excellent teachers.

Brianna had dilly-dallied with her major geography project, saying every day she still had plenty of time. Neither Mom's nor Dad's pointed questions about her progress made any impression. She tossed them off with a flick of her head and a "Don't worry. I'll get it done on time." Mom and Dad decided to say no more.

The night before the project was due, Brianna got out the materials, looked them over, and groaned. She couldn't possibly finish even if she stayed up all night. Teacher had promised an exciting field trip for everyone who turned in a completed project on time. What could she do? She really wanted to go on that field trip. No one offered to help. They were all busy with their own responsibilities. By 3:00 in the morning she was exhausted and nowhere near finished. She fell asleep at her desk and woke up with a splitting headache. The day of the field trip Brianna had a lot of time to think while she sat in study hall all day. Next time she'd plan ahead and make wiser decisions about time and preparation.

Brianna complained loudly about the unfairness of such a long assignment. She needed a lesson in time management and organization. She also needed to learn not to blame others for problems she herself had created. So her parents stepped in with a few pointed questions. How long had she known about the assignment? How should she have handled the assignment? Dividing it into parts and doing one part each week would have gotten it done on time. They went over the assignment with her and helped her divide it into reasonable sections that could have been done in a week. With that practice, next time she would be ready for a biggie.

Sometimes the consequences of a wrong decision are too important to allow a child to stumble along blindly trying to deal with the aftereffects or ignoring them completely. Josh wanted to play ball near the neighbor's house. Tim was reluctant because he had been warned many times not to play there. "It won't make any difference," coaxed Josh. "We can control the ball." But they couldn't or didn't, and the ball crashed through the neighbor's kitchen window. Tim's parents believed in responsibility, so they insisted he pay for the window. Tim needed a lot of parental support and encouragement as he worked every day after school to earn money to pay for the broken window. He learned an important lesson about decisions and responsibility.

Wrong decisions can be very valuable learning tools. Be sure your child knows you are there to support and encourage. Although you won't remove the consequences of the decision, you are there to help him through.

Sometimes a wrong decision can be changed midstream. Be there to offer encouragement and discuss the alternatives at the faintest indication your child sees her mistake and wants to change. *Never* say "I told you so. That was a stupid decision you made! About time you caught on!" Pride can often get in the way of admitting an error in judgment, and cutting words never help. Your encouragement can make the difference between learning from a mistake and stubbornly refusing to change.

CHECK UP ON SKILLS

Check up on your child's decision-making skills by circling the number that describes her skill level. Then help her grow by teaching and practicing the needed skills (next page).

CHECKING UP ON DECISION-MAKING SKILLS

Skill	Beginner						Skilled
Knows how to collect facts.	1	2	3	4	5	6	7
Knows how to test the facts.	1	2	3	4	5	6	7
Thinks logically from facts to future consequences.	1	2	3	4	5	6	7
Can make a plus and minus list in priority order.	1	2	3	4	5	6	7
Knows how to weigh the facts.	1	2	3	4	5	6	7
Knows how to determine right and wrong.	1	2	3	4	5	6	7
Looks realistically at key issues and reality of situation.	1	2	3	4	5	6	7
Connects values with decisions to be made.	1	2	3	4	5	6	7
Controls impulses and considers danger.	1	2	3	4	5	6	7
Considers God's Word when making decisions.	1	2	3	4	5	6	7
Understands cause and effect and links it to own actions.	1	2	3	4	5	6	7

CHART CONTINUES

Skill	Beginner						Skilled
CHART CONTINUED							
Considers the "fence" when making decisions.	1	2	3	4	5	6	7
Looks for undercover issues and principles.	1	2	3	4	5	6	7
Considers how other people will be affected.	1	2	3	4	5	6	7
Prays about decisions.	1	2	3	4	5	6	7
Combines thinking and feeling when making decisions.	1	2	3	4	5	6	7
Analyzes mistakes and learns from them.	1	2	3	4	5	6	7
Knows and feels God cares and will help with decisions.	1	2	3	4	5	6	7
Responds automatically to some values decisions because of much practice in making wise decisions in that area.	1	2	3	4	5	6	7
Welcomes the challenge of decision-making.	1	2	3	4	5	6	7
Is growing in ability to make wise decisions.	1	2	3	4	5	6	7

FAMILY ACTIVITIES TO STRENGTHEN DECISION-MAKING SKILLS

Fact Finding: Have a fact-finding night once a month. Work together to collect facts about an important decision area.

What-if Game: Make up lifelike situations that demand real thinking to resolve. "What if your best friend asks you to show her the answer to a question on a test when the teacher steps out of the room?" "What if another kid at day care comes along and knocks down the tower you had so carefully built with the Legos blocks?"

Guidelines: Talk about guidelines for choosing personal and family activities. Make a list of different activities that meet your family's guidelines.

Test the Facts Game: Each person gives a fact, either made up or true. The rest of the family tries to decide whether it is true or false and where it came from. Is it a reliable source?

Weigh the Facts Game: Use a list of pluses and minuses about a decision your family is dealing with. The family decides how much weight to assign each fact. Use a balance, if you have one, and place the facts in the balance. Each fact could be taped to a weight or block of different sizes as a visual demonstration of weighing facts.

Role Play: Act out a difficult decision your children might confront, including the consequences of different decisions.

Moral or Not? Game: Toss out different kinds of decisions, ones that are strictly personal preference and others that have a clear right and wrong or moral implication. The children can place each decision where it belongs. Anyone can suggest decisions.

Who's Affected? Game: Describe different kinds of decisions and ask, "Who is affected by this decision?" Cut out people from a catalog and glue on cardboard or use paper dolls or felt people figures. Ask the children to pick the people who are affected by this decision, if any. Arrange the people in a visual representation of who is affected by this decision and to what extent. Make places for "No one is affected," "Affected a little bit," and "Affected a lot" or whatever labels your family's creativity can dream up.

Guidelines: Find Bible verses that provide guidelines for various types of decisions. Copy them on cards to post around the house.

KEYS TO DECISION-MAKING

1. Make a fence, appropriate to your child's age, within which decisions can be made.

2. Provide many opportunities to practice making decisions.

3. Teach your child decision-making skills: how to collect facts, test the facts, and weigh the facts.

4. Teach your child how to find out if there is a clear right or wrong according to God's Word.

5. Practice finding the principle that should guide a decision.

6. Consider other people who might be affected by this decision.

7. Pray with your child about the decision.

8. Provide plenty of encouragement and support.

9. Handle mistakes carefully. Allow natural consequences to take over. Provide guidance so your child will learn from the mistake.

10. Encourage family activities that will strengthen decision-making skills.

It's not hard to make decisions when you know what your values are.
                                                    —*Roy Disney*

GOD

LIVE the values

TEACH the values

PROTECT your child's mind

MAKE right and wrong very clear

DEVELOP self-respect and confidence

GIVE lots of practice in making decisions

SHOW your child how to deal with peer pressure

MAKE

GOD

REAL

CHAPTER 9

Show Your Child How to Deal With Peer Pressure

When Peter saw him, he asked,"Lord, what about him?" Jesus answered, "If I want him to remain alive until I return, what is that to you? You must follow me." John 21:21, 22.

Peer pressure is a lot like the hurricane Georges that hit the Caribbean in 1998. The storm caused at least $2 billion in damages in Puerto Rico alone, where our son lived. Very few lives were lost on the island, however, because they were prepared. In recent years Puerto Ricans have worked very hard to build themselves cement block houses on strong foundations. Almost all houses have metal louvers at the windows, which can be used to shut out storms. The windows in our son's new home were guaranteed to withstand hurricane-force winds. When we lived there 30 years ago many people lived in wooden houses, easy prey to the destructive forces of hurricanes.

A hurricane watch sends people scurrying to board up their homes. Many people have boards especially prepared to cover large areas of glass, with places to screw them into the frame of the house. Water, candles, and food are stored. Some people have their own gasoline generators for emergency power supplies.

The eye of the hurricane hovered over Mayagüez on the western end of the island for several hours. Many people had no electricity, water, or telephone for months following the hurricane. Yet very few lives were lost. Inconveniences? Yes. Loss of trees and gardens? Yes. Loss of life? No. The secret—preparation.

Peer pressure hits kids just like a hurricane—with full force and the potential to "kill" emotionally. But families who have prepared their kids by building a solid values foundation and specific skills to divert peer pressure will withstand the onslaught. A few tumbles? Yes. Loss of character and life's vision? No.

Peer pressure begins in preschool, and the pace accelerates on through childhood, adolescence, and youth. While the intensity does lessen after youth, adults sometimes feel peer pressure, too. Peer pressure is not an invention of the twentieth century or a special trick for the twenty-first century. It has been around since Cain and Abel, but many experts feel it has escalated during the past three decades. What can you do to help your child deal with the increased peer pressure he or she is feeling every day?

How vulnerable is your child to peer pressure? Many factors make a difference, including your child's personality. The children most vulnerable to peer pressure are those alienated from their families. They act bored or apathetic, and they have a poor self-image and lack self-respect. They also are not really plugged into school. They are marginal students on the fringe of the school community, not really involved.

If your child has been in day care with many other children most of her waking hours since she was very young, she probably looks to her peers for approval for her actions. She is more vulnerable to peer pressure than children who have spent more time with adults.

Changing schools, moving to a new location, or changing cultures makes children easy prey to peer pressure. They want to fit in and find friends, so are likely to do anything anyone else suggests. Children from dysfunctional families who do not support them are easily persuaded to join a gang. They yearn to "belong," and the gang gives them that feeling.

Some children seem to need significant doses of approval of other children. Others shrug their shoulders and couldn't care less. Our son was perfectly happy with a few good friends. He didn't seem to care what the rest of the world did. He had good friends and they supported each other.

On the other hand, our daughter wanted to know and be liked by everyone. She was definitely more vulnerable to peer pressure. However, she came to high school with a reputation as a "good girl." Although some students at her Christian school experimented with drugs, she told me no one ever offered her any. Even her closest friends didn't suggest she do some activities they knew she wouldn't want to do. A child's reputation, acquired earlier, can be very protective. Helping your child deal with peer pressure begins very young.

INCREASE FAMILY INFLUENCE

Family influence is an important key to preventing peer pressure. Sharon Scott, a nationally recognized expert on peer pressure and author of *Peer Pressure Reversal*, suggests that the following societal changes have increased peer pressure by decreasing the influence of the family on the developing child. These trends have lessened the quality and quantity of adult-child interaction. In other words, kids don't spend as much time with adults as they used to. When kids spend most of their time with other kids, peer pressure is stronger. Time with adults helps to moderate peer pressure.

Families are more mobile, so neighborhoods lack unity. In former times neighbors watched out for everyone's kids. Fewer families live near their extended families. Once grandparents, aunts, uncles, and cousins all took care of each other. It was harder for kids to get away with something when so many people might know about it.

The increase in single-parent families and dual-parent working families has sharply decreased the amount of time children spend with their parents. Moms and dads are simply too busy to be with their kids very much. Consequently kids find themselves on their own with their peers. The average workweek in the United States has increased several hours during the past two decades. Parents want independent, self-reliant kids who can take care of themselves so they won't have to pay too much attention to what is going on. Every popular magazine talks about self-reliant kids who can take care of themselves. That seems to be the primary goal of parenting right now.

Teens—and younger—on TV provide predominantly negative models. Real teens—and younger—feel pressure to be like the kids on TV. Rock stars, movie stars, and sports stars in general do not provide positive role models for kids today. Greed and unrestrained and irresponsible sex are the norm. The easy availability of alcohol and other drugs increases the pressure to be part of the gang.

Scott points out that even some positives can carry negative vibes for family life. Electrical devices—dishwashers, computers, video games, TVs, and Walkmans—separate families. We did not have a dishwasher when our children were in the elementary school, and so we washed dishes together. While washing dishes we talked, learned songs, made up new words to songs we knew, and tried to have fun doing this daily chore. Most of the time it was definitely quality time together. It doesn't take several people to tidy up the kitchen and load the dishwasher. It can be done in a few minutes.

In homes full of electronic gadgets and labor-saving devices, each person lives in his or her own world, not interacting with other members of the family, thus decreasing time with adults. Lost—valuable time that could be used to pass on your values.

Decreasing such societal influences is an important part of helping our children cope with peer pressure. What can Christian families do to decrease their impact? What can your family do? Go through the previous paragraphs once more and think about each area. What can you do to lessen the impact of such changes on your family? What can you do to increase the amount of time your children spend with adults and lessen time spent with their peers? Sharon Scott feels this is an important key to reducing the power of peer pressure.

Recently I talked with some former students who told me they were moving. Why? They liked their jobs and where they were living, but they decided they wanted their children to grow up near their grandparents. They wanted the influence of their extended family, so they found jobs near their family. They had made a decision to increase family influence, and I congratulated them. What can you do to increase family influence?

When your child goes out to confront the world, how quickly he or she caves in to peer pressure will often be the bottom line. You need a planned program to immunize your kids against peer pressure.

Begin early with the idea that sometimes we cannot do what everyone else is doing. We choose to be different because God wants us to. Explain that following the crowd is often not God's way. He has warned us about the crowd. Jesus said huge crowds walk the road to destruction, but very few walk the road to eternal life. We are individually accountable to Him. Sometimes we will choose to be different.

Most Americans want their children to be outgoing and popular and spend lots of time with their peers. Many parents measure their success as parents by how popular their children are with their peers. Yet some children don't fit that mold. They are different. Their interests don't mesh with those of other kids their own age—they'd rather read a book or develop a computer program than hang out with the crowd. Actually, peer pressure is much less for those children because they have already chosen to be different and not do what everyone else is doing. Be grateful your child wants to walk to a different drummer. Many families home school their children for this very reason—they don't want them to do what everyone else is doing.

Make your propaganda early! Talk about teenage activities before your child is a teenager. Establish what you expect for her behavior before the turmoil arrives. Discuss peer pressure and its effects. Talk over boyfriends and girlfriends, clothes, cars, and dates long before the hormones transform your child into a stranger. Explore principles to guide entertainment selection. Consider how to choose friends. Get ready for plunging into the river that separates childhood from adulthood before your child arrives at the water's edge. Then it's too late to give swimming lessons. Prepare, prepare, prepare!

Encourage family rather than peer orientation. Research on substance abuse has pointed out that young people who have a stronger family orientation are less likely to abuse alcohol and drugs or to succumb to peer pressure in other areas. The stronger the child's ties to the family, the more influence the family has in establishing values. If your family structure is weak—and you know it—run, don't walk, to the nearest Christian counselor and begin to change today! For the sake of your children's future you need a strong family now.

If your basic family structure is sound, but you've unthinkingly bought into the idea that kids need to be with their peers most of the time, try some of the following (next page) suggestions to strengthen family ties:

Encourage active involvement in worthwhile activities. The child who participates in extracurricular activities at school—plays in the band, serves on the staff of the school paper or as

STRENGTHENING FAMILY TIES

1. Be interested in what your child is doing. Ask. Participate.

2. Cultivate family hobbies and interests.

3. Be one jump ahead. Plan many interesting family activities. Encourage the children to plan family activities.

4. Limit time with peers in favor of family activities.

5. Invite other children to do things with your family. Welcome your children's friends.

6. Stock your home with kid-friendly activities—games, ping-pong, basketball, crafts, hobbies, CDs. Buy family memberships to interesting places so your children can take friends with them.

7. Cultivate your children's friendship. At least once every two weeks have a "date" with each of your children.

8. Be creative in finding time to be with your children.

9. Respect your children's growing maturity.

10. Make home the most attractive place in the world. Keep things picked up and the cookie jar and the refrigerator full. Send out a message of warmth and welcome.

a peer counselor or mentor—and is active with a church or community volunteer service program will acquire friends also involved in those same activities. They will usually be the kids who have a positive influence on others.

While your child is still in grade school, help him learn some skills that will open doors for worthwhile activities in high school. Such skills will give status, satisfaction, and involvement in constructive activities, and provide opportunities for friendships with the "good kids." The person respected for his/her ability in some area is more often respected in other decisions also. After-school jobs—mowing lawns, baby-sitting, a paper route, or selling a product—teach responsibility and give kids confidence. They teach a child how to deal with people situations.

Help your child learn to dress attractively and know what to do in social situations. The child who feels confident in social situations will be much less likely to find herself overwhelmed with peer pressure. She knows how to handle things. Respected by the other kids, she "belongs," even though she doesn't always agree with what the crowd wants to do.

Help your preteen learn how to select attractive clothes that suit her personality and body type. Use family activity nights to practice manners and how to get along on dates. Older kids can coach younger siblings. Look for good books on these topics at the library. Model social skills at home.

Establish clear guidelines for your child's behavior. "My dad said I can't" is a good backup for a child's decision. The family is the guardian of standards. Research from Search Institute points out that teenagers with mature faith and positive attitudes toward the church generally come from families that have clear standards for behavior and enforce them. Their research shows that teenagers accept standards from their family much better than from either the church or the school. Moms and Dads, it's up to us!

It takes a lot of time on our knees and with His Book to be able to tell the difference between moral issues on which we should take a clear position and passing cultural fads with no real moral implications, even though they're different from the way we did things. And it demands a lot more time on our knees to acquire the patience and stamina to stay by our convictions and make the consequences stick. Parenting is not for weaklings! It's the most challenging job in the world.

Encourage your child to make values commitments ahead of time. As your child is looking toward seventh and eighth grades, have some serious talks about the pressures of the teen years. Take your child out to eat with just Mom and Dad. Have a heart-to-heart talk about sexual purity and the joys of saving yourself for your wedding night. If you came to marriage a virgin, what you say will have a ring of authenticity. If you didn't, think carefully about how you are going to respond if your child asks, "Were you virgins on your wedding night?" An honest response is in order: "No, and I've always regretted it. I want you to have the joy I missed." Give your child a visible token of that purity (for a girl, perhaps a heart pin with her initials and the date engraved on the back that she can give to her husband on her wedding night as a sign of the purity she brings to their relationship). Prepare an attractive card (easy to do on computers) with a Bible verse and a commitment to virginity that your child can sign. Suggest to your child that you go out for a date every year on her birthday to renew the commitment. Family accountability reduces a lot of pressure from peers.

A commitment ahead of time helps immensely with some of the toughest decisions: I will not do drugs. I will not smoke cigarettes or use alcohol. Firm decisions made beforehand make it much easier at the moment of pressure. Don't leave these decisions to chance. Do everything possible to encourage your child to make some firm promises based on solid values.

Teach your child how to recognize and respond to peer pressure. Sharon Scott, in *Peer Pressure Reversal*, suggests that a child, after recognizing that he is in a peer pressure situation, needs to have the tools to get out of the situation in 30 seconds. Otherwise he will succumb to the pressure. Escaping a bad situation in 30 seconds means your child requires some automatic responses that he can use almost without thinking. He must practice them ahead of time in order to make them automatic.

Kids feel the most pressure from their close friends or boyfriend/girlfriend. Such situations are the hardest to refuse because your child fears losing the friendship. The tools for getting out without losing the friendship will really pay off here.

Step 1: Teach your child to recognize pressure tactics. Starting when your child is around 6 or 7 years old (or younger), teach him the signs to look for that suggest the other kids are trying to get him to do something he shouldn't. Have your child listen on the playground or when with friends to see if he can figure out when someone is pressuring other kids. What does he himself say when he wants to persuade a friend to do something?

The exact words vary with each generation of kids and each culture, but the underlying message is the same—"Do what I want or else I'll make fun of you! You won't be my friend anymore!" Figuratively the kid is saying "I'll blow you up!" If your child can't think of any "dynamite" words, suggest some from your childhood or ones you have heard recently . . . chicken, baby, fraidycat, Mama's boy. Usually this will get him thinking. Make a list of these "dynamite" words or phrases. Go over these pressure tactics many times until your child recognizes them quickly. Practice by making pressure and nonpressure statements. See how quickly your child can recognize the "dynamite" ones. A bell should go off in his head immediately—"Dynamite! Gotta watch out!"

Body language and tone of voice are also big clues to "dynamite" situations. Figure out with your child how other kids act when they are pressuring—changing their tone of voice, huddling together so an adult won't hear, looking around furtively, etc. Role-play some of these situations so your child will immediately recognize "dynamite situations" by the words said, the tone of voice, or the body language.

As soon as she recognizes a "dynamite situation," she must think about the consequences if she gives in. Will she get into trouble with anyone? Is there a rule she might be breaking? Is this forbidden by God's commandments? She has to think this through very quickly and come to a conclusion: I don't want to do this, or This is OK.

Step 2: Teach your child how to respond to pressure tactics. Remember, she has 30 seconds to get out of the situation, or it's likely she'll succumb to the pressure. She has only two chances to say no. After that she needs to leave the scene, according to Scott. The response techniques need to be practiced until they become automatic. (See Scott's book for more details on how to teach and rehearse the responses.)

Your child's response to pressure needs to fit her personality. Some kids can defuse a bad situation with a joke, but others would fall flat on their face if they tried a humorous approach. Know your child and what might be most comfortable for her. Be sure she has at least four or five options. Basically her options fall into three categories: Say No, Be Funny, or Toss It Back.

Let's take a quick look at these responses. There are many ways to say no. Your child can just say "no—nah, not now, can't, nope, forget it, not today." He can also just leave the situation. Walk away. Act offended. Leave casually. Leave with confidence. She can pretend she didn't hear, ignore the whole suggestion, and move on to something else. She can also say no by making an excuse—my folks won't let me, I have other plans, I don't feel like it, I've got chores to do. 'Bye.

Being funny takes a little more skill, but humor is a skill that can be learned. Kids respond well to humor. He can be funny by offering a really crazy excuse—I've got to talk to my plants or brush my canary's teeth! Can't—the FBI is consulting me about a deal, or the principal is consulting me about how to run the school. Or he can act really shocked—I can't believe you'd do that! Jokes are obviously ridiculous. Other kids laugh and the tension eases, but they get the point—he doesn't want to do what they have suggested.

She can toss it back by abruptly changing the subject—Hey, let's go to my house and listen to my new CD. She can also throw the pressure tactic back—Chicken? It takes one to know one. If you want to be my friend, you'd better not ask.

Any type of response takes practice until the child feels really comfortable giving it. He needs to pull it off with aplomb and confidence. Repeatedly go over the steps of how to escape a bad situation—make your statement (not more than two responses), then turn around and depart without any further comments or arguments. Leave with dignity and confidence and go on to another activity. Emphasize the 30-second rule—in and out of the bad situation in 30 seconds!

The research on how we influence others' thinking suggests that it is easier to sway a group if you state your conviction at the beginning. If you present your ideas positively, others will probably follow along. Teach your child this technique. Give her a repertoire of positive ideas for activities that she can suggest instead of the negative ones. Practicing the ideas at home until they've become almost automatic will prepare your child to successfully confront negative peer pressure. And be sure she knows how to reach you and always has coins to make a phone call. "Come get me!" should send you on a rescue mission with no questions asked.

Inspire your children with high ideals from God's Word. They need a clear "Thus saith the Lord" to back up the principles you've taught them. Search together in God's Word for guidelines for the situations your child must confront. Challenge him to live in relationship with God every day. Demonstrate yourself how to do this. Share your own walk with the Lord, the difficult moments as well as the glorious ones. When Jesus is your best friend, it's a lot easier to say no to other friends who want you to do something that would offend your Best Friend.

FAMILY ACTIVITIES

Culture: Have a heart-to-heart chat with your spouse (or yourself if you are a single parent). Look at the cultural things that separate children and adults. What can you do to increase their time with adults and lessen time with peers? Decide on one thing you will do to give you and your children more time together.

Propaganda: Select a "propaganda" topic to discuss during family night: What is peer pressure? How does it affect kids? What's it like to have a boy/girl friend? What do kids do on dates? What do you have to know before you can drive a car? What kind of entertainment (spelled recreation) will really recreate our bodies and minds? What kinds of kids make good friends?

Teen Intro: On your child's thirteenth birthday, arrange a private time with Mom and Dad. Have a special treat. Talk about the responsibilities of becoming a teenager and growing up. Make a list of the skills he will need to develop before he graduates from high school and goes out to work or on to college. Decide which ones are appropriate for this year. Develop a plan. Each year check up on progress and add skills to the plan.

Family Hobby: Take a family vote on a new hobby you would like to develop together. Set aside time to begin.

Date Time: Have a "date" with each child at least once every two weeks. On that date, the child gets to choose what to do and where to go.

Personal Appearance: Have your colors done as a family or go to a workshop on color coordinating. Then learn how to choose clothes that fit with your colors. Secret tip: When all your colors go together you need fewer clothes, but appear to have more.

Peer Pressure: Teach peer pressure skills. Do this as a family, including younger and older children. Use the ideas of this chapter or follow a book on peer pressure. Check with your local Christian bookstore.

Friendship With Jesus: As a family read a book about effective prayer. Practice what you have learned. Start a family prayer diary in which you write prayer requests and answers.

Friendship With Jesus: Decide on a time of the day when all family members will have their personal, private time with Jesus. The first 15 minutes after waking up works well for many families. Talk about what to do during this time. Help each child prepare a basket with supplies for their time with Jesus—tapes, books, Bible, journal. Even very young children can enjoy a special time with Jesus.

KEYS TO DEALING WITH PEER PRESSURE

1. Increase family influence.

2. Begin early with the idea that sometimes we cannot do what everyone else is doing.

3. Make your propaganda early.

4. Encourage family rather than peer orientation.

5. Encourage active involvement in worthwhile activities.

6. Establish clear guidelines for your child's behavior. Hold to them. Provide consequences for deviance.

7. Encourage your child to make values commitments ahead of time.

8. Teach your child how to recognize and respond to peer pressure.

9. Inspire with high ideals from God's Word. Encourage a personal relationship with Jesus.

Birds of a feather flock together.

—American proverb

PART 2

FRUITS OF THE VALUES TREE:

How to Help Children Learn Specific Values

VALUES BEGIN WITH GOD

All values grow in the soil of love.
God's love planted in your heart expresses itself in these values.
They give substance to love.

Love rejoices with truth Love does not delight in evil. Love always trusts	Faith in God
Love is not rude	Respect
Love always protects Love never fails	Responsibility
Love is kind Love keeps no record of wrongs	Kindness and compassion
Love rejoices with truth. Love does not delight in evil.	Honesty and integrity
Love does not boast Love is not proud Love is not self-seeking	Humility
Love is not easily angered	Self-control
Love is patient Love always perseveres	Patience and perseverance
Love does not envy	Contentment and thankfulness
Love never fails Love always hopes	Loyalty and commitment

—1 Corinthians 13

CHAPTER 10

Faith in God

So then faith cometh by hearing, and hearing by the word of God. Rom. 10:17, KJV.
The fruit of the Spirit is . . . faith. Gal. 5:22, KJV.

Three-year-old Alisha wore a puzzled expression as her family settled themselves on a church pew, waiting for the service to begin. Soon Mother felt a tug on her sleeve and heard Alisha's whisper, "Mommy, teacher said the church is God's house. Where is His bed? Where does He cook?" Mommy tried to hide her amusement behind a smile as she replied, "I'll explain it after church."

Nine-year-old Allan cried disconsolately. He'd lost the special hunting knife his dad had made for him from hard steel and leather. When he started across the alfalfa field next to their house, the knife was securely in his holster fastened to his belt. But when he reached for it on the other side of the field, it was gone. How could he ever find it in a field of alfalfa? Mommy hugged him and said confidently, "Let's call the whole family, and we will all pray that God will help us find your knife. He knows exactly where it is right now." So the family gathered, and everyone prayed that God would help them find the knife. Then they all went out looking, trying to cover all the steps Allan thought he had taken. A shout of triumph! Dad had found the knife hidden among the alfalfa plants. Another family gathering. More prayers. But this time broad smiles lit every face, and all the prayers echoed "Thank You, God."

Liza, our 14-year-old granddaughter, is facing a major move. She has lived all her life on a beautiful Caribbean island. Now her parents have decided to move back to the United States. Recently she sent me this e-mail message: "The thought of moving scares me. I keep asking myself if they'll like me and I'll make friends. This all scares me, but I know that I'll like it when I get up there. God will be with me, and I'll do all right." Clearly she is depending on God to see her through this major upheaval. Her parents have passed along their own faith in God to her. I have heard them say, "God will lead us. He has everything under control."

Three, 9, or 14. Age doesn't matter. It's all part of passing along our faith in God to our children—one of the greatest joys, and sometimes one of the greatest puzzles, of parenting.

Faith in God is the most important value you can pass along to your children. It undergirds all the other values. Without it, values lack meaning and substance. They become things we do—actions on the outside—rather than flowing naturally from God in our hearts and minds. Values begin with God. Give your best effort to guiding your children toward faith in God. To begin, consider What does faith in God look like in everyday life?

WHEN I HAVE FAITH IN GOD . . .

I believe that Jesus died on the cross to save me because He loves me and wants me to be with Him always.

Hope

Trust

Belief

Confidence

Conviction

I believe what God tells me in His Book—the Bible. I know He wants me to obey His words.

I trust God to lead me and to guide my life.

I know God will help me when I am in trouble. I am confident He will show me what to do.

I know Jesus will forgive anything wrong I do and He will cover up all my sins with His perfect life.

I want Jesus to be my very best friend. I want Him to walk with me every day, to hold my hand, and to pick me up when I stumble or fall.

Jesus gives me the courage to live my convictions, even when it is tough, because He is always with me.

GOD'S VIEW OF FAITH

Faith is a gift from God to each person. He promises to give us faith, if we ask for it. We can't make up faith on our own—God gives it to us. Faith means believing God will be with you even when you can't see what's around the next corner in your life. God will honor your faith.

Bible People

Use this guide with your children:

Hebrews 11 is called the faith chapter. It tells about many people who did outstanding things because of their faith in God. How many people are mentioned in Hebrews 11 because of their faith? Make a list of these people. Then look in the Bible to see if you can find the whole story. Talk about their faith. Their faith gave them great courage, and many did extraordinary things for God. What other things did they do in faith that are not mentioned in this chapter? Were there times when these people forgot about their faith in God? What happened? What did God do when they forgot? Pick out your favorite "faith" person. Find out all you can about that person. Look in a Bible dictionary or concordance or encyclopedia. Maybe your library has a book about that person. Create something about that person—a drawing or painting, sculpture, story, drama, poem, craft, etc.

Now faith is being sure of what we hope for and certain of what we do not see. Heb. 11:1.

I live by faith in the Son of God, who loved me and gave himself for me. Gal. 2:20.

Take up the shield of faith, with which you can extinguish all the flaming arrows of the evil one. Eph. 6:16.

Fight the good fight of faith. 1 Tim. 6:12.

Be strong and of good courage; do not be afraid, . . . for the Lord your God is with you wherever you go. Joshua 1:9, NKJV

Trust in the Lord with all your heart, and lean not on your own understanding; in all your ways acknowledge Him, and He shall direct your paths. Prov. 3:5, 6, NKJV.

HOW TO HELP CHILDREN DEVELOP FAITH

While faith is a gift from God, there are many things you can do in your family to help your children accept that gift.

GENERAL GUIDELINES

1. Carefully design the atmosphere of your home to lead toward God. Children absorb the atmosphere around them. Atmosphere can be felt as soon as you step into a home. Make yours palpably spiritual and faith-oriented. Ask yourself, *If a stranger came to our home, would he know we are people of faith in God?* Chapter 5 has some suggestions for atmosphere designs.

2. Share your joy in the Lord. Children gravitate toward joy and happiness. Talk about the special things God has done for your family. Thank Him daily for His blessings. Make a "Joy From God" notebook about your family. In it record special joys from God that you and your family have experienced. Share God's love and forgiveness. Share His grace. Share the JOY! If you can't think of any joy to share, ask God to show you His joy. Write down every insight. Little by little His joy will fill your heart and you will naturally pass it on to your children.

3. Pray *for* your children and *with* your children every day. Pray many short prayers during the day to communicate your joy or sorrow or need to God. Converse with God all day. Your children will quickly pick up the idea, and God will become their confidant and friend too. Make prayer an established tradition to begin and end every day. Gather your family around you before you send them out to confront the world each morning. Pray for angel protection and the Holy Spirit to be with each family member during the day. Do the same each evening, thanking God for His blessing and care during the day. Pray about any problems that have come up that day or are a continuing concern for your family. Pray about decisions, wrongdoing, special events and temptations, and friendships, and pray for others. Ask the Holy Spirit to be with your children all the time.

4. As a family, read and study from God's Word every day. Choose a time of day when everyone can be relaxed and enjoy the experience of God's Word. Use a modern version so the children will understand better. Explain difficult phrases. Select short passages that have meaning for the children and that will be a guide for their behavior. Whatever you do, don't use God's Word as a hammer over their heads. You will turn them off, and they will reject God. Instead, let them wrestle with the meaning of the Bible verse and come up with their own ideas. Trust the Holy Spirit to speak to your child.

5. Share your personal faith experience with your children. Remember to "live the values." Your own model speaks the loudest! Share your faith experience with its ups and downs with your children. They will learn that faith is a real part of your life, and they will want that faith, too. Demonstrate in your own life the power of God's grace.

6. Be open to talking about faith and God with your children and discussing their questions and concerns. Don't let your faith and belief in God be one of your family's best-kept secrets. Talk openly and freely about God. Listen carefully for your child's needs and unspoken questions. Respond with love and concern, not criticism. Children can be gently led, but not driven, toward faith in God. Lead with your faith.

7. Help your child develop a growing personal faith connection with Jesus and God. In the end, what counts is your child's own faith. All of the above ideas should focus on helping your child develop a personal faith connection with Jesus and God.

FOCUSED GUIDELINES

I have chosen two important areas for focused guidelines: God's Word and prayer. They are crucial for helping your children develop faith in God as their most important guiding value for life. They will make an unbreakable foundation for all other values.

God's Word

God's Word is the reason for our faith—it undergirds faith; it provides answers for life's dilemmas, assurance in difficulty, connection in times of stress, and promises for the future. Without a real connection to God's Word your child will not develop faith in God. Follow these guidelines to help your child connect to God's Word:

Show your own love and respect for God's Word. Use the Bible every day, lovingly and reverently. Turn to the Bible for help in daily affairs; claim promises for your family's needs. Have a special place of honor to keep the family Bible. Share your own insights from Bible study, as well as your joy in God's Word.

Associate Bible learning with your love and care. Make Bible learning a special family time of closeness. Learn about God's Word within an atmosphere of loving support. Avoid angry confrontations or put-downs associated with the Bible. Associate the Bible with cheerfulness, happiness, love, tenderness, and sympathy.

Make Bible learning fun and interesting. Create happy memories around God's Word. Use Bible games, role playing, audiotapes, videotapes, and pictures. Give your child a special Bible. Make it a remembered occasion when she receives the Bible. Create many opportunities to use the Bible at home. Make the Bible interesting by introducing extras, such as Bible customs, geography, or history. Avoid long speeches, tedious remarks, and hard words.

Teach Bible principles that will help your child deal with life. Emphasize positive principles. Show Bible reasons for faith. Go to the Bible for answers to everyday twists and turns. Help your child think independently about what the Bible says—what action should she take? Encourage your child to memorize key guiding verses that will be a comfort and guide to him in the future. Make memorizing Scripture fun and interesting. Personalize the Bible by relating it to your child's interests, needs, and puzzling situations.

Teach your older children how to use Bible study tools. When teens or preteens say the Bible is "boring," challenge them to learn something new: different views of Bible inspiration; how and why the Bible was written; how we got the Bible; how to use reference books (concordance, atlas, dictionary, commentary, encyclopedia, source book); beginning principles for Bible interpretation (such as the context, the unity of Scripture, important themes of the Bible, the Bible as final authority); referencing or cross-referencing subjects; overview of important historical events period by period; the most important key texts for Bible doctrines. Don't assume that because your child is attending a church-sponsored school he will learn all of these things. Many adults have no idea how to study God's Word. Scripture study can provide an unending depth of new understanding. Challenge your children to dig deeply.

Prayer

Prayer is your child's connection with God, a telephone line direct to the King of the universe. Young children are natural believers, so they will grasp prayer with open arms. Nothing is too hard for God!

Pray regularly with your children. Begin with your tiny baby. I believe the Holy Spirit surrounds the infant with the love of God and the baby feels something different when parents pray with the baby. Be regular about prayer for meals and bedtime so that prayer becomes an expected part of your toddler's life.

Begin teaching your child with simple spontaneous prayers. As soon as your toddler can talk, she can repeat one or two word prayers after you. As her vocabulary increases, she will begin to pray spontaneously. Children don't need to know memorized prayers. Let them pray what is on their heart in unrehearsed prayers. "Bless Mommy and bless Daddy and bless the cat and bless the dog."

Gradually introduce more aspects of prayer. As your child matures, introduce the different parts of prayer: Love You, God! (praise); My day (sharing with God); I'm sorry, I goofed (confession); Thank You! (thankfulness); Help! (requests). Introduce only one part at a time. Use that in prayer. For example, teach your children to tell God that they love Him each time they pray. Be sure to do this when you pray. Children are really good at the Help! part of prayer—they have lots of requests, and their prayers may consist of only requests. Gradually your children will learn to express their love to God, share their day, confess their faults, be grateful, and tell God what they need.

Help your children experience prayer as a friendship with Jesus. Prayer is like talking to a friend. Jesus is their special friend who never leaves them or quarrels with them. He's always there and wants to be their friend and helper. During the elementary school years children mature in their thinking about friends and in their friendship. Jesus as their friend suits their more mature thinking perfectly. Their friendship with Jesus can mature into an experience of real joy and security. This is what your teens need to see them through the turmoil of those years.

Model the kind of prayers you want your children to experience. When children are very young, pray simple prayers they can understand. As they grow, make your prayers match their new mental abilities. Your older children and teens need to know what prayer really means in your life—the struggles, the heartfelt confessions, the faith that is the heart of your communication with God. Give your children a taste of real communication with God, and they will want more. They have met the King.

TROUBLE WITH FAITH AND TRUST?

Faith in God emerges from the first building block of personality—trust. If that block is missing, a person—even an adult—has a very hard time trusting God. Babies learn trust very early. If they are fed when hungry, comforted when distressed, talked to and cuddled, and generally made comfortable, they learn to trust their world. During the first year of life they learn that their caregivers will respond to their needs. They come to feel that the world is a pretty good place. Enter trust! All the rest of personality is built on the trust foundation.

Some babies don't experience a caring environment during their first years. Some are actually abused, rather than loved. Others experience trust early on, but have some bad experiences later—Mom abandons the family or a neighbor boy sexually abuses the child. Exit trust.

Some children have trouble with trust and faith in people (and consequently God) for other more easily fixable reasons. They can't count on their parents' word. Promises don't mean anything, and threatened punishments never happen. The adult's words are meaningless, and their actions unpredictable. Dad promises to come for a visit and never shows or calls. One day Mom is loving and caring, the next bitter and hostile. The kid never knows what reaction he'll get. Exit trust.

Trust and faith in God begins with trusting earthly caregivers. Trust is a fragile flower that requires loving care. Kids who have lost trust—or never learned it—often become mean spirited, angry, defiant, and uncooperative. Or they simply do their own thing and ignore what the adults in their lives want them to do. Sometimes they become sly and deceptive, while outwardly charming. They hoard their things. They don't have any friends because friendship is based on mutual trust.

What can you do if you recognize that your child has serious trouble with trust? If the reasons run deep, immediately see a Christian counselor who can help you deal with the deep-seated issues. If the reasons are easily understood and changed, listen to what happens in your family. Do you keep your promises to your children? Do you do what you say you will do? Ask God for help to change so your children can get a glimpse of His trustworthiness through you. Change takes time, but you can rebuild trust in your children. As you rebuild trust with your children, trust and faith in God will begin to show through.

If an adult has been particularly unworthy of trust, the child can feel a real sense of joy and marvel at finding Someone who can be trusted— God. Emphasize how God loves the child, cares for her, and can always be trusted. God is the friend who never leaves and the parent who never abandons. The Holy Spirit is the comforter every child needs when in distress. Read many Bible stories about God and help your child learn promises that emphasize trust in Him.

Faith in God can be more difficult for children reared in families that place great emphasis on "thinking for yourself" and having "scientific proof" for everything. Highly educated parents may have been trained to discount faith in God and rely on their own thinking. Sometimes this attitude leaves very little room for trusting God and His leading. Everything has to be known ahead of time and explained. God's leading is seldom mentioned or even considered. It's a hazard of a high level of education.

If your home has a "discount faith" atmosphere, you will have to nurture faith in a special way. Pray for faith. Faith can be combined with solid thinking. Your child needs your model of a thinking person with faith. Make a strong effort to rely on God. Discuss the situation with your spouse. Begin to talk about faith. Give God credit and help your children acquire faith in Him. As Kant said, sometimes we have to deny knowledge to let faith in. What does that mean to you?

FAMILY ACTIVITIES

Trust Walk: Blindfold a child. Another child or an adult will be the blindfolded child's guide. Guide the child through different parts of the house, especially places where a guide is really needed because of small passageways or obstructions. The guide talks to the blindfolded person to lead him. Other family members can try to be distracting, by giving false directions or making lots of noise. Then reverse roles until every family member has had a chance to lead and to follow. If the children are very young, eliminate the distractions.

Debriefing: How did it feel when you couldn't see where you were going? Did you trust your guide? Did your guide get you back safely without running into anything? Did you get tricked by some of the bad directions? What did you have to do to get through without running into anything? How is trust in God like this game?

Do you know what will happen to you tomorrow? None of us do. We trust God to be with us. He will be our guide. Who tries to get us off track by shouting bad directions? What can we do about that?

Lions' Den: Look up 1 Peter 5:8. According to God's Word, we live in a lions' den. Wow! Remember Daniel and his night in the lions' den? How did he get out alive? (See Daniel 6 for the story.) He spent only one night in the lions' den, but God says we live in a lions' den all the time. Satan wants to eat us up and destroy us. How can he destroy us?

Get out some newspapers and look for articles that describe Satan as a roaring lion. (Murder, dishonesty, hatred, cruelty, greed, etc.) Look at the listing of movies. Family members can tell what they've heard about the movies—nudity, sex, violence, bad language, disrespect, etc. Satan is trying to get everyone.

If your children like to draw, draw some lions. On each one write one of the ways Satan, the roaring lion, tries to get kids. It takes courage to live in the lions' den. Who keeps us? Who gives us courage to say no? Who protects us from the lion? At the end, finish the picture (or bulletin board display) by placing a photo of your child in the center with a picture of Jesus in front of the child protecting him or her from the surrounding lions. Jesus is the lion tamer. He protects us from Satan, the roaring lion. He will keep the lion from getting us.

For younger children: They will not understand the symbolism of the lion's den, but you can make the game fun for them by letting them act as lions. Give each "lion" a name of a bad thing Satan tries to get little kids to do—disobey, sass, lie, etc. Let the kids suggest these names. The children can "roar" around the floor trying to "eat up" a sibling or a teddy bear or doll. Mom or Dad could be Jesus, who protects the child from the lions.

Family Prayer Book: Make a family prayer book about the different parts of prayer (Love You, God! My Day. I'm Sorry, I Goofed. Thank You. Help!). Do this as a family activity. In the Thank You section, your children could take pictures of things they are especially thankful for to put in the book, including themselves with the item. The children will have fun posing for pictures for the I'm Sorry, I Goofed section and the Help! section. A beautiful picture of Jesus completes the book.

Family Prayer Journal: Start a family prayer journal. In the journal record your family's prayer requests. Older children can write in their requests, while younger ones can draw pictures. Pray for each of these requests. Be sure to leave space for the experience of how God answers the prayer. Date each entry. Children who have experienced a family prayer journal usually want to have their own prayer journal as their faith in God increases.

QUOTABLE WISDOM

Ever since the beginning of the world, wise people have been passing on their wisdom. Storytellers told the wisdom to the next generation. Eventually the wisdom stories and proverbs became part of a culture and were quoted widely by parents to their kids. Deep thinkers wrote thought-provoking sayings.

What did your parents say about faith in God and courage? Pass their wisdom on to your children, or let your children pick a favorite from the following wisdom quotes, or make up one of their own.

"He who is small in faith will never be great in anything but failure."

"A soul without faith is like an observatory without a telescope."

"I have therefore found it necessary to deny knowledge, in order to make room for faith" (Immanuel Kant, 1787).

"Trust in God, but tie your camel."

"Go as far as you can see. When you get there you will see farther."

"When God holds your hand, you cannot fall."

"If you don't stand for something, you'll fall for anything."

"In matters of style, swim with the current; in matters of principle, stand like a rock" (Thomas Jefferson).

NATURE TRAILS TO FAITH

"But ask the animals, and they will teach you. Or ask the birds of the air, and they will tell you. Speak to the earth, and it will teach you. Or let the fish of the sea tell you" (Job 12:7, 8, ICB).

God speaks to us through nature, His second book. Your family can learn much about values from nature. Keep your eyes open for nature trails to faith.

Butterflies provide a wonderful illustration of what faith in God does for us. Find a caterpillar, observe it turn into a chrysalis, wait for the transformation into a beautiful butterfly—a new creature completely different from the caterpillar.

Faith in God will make you a new creature with His values. You will want to be like Him and live as His friend every day. You will be a completely new person.

Trees come in many shapes and sizes—palms, oaks, maples, flamboyants, pines, redwoods. Some have very deep root systems and are flexible. They can withstand hurricane-force winds and great storms because their roots are anchored deep into the earth. The trees with shallow root systems or growing in rocky, thin soil are easily destroyed by the storms. Look in a science encyclopedia to find pictures of different trees and their root systems. Draw the root systems of the trees that grow near you. Compare the soils they grow in.

When you study God's Word and learn about Him, you are planting your heart roots into deep soil. When you grow your roots deep into God's Word you will not be destroyed by the temptations of evil. You cannot be upset and thrown about. You are protected by your faith in God.

Birds often show great courage in defending their young. The gray kingbird will peck and dive repeatedly at an invading hawk, a bird many times its size, until the hawk finally leaves its territory. The invading hawk seems invincible against a gray kingbird, which is only about the size of a cardinal. But the gray kingbird doesn't pay any attention to the size of the invader. She defends her young with great courage—and wins in the end!

God gives you courage too, even when the other kids are bigger and really nasty. He will help you defend your faith in Him. You and I will come out winning with God!

EVERYDAY TRAILS TO FAITH

Jesus usually taught values by using stories about everyday things that the people He spoke to saw or experienced all the time. Do the same with your children. Use what happens to them or to other children to open the door to what your child is thinking and feeling.

1. Ricardo: I studied hard for the test, and I prayed that God would help me remember, but He didn't. I failed a whole section because I couldn't remember what I had studied. How come God didn't help me, like He said He would?

2. Josh: I'm really shy, and it's hard for me to stand up for what I believe. I don't seem to have much courage. It seems so easy for some other

kids. Do they have more faith? How can I get some more?

3. Adriana: My friend Daleela has so much confidence. She goes anywhere and talks to anyone about anything. Does it mean I don't have faith in God because I don't have confidence like she does? I'm scared, and I'm afraid the other kids will make fun of me. What can I do to get confidence?

4. David: I always think of the worst thing that can happen. It's hard for me to have hope that things will turn out good. I always think they'll turn out bad, no matter what I do. Is hope part of faith in God? How can I be hopeful when I'm sure things will turn out bad?

5. Marijane: Sometimes I feel really discouraged and down in the dumps. I do so many bad things that I think Jesus can't forgive them all. I'll never be like Him. I might as well give up right now. Does Jesus really forgive everything bad I do? Does He really forget all those things? Will He really save a kid like me? How can I know for sure?

6. Estrellita: My teacher at church talked about something she called "grace." I didn't understand. Is grace about God? What does it have to do with me?

KEYS TO FAITH IN GOD

1. Carefully design the atmosphere of your home to lead toward God.

2. Share your personal faith experience and your joy in the Lord with your children.

3. Pray *for* and *with* your children every day.

4. As a family, read and study from God's Word every day.

5. Be open to talking about faith and God with your children, and to discussing their questions and concerns.

6. Help your child develop a growing personal faith connection with Jesus and God.

CHAPTER 11

Respect

Show respect for all people. Love the brothers and sisters of God's family. Respect God. Honor the king. 1 Peter 2:17, ICB.

Respect is in short supply these days. Children mock their teachers and plan ways to get even if they are disciplined or their grades are what they really deserve. Children are disrespectful to parents. People argue with the police. Clerks ignore customers and treat them with disdain. Robberies and murders fill the pages of our newspapers. Angry drivers threaten other drivers at gunpoint. Youth and adults destroy their bodies with drugs, alcohol, and tobacco. Adults abuse children, and children abuse adults. People fight ethnic wars and mock God. What has happened to respect?

When I give workshops for parents on values, I ask each small working group to decide on the six most important values to teach children. Respect has been on almost every group's top-six list of important values. Clearly it is one of the most important values. It carries many other values on its shoulders. How can you help your children learn to respect God, others, themselves, and nature? How can you teach them to live respectful lives in a world gone mad with disrespect? How can you teach them to live by the golden rule—to treat others as they would like to be treated?

What does respect look like in everyday life?

WHEN I AM RESPECTFUL . . .

I worship God with reverence. I help take care of the church, and I listen carefully to the minister and my teachers.

Esteem
Regard
Honor
Reverence
Worship
Adoration
Love
Courtesy

I respect myself too much to harm my body or my mind. God created me as a unique person. There's no one else just like me.

I am polite. I do not behave rudely. I do not force myself on others because respect is based on love.

I care about other people's needs. I let other people go first. I do not have a "me first" attitude.

I take care of my things. I do not damage other people's property.

I give my seat to older people. I help them carry heavy packages and I greet them cheerfully and politely. I listen to what they say.

I never make fun of people who are different from me.

I will do what I can to help someone who is being picked on because he is different. I have friends of many different races and cultures. I like to learn how they live. I do not try to force them to be like me, because I respect our differences.

I do what people in authority ask me to do—the police, my teacher and principal, my parents. I am never rude to them.

I obey the rules of my community and my school. I also obey my family's rules. I do what I can to take care of the natural world. I do not harm living things or the environment.

GOD'S VIEW OF RESPECT

God created the world and every living thing in it. He loves His creation with a love we as mere humans cannot comprehend. Each person is unique, created for a special purpose, created with a spark of the divine image. God cares for His creation, lavishes His love on each person, and seeks our love and friendship in re-

*Holy and reverend
is his name.
Ps. 111:9, KJV.*

*At the name of Jesus
every knee should bow.
Phil. 2:10.*

*Now we ask you,
brothers, to respect those
who work hard among
you, who are over you in
the Lord and who
admonish you.
1 Thess. 5:12.*

> *Honor one another
> above yourselves.*
> Rom. 12:10.
>
> *Honor your father
> and your mother.*
> Ex. 20:12.
>
> *You were bought at a
> price; therefore glorify God
> in your body and in your
> spirit, which are God's.*
> 1 Cor. 6:20, NKJV.
>
> *Whether you eat or drink,
> or whatever you do,
> do all to the glory of God.*
> 1 Cor. 10:31, NKJV.
>
> *You shall not murder.*
> Ex. 20:13, NKJV.
>
> *The earth is the Lord's.*
> Ps. 24:1, NKJV.

turn. He respects us and our free will to choose a friendship with Him. He wants us to give Him, our fellow human beings, and the natural world this same love and respect. If God, as the king of the universe, loves and respects His creation with such depth, how can we do less? We must respect ourselves as His creation and the object of His love. We were, after all, created in the image of God.

Bible People

Throughout Scripture God clearly indicates that He expects us to respect Him as the king of the universe. His laws are to be respected, also. God made this very clear at Mount Sinai (Exodus 20:18-20). He gave very specific instructions about the sanctity of the desert tabernacle (Ex. 25-27) and the Temple in Jerusalem (1 Kings 5-8) and the reverence due the structures, the priests, and the ceremonies (Ex. 28-30). When young men mocked Elisha, one of God's prophets, He immediately showed His displeasure (2 Kings 2:23-25).

God's Word contains many stories about respect for persons in authority. When called into his presence, Daniel showed great respect for the king (Dan. 2:27-45). Joseph showed the same respect for Potiphar and the Egyptian monarch (Gen. 39; 41). Abigail respected David as her king, and provided for the needs of him and his soldiers (1 Sam. 25:14-35). David refused to kill King Saul, his enemy, when he had a perfect opportunity, because he respected the king (1 Sam. 24:6).

God also shows infinite loving care and respect for individuals. When Peter denied his connection with Jesus, he was not abandoned by the Lord. Instead, Jesus reassured Peter three times that he was accepted and restored (John 21:15-19). An angel provided food and encouragement for Elijah when he was discouraged and depressed (1 Kings 19:1-9). God restored King David after he committed adultery and murdered a man (2 Sam. 12:13, 14). God sent a messenger to instruct an Ethiopian on a desert road who was open to learning about the Saviour (Acts 8:26-40).

The above stories are only a few suggestions. The Bible contains many more examples of respect. When you focus on teaching respect to your children, select some of these stories. Read them, dramatize them, talk about them, and draw out your children's thoughts. Draw or paint a collage; write a lead story for a newspaper, or write a paraphrase of the Bible story, adding a modern application. Make up a song; make a model of the story from paper, wood, clay, or Legos. Reenact the story as a skit. Play with the story until it becomes part of your children's thinking and feeling, until it enters their very being.

HOW TO HELP CHILDREN DEVELOP RESPECT

Respect is founded on the worth of every human being in the eyes of God. Once we understand that worth, we will look at each individual with respect. This is the main message of respect. Respect yourself and others because God loves you and everyone else in the world. Respect conveys God's love to everyone. Love is the foundational core of respect.

GENERAL GUIDELINES

1. Convey a powerful message of love and respect to your children. The most convincing thing you can do to teach your children respect *is to treat them with respect.* A respected child or adult will pass along respect to others. No sense of being respected, no respect for others. It's as simple and as complex as that. Share large amounts of love and respect with your children. Many parents love their children, but do not respect them. What does respecting your children include?

Really listen to your child. Stop what you are doing and listen. Make appropriate comments. Show that you value his ideas.

Respect your child's feelings. Children do have feelings, you know. Their feelings are real. In fact, their feelings are stronger and more dominant in their lives than the feelings of adults. Their feelings are more easily hurt. Sometimes adults talk about children in their presence, as if they had no feelings. Be careful not to hurt their feelings with sarcastic or snide remarks about their failings. Never use verbal put-downs. Ask yourself, Would I say this about my best friend or a coworker in their presence? If the answer is no, then don't say it about your child, either.

Respect your child's individuality. Avoid comparisons. Even siblings are not alike. God made everyone different. Help each of your children develop his or her own abilities. Give children the latitude to make choices appropriate for their age. Respect their choices. (See chapter 8 for ideas about how to help children learn to make choices.)

Respect your child's privacy. Don't read her letters. Knock before opening a closed door. Don't borrow her clothes without asking. Each family member deserves the right to keep their prized possessions in safe keeping where others will not intrude.

Respect your child's growing abilities to manage and direct his life. Don't treat Mr. Thirteen the same way you treat Miss Nine. Don't try to direct every minute of your teen's life. Sure, he'll make some blunders, but he will learn from those experiences and will do better in the future. And he will feel respected.

If you treat your child with respect, she will faithfully mirror back that respect to you and others. Your own example holds the key to a respectful child.

2. Treat your spouse and extended family with respect and love. Respect your spouse and extended family in all of the above ways. These guidelines work for adults, too: Listen. Respect feelings, individuality, and privacy. Don't try to manage everyone's life to your taste. If you and your spouse, or other adults who live with you, frequently quarrel and shout insults to each other, your children will learn deeply ingrained lessons of disrespect that will be almost impossible to erase.

3. Focus on finding the good in people. Don't criticize and berate people. When you consistently look for the good in people and talk about it, your children will catch on. They in turn will focus on the good in those around them. But if you constantly criticize and berate people you know, expect the same from your kids. How can you expect your child to respect the minister and religious education director when all you have to say about those individuals is negative? Yes, I know, some leaders don't deserve respect, but most do. Keep your thoughts to yourself. Go personally to the weak leader and try to support and strengthen their work. If you have nothing but criticism for Grandpa and Grandma—or other relatives—how can you expect your children to connect with their family and respect their heritage?

4. Show respect and honor to the elderly. People who treat the elderly with respect usually treat everyone with respect. The elderly are vulnerable. They are often the first target of disrespectful children and teens. From the time they are young, teach your children by example and positive teaching to respect and honor the elderly. The elderly should be valued for their wisdom and contributions to life. A child should always offer his seat to an older person. Take the time to help carry packages when you see someone who needs assistance. Offer an arm if needed. Listen to their stories with interest, *even if you've heard them before.* They are experiencing a lot of pleasure from telling them. Remember, you too will one day be elderly and your children will treat you just as you have treated their grandparents.

5. Show caring concern for those who have disabilities or are disadvantaged. Do what you can to help. Introduce your children to individuals with disabilities. Stop and talk a bit, smile, and offer to help, if needed. Many children from middle class homes live such protected lives that they do not realize there are children who really suffer from hunger and cold—maybe in your own city. Pictures on TV don't take the place of actually seeing a homeless person. If there are homeless in your city, take your children to areas where they can be seen. Then plan what you can do to help. Maybe volunteer at a soup kitchen or collect blankets to distribute to the homeless. I read a story in *Reader's Digest* about a preteen boy who collected or made dozens of sleeping bags for the homeless in his city.

6. Include people from different races and cultures in your family's circle of friends. This may take some extra effort because our comfort circle often includes only people of our own race, culture, and religion. Step out of your family's comfort zone. The effort will be worthwhile. You will learn about different cultures. Your children will become "international persons" with an expanded view of the world and curiosity about people and how they live. They will feel comfortable around people who are different from themselves. They may even be inspired to learn another language—a real advantage on a future résumé. However, you can negate all this effort if you make snide remarks and speak of them with insulting names. Always speak about everyone with respect. Make it clear to your children that you will not tolerate rude or disparaging remarks about anyone.

7. Teach your children how to be courteous to everyone they meet. Courtesy rides on the shoulders of respect. It is not a series of rules posted by some courtesy guru. Emily Post's granddaughter, who currently writes a column on courtesy for *Good Housekeeping* magazine, often reminds her readers that courtesy is really just respecting the other person and treating them as you would like to be treated. "Please," "Thank you," and "You're welcome" proclaim a thoughtful person. Thank-you notes are cherished by gift givers.

However, children are not naturally courteous. They will be more so if they are treated with respect and courtesy by their parents, but your example alone probably will not be enough to teach a courteous way of living. You will need to be explicit about how you want the children to act and insist on compliance. Practice being courteous. Insist on the "magic words" every day. Help with thank-you notes. It takes time to grow a courteous child, but it *is* possible. Courteous children receive many "warm fuzzies" from others. Everyone likes them. And, of course, they in turn feel good about themselves. It's a rewarding circle.

8. Support and respect the leaders and laws of your community. When you tell your kids "Watch out for any police and let me know" as you drive 10 miles over the speed limit, you're giving a powerful message of disrespect for the laws of your community and country. Your children catch on quickly. Don't be surprised if you experience a repeat when your teenager starts driving. Ignoring the laws is all too easy for an adolescent anyway, but more so if they've grown up with disrespect and disdain for law and order.

Your example plays a big role here, but you also need to explain what you are doing and be sure the kids obey, too. "We will walk in the crosswalk because it is safer and because it is the law." "We will wear our seat belts all the time. Obeying the law keeps us safer." Traffic laws are the ones we run into every day, but what about curfew laws, leash laws, and respect for others' property? What about church and school rules, and rules of leaders and teachers? Respect for leaders and laws makes living together much easier. If you respect the leaders at church and school, your children will be much more likely to do so also.

9. Teach your children to respect themselves and their bodies. Start to teach your children habits of healthful living and respect for one's body when they're young. Teach them to eat good foods, get plenty of rest and exercise every day, avoid harmful substances, and keep their bodies clean. Teach them to respect themselves—don't say disparaging things about themselves or accept those kinds of statements from anyone else. Of course, you set a good example by encouraging and supporting, not berating, them. Teach them to recognize the signs of potential abuse and how to avoid getting caught in that trap. Sex education is part of this package of respect for yourself, too. Visit your nearest Christian bookstore, where you will find books to read with your child and for your teenager to read. Be open to discussion of this topic. Better your children learn from you than from their friends or the TV set.

10. Teach your children to treat others the way they themselves would like to be treated. The golden rule is the essence of respect. It applies to friends and nonfriends, people you love and people you have a hard time with, family members and strangers. It's a simple question for every situation: How would I like to be treated if I were that person? Very young children are just learning to understand how other people feel. They are beginning to experience empathy. They need lots of practice thinking about how others feel before they will be able to apply the golden rule. (Chapter 15, on kindness and compassion, has suggestions for helping your child develop empathy.)

Your grade schooler should understand better because he's older. Ask, "If other kids were making fun of you, how would you like to be treated?" ("Have another kid come up to defend me and be my friend.") "If your friend borrowed your Rollerblades, how would you like to be treated?" ("Return them promptly and in good condition.") And for your teen, "Your girlfriend refused your desire to kiss and make out, and you're mad at her. If you were in her place, how would you like to be treated?" ("Respect my wishes and continue the friendship.") "You were playing ball with your friends, and the ball crashed into the bathroom window of the house next door. If you were the neighbor, how would you like to be treated?" ("Come and tell me you did it and offer to pay for the replacement glass.") The golden rule works every time.

11. Show your children how to be reverent in God's presence and to worship Him with adoration. Today many people show very little respect for God, the king of the universe. They speak slang to Him, go to church in everyday clothes, use His name as a swear word, and toss His Word in a pile with a bunch of other books. If you were invited to an audience with the king or queen of a modern country, how would you prepare and how would you act? I imagine you would study the appropriate manner of addressing royalty. You would learn proper manners for the occasion and carefully select your clothes. You might be in a bit of a dither over the occasion. All this to show respect to an earthly monarch! What about the King of the universe? Do you prepare as carefully to meet Him in His earthly dwelling place? Do you act respectfully and reverently in church? Do you worship with reverence and adoration? Your children need to learn respect and awe for the real King, to walk softly in His presence, and to worship in their hearts.

12. Respect God's Word, the Holy Scriptures, as your family's guide for living. Worship and reverence for God begins with respect for God's Word. Read the Bible daily with your family. Treat the Book itself with respect by keeping it in a location of honor. While your family may have many Bibles, a family Bible kept in a place of honor speaks of your values to anyone coming into your home. Turn to God's Word for direction, consolation, and happiness. It will never fail you. (See chapter 10 for ways to help your children learn to love God's Word.)

FOCUSED GUIDELINES

I have selected healthful living for focused guidelines. Every child needs to develop habits of healthful living. They don't come naturally, but are invaluable for all of later life. My husband, a pediatrician for 25 years, helped with these guidelines.

Healthful Living for Kids

Diet

1. Start early with breast feeding, if possible. Add solid foods slowly, beginning around 5 months. Start with cereals, then vegetables, finally fruits.

2. Keep mealtimes regular. In general, don't allow snacking unless they are healthful snacks, such as carrots, celery, wheat crackers, dried fruit. Many children do need a small picker-upper when they get home from school, especially if the evening meal is rather late. But if children snack on junk foods, they will not eat enough nutritious food for their body needs. If your child never wants to eat at mealtime, you can be sure he is snacking in between meals.

3. Offer nutritious and attractive foods. Use desserts, sugar, and juices sparingly. Avoid junk foods, especially candy and pop. Most soft drinks have almost as much caffeine as coffee. Use a variety of natural foods from basic food groups.

4. Teach children how to select and prepare healthful meals.

5. Cultivate mealtime as a happy family time.

6. Offer children lots of water. It is the perfect beverage. Make getting a drink easy. Avoid large amounts of fluid at bedtime and mealtime.

7. Watch children's attitudes toward food. Don't give children food, particularly sweets, to console them when they are hurt or upset or as a reward for good behavior. It establishes the habit of using food for consolation, which can lead to later obesity. Don't give infants a bottle to go to sleep. It can be damaging to their teeth.

8. Avoid emphasizing dieting or the weight of family members. If you yourself are dieting, don't make a big deal of it. Just go about your dieting quietly and without comment. Children are amazingly sensitive to messages about size. The media overemphasizes thinness for girls and women, and when they also hear it at home the emotional message turns sour. A surprising number of girls under the age of 10 have already developed anorexia. They are not eating enough to ensure proper growth. They have internalized the message that to be lovable they must be thin. Don't think, *That can't happen to my child.* It can! Watch the food messages.

Exercise and Fresh Air

1. Beginning in infancy, see that your child spends some time outdoors daily. Sunshine and fresh air are important health advantages.

Everyone needs at least 15 minutes of sunshine daily for vitamin D absorption. Some schools do not have recess anymore, or children play in a gym and get almost no time outside during the school day.

2. Play and work with your children to provide an adult model of the active life.

3. Teach coordination early. High school is too late. Be sure your child learns to run, skip, climb, throw, lift, and tumble.

4. Deemphasize organized school sports, and encourage lifetime leisure activities such as swimming, hiking, running, skiing, tennis, golf, or cycling.

5. Play down competition, and encourage physical development and social enrichment.

6. Encourage useful exercise, such as gardening, carpentry, mechanics, and housework.

7. Avoid many hours of TV, reading, and sedentary activities. Children who spend many hours watching TV or reading do not develop needed physical or social skills.

Rest

1. Encourage regular times for sleeping, according to the child's needs. Sleep needs vary widely.

2. Provide a quiet peaceful environment for sleeping. Avoid before bedtime excitement or TV.

3. Make bedtime the spiritual and social highlight of the day. Establish a routine with younger children (e.g., bath, story, cuddly time). Give each child a special time with you just before they go to sleep.

4. Avoid using bed or sleep to punish a child.

5. Give each child their own bed. Avoid children sleeping together or with parents. Maybe occasionally, but not as a rule.

6. Avoid drugs or medications before sleep time.

7. Avoid bedtime snacks.

Personal Care

1. Keep your child's clothes repaired and clean.

2. Be sure clothes are the proper size. Children grow fast and garments that are too tight are irritating.

3. Teach cleanliness: regular bathing, washing hands before eating, brushing teeth, using clean clothes, deodorants, etc.

4. Discuss body changes during preadolescence and adolescence.

5. Help children learn to keep their hair and skin attractive. If your teenager has acne, get some professional help.

6. Help your children learn how to dress attractively without depleting the U.S. Mint or being overly invested in what everyone else is wearing. Teens naturally want to look in style, but they do not have to be slaves to every whim of the crowd. Help with poise and posture and how to handle their bodies. Knowing you look OK and can handle your body with poise helps build confidence and self-respect.

PROBLEMS WITH RESPECT?

Eric refuses to cooperate with anything his parents ask. He is defiant and disrespectful. He kicks and screams when crossed. His automatic response is "No!" He has few friends because he fights with everyone. He argues with everyone about everything. He is uncooperative at kindergarten, refusing to obey classroom rules or do assignments. He is disrespectful and argumentative with adults and children alike. His mother is at her wit's end, and his father throws up his hands helplessly and retreats to his office. How can a 5-year-old be so defiant and disrespectful?

William Lee Carter, in his book *KidThink*, offers some excellent suggestions for understanding and dealing with the oppositional child. I have adapted some of his ideas for dealing with Eric.

Eric has a difficult temperament. His parents didn't make him difficult—he came that way. He is very emotional and wants to be in control of everything, including his parents. He doesn't like changes in routine or any surprises because they make him feel he doesn't have control. Power and control are what motivate him. While most children will learn from reasoning, Eric persists in seeing only his own viewpoint. He sees only the immediate consequences of an action. Talking and reasoning with him only escalates into arguments.

Eric has learned that he can control his parents by getting them emotionally upset. He is fast becoming addicted to the sense of power and control he feels when his parents get upset. What can they do?

If they are to help Eric, his parents must first learn some detachment from his problems. They must remain calm, cool, and collected at all times. Eric must remain in control of his problem. As soon as his mother gets angry, Eric no longer has to change his behavior. He has won and doesn't need to change his behavior, because he controlled his mother. Thus she should not get involved emotionally, and should let him own the problem.

Eric's parents must provide firm boundaries for him. These boundaries need to be stated clearly and positively: "A temper tantrum will cause you to be isolated in your room. Controlling your feelings will allow you to be with other people where you can be involved in what is going on." His parents need to follow these boundaries explicitly and promptly. Trying to persuade Eric to behave differently or think differently is futile. Mom and Dad (and caretakers) should act immediately according to the boundaries previously set.

They should not try to reason with Eric. His thinking is different from that of other children, and reasoning doesn't work. He is a child who must learn from his own experience. Most children recognize that adults have more experience, and want to be cared for and helped by adults. Not Eric. He thinks he knows everything and doesn't need adults to help him. He wants to be in control. He has to learn for himself.

Eric's parents can be more effective in helping him mature if they listen to him and give him individual time doing pleasant things together. He will cooperate better if he feels understood and liked. They need to pick their timing carefully when they want to instruct Eric. Timing is everything for this child.

Eric is not an easy child to help. He probably will experience more hard knocks in the school of life than most children because he insists on learning everything firsthand. But if his parents remain in control by not joining the argument, he will learn more quickly.

FAMILY ACTIVITIES

Visit the Elderly: Visit elderly persons your family knows, beginning with relatives. If none live near you, take your children to visit a retirement home or assisted living center. They can take homemade pictures, flowers, goodies to eat, and good cheer to distribute. Go regularly so your family gets acquainted with individuals.

Adopt a Grandparent: If your parents don't live nearby, adopt a grandparent. Many elderly people live very lonely lives and would welcome being adopted into a family. Bring the adopted grandparents to family gatherings and special occasions at your home. Help the children make little gifts for them and write notes about their lives. Mail is a highlight of the day for the elderly. Your family will be rewarded with far more than you give, and your children will learn respect for older people.

Family Genealogy: Investigate your family's heritage. Tell stories about your family. Visit cemeteries where family members are buried. Find out all you can about your ancestors. Genealogy chasing resembles solving mysteries. Your children will love it, and they will feel connected to something larger than themselves. They will also learn to respect all kinds of people. Who knows what kind of people are part of your family tree!

Card Connections: Make cards to welcome new babies and to express get-well wishes for people whose names are published in the local paper under births and hospital admissions or for people you know. Duplicate a little note to include in each card explaining that your family is reaching out to people hoping to make a friendlier community. Ask the person receiving the card to pass along the friendship by sending a get-well or welcome baby card to someone they know. This is not a chain or a pyramid, just one family's outreach to people.

Making cards is quite easy with a computer. Plain paper will do. Younger children can draw pictures on the cards on which the older children have written a message. Pick out one or two names each week. And during the week, as a family, pray for the people you sent the cards to.

QUOTABLE WISDOM

Pass along some quotable wisdom to your children.

"The more things a man is ashamed of, the more respectable he is."
—*G. B. Shaw*

"If you like yourself and who you are, then you'll probably like almost everyone you meet regardless of who they are."

"If you judge people, you have no time to love them."
—*Mother Teresa*

"I will speak ill of no man, and speak all the good I know of everybody."
—*Benjamin Franklin*

"This is the final test of a gentleman: his respect for those who can be of no possible value to him."
—*William Lyon Phelps*

"No one can make you feel inferior without your consent."
—*Eleanor Roosevelt*
"The light that shines farthest, shines brightest at home."
"Deeds are love and not fine speeches."
—*Spanish proverb*
"Love warms more than a thousand fires."
—*English proverb*

NATURE TRAILS TO RESPECT

Keep your eyes and ears open for nature trails to values. You don't have to be a biologist to learn values from nature. Even city dwellers can observe nature in zoos and nature preserves. Libraries lend nature books and videos. Help your children go beyond the facts to their meaning and connection to values. You might ask: What can we learn about respect from this video on African antelope? With a little prompting, your children will catch on and come up with plenty of ideas connecting nature with values. The more you do it, the more easily the connections will come.

Ocean Waves: Ocean waves are a powerful force to be reckoned with. Sailors respect their strength and what they can do. They have been recorded at 100 or more feet in height. Even the Great Lakes have recorded waves 20 to 30 feet high. A 1955 earthquake in Portugal sent waves crashing into the West Indies, one wave following another across the ocean. (Get a map and see how far the waves traveled.) One wave doesn't go all the way across, but the succession of waves carries the tide across an entire ocean. The waves deserve our respect, and God, the Creator of the oceans, surely deserves our respect.

Animals: Animals have an instinct to preserve their bodies and to protect their young. They will search for food for their young and for themselves. They will eat only enough to keep up their strength. In cold climates animals stockpile food to get through the winter, or they eat enough to provide fat to burn during months of hibernation. Obese animals are unknown in the wild. Only household pets become lazy, do not exercise, and overeat. Animals in the wild do not self-destruct. Only humans eat what is not good for them, destroy their infants through abuse, and self-destruct through bad habits of living. In the wild many animals live in social groups. Each group has a leader who is respected by all members of the group. The leader is responsible for the safety of the group and for finding an adequate food supply to care for the group's young. We can learn many lessons about respect for ourselves and our leaders from the different animals.

EVERYDAY TRAILS TO VALUES

Everyday situations your child confronts are the best way to teach values. Use these little stories, or similar experiences, to open the door to your child's thinking.

Early Childhood: Spitting

Two-year-old Jacob and his mother went to visit their neighbor, Janelle. When they got there, Janelle picked up Jacob to play with him, but Jacob did not want to play. When Janelle persisted in trying to play with him, Jacob purposely spit on her face. Then he hit her. Was that a nice thing to do? How do you think Janelle felt when Jacob spit on her? What could Jacob do now to make Janelle feel better? What should Jacob's mom do?

Late Childhood: Name-calling

One morning in class Ben was making fun of Mario—calling him names and throwing paper at him. Ben thought it was funny, but Mario did not. When the other kids started laughing at the jokes that Ben was making about him, Mario started crying and walked out of the class muttering "Leave me alone." When the teacher realized what had happened, she sent another student after Mario and asked Ben to come to the front of the class. What can the teacher say or do at this point to teach Ben (and the other students) that what he (they) did to Mario was not funny, but was very disrespectful?

Adolescence: Back Talk

One evening Alfred invited his best friend, Samuel, over to his house to play football on his new Sega Genesis video game. As they got ready to play, Alfred's mom came into his room and kindly asked him if he would go to the store to buy something for her. Alfred immediately snapped at his mother for interrupting him and concluded his rude speech by saying, "Leave me alone! Why don't you go buy it yourself?"

Samuel was shocked at the way Alfred replied to his mother's request. He felt that Alfred had been very disrespectful to his mother. What can Samuel say to his friend (without upsetting him too much) to help him realize that he was disrespectful to his mother? How can Samuel help his best friend develop more respect for his mother?

KEYS TO RESPECT

1. Treat your spouse, children, and extended family with love and respect.

2. Focus on finding the good in people.

3. Show respect and honor to the elderly.

4. Show caring concern for those who have disabilities or are disadvantaged.

5. Include people from different races and cultures in your family's circle of friends.

6. Teach your children to be courteous to everyone they meet.

7. Support and respect the leaders and laws of your community.

8. Teach your children to respect themselves and their bodies.

9. Teach your children to treat others the way they would like to be treated.

10. Show your children how to be reverent in God's presence and to worship Him.

11. Respect God's Word as your family's guide for living.

CHAPTER 12

Responsibility

*Whatever your hand finds to do,
do it with all your might. Eccl. 9:10.*

Brandon's grandparents were planning a drive around the island during their holiday visit, stopping at interesting places along the way. Brandon's sister was going and so were his cousins and aunt and uncle. But—and a *big* but—Brandon had accepted the part of an angel in the musical his church would be presenting Christmas weekend, and the last rehearsal was during the trip. It would be so much fun to go, but he was supposed to be at the rehearsal. Why did everything have to happen at the same time? In the end, responsibility won out, and Brandon stayed. He and his parents joined the trip on the last day, after the rehearsal. They had a great time at the new observatory museum. And the musical went very well.

Ask any teacher or boss or church pastor. Ask any parent. Responsibility is the one indispensable character trait that many kids—and adults—don't have. Everyone's willing to help if it doesn't inconvenience them. "I'll teach a class the weekends I'm not camping." "I'll play the piano if I wake up in time." To teacher: "I didn't have time to finish the assignment." Later, to a friend: "Wasn't that movie on TV last night great?"

Responsibility will put your children at the head of the line, in school and on the job. Everyone's looking for a really responsible person, someone who can be counted on all the time.

How can you teach your child to be responsible? Kids seem so irresponsible. Of course, because they're kids. Nobody's born responsible, although some kids learn responsibility quicker than others.

What does responsibility look like in real life?

Conscientious

Faithful

Dependable

Reliable

Trustworthy

WHEN I AM RESPONSIBLE . . .

I can be trusted to keep my commitments.

I am dependable. I will finish the job and even do a little extra.

I do my part to make a happy family.

You can count on me. I will do my jobs well and keep my promises.

I really think about my actions and what they will mean to me and others. I make decisions based on careful consideration and prayer about what God wants me to do. I can postpone pleasure right now because I know God has a better plan for me in the future.

GOD'S VIEW OF RESPONSIBILITY

God wants me to do my work to the best of my ability and to hang in there to the end. *Faithful* is the way God says it. My faithfulness honors God, my Creator and Saviour. Oooo . . . I want to honor God, but sometimes I forget and goof. Sometimes I don't want to do my best. How can I be faithful and responsible? God says: "I'll be with you. I will put my love all around you like a blanket. I promise to always be there when it's tough to be responsible. I will be faithful to you because I want you to be faithful to the end." Aha! I see. Responsibility isn't just doing my job well and keeping my promises. Christian responsibility is having Jesus at the center of my life keeping me faithful.

When we were with you, we gave you this rule: "If anyone will not work, he will not eat."
2 Thess. 3:10, ICB.

You were faithful over a few things, I will make you ruler over many things.
Matt. 25:21, NKJV.

If you are faithful, I will give you the crown of life.
Rev. 2:10, ICB.

Bible People

Some Bible people who were responsible and faithful: Abraham (Gen. 14:14-24), Joseph (Gen. 47:1-12), Moses (Ex. 19; 20), Esther (Esther 4:15,

16), Daniel (Dan. 1), Mary and Joseph (Luke 2:39, 40), Paul (Acts 27), Hanani (read about him in Neh. 7:2).

How did each of these people show his or her faithfulness? Read about each one. Talk about their faithfulness and responsibility. Did they goof sometimes? What did God do then? How did God help them learn? Make a poster, collage, or booklet about each person you discuss. Draw pictures or write stories about how each one was responsible and faithful. Make up a song or do a skit about one of the stories.

HOW TO HELP CHILDREN DEVELOP RESPONSIBILITY

By the time children start school they have learned many lessons in responsibility or irresponsibility. It shows. When I taught first grade, by the end of the first week of classes I already knew which children came from homes where responsibility was stressed.

GENERAL GUIDELINES

1. Model responsibility in your own life. Show that responsibility is very important to you by living it. Keep your promises to your children. If you say you're going to get them an ice-cream cone if they behave during your trip to the mall, do it. Don't say, "It's too late now. We'll do it next time."

Show you're responsible in the things *you* have to do. Don't sit and read a book or watch TV when the kitchen sink is running over with dishes and food and the children need help with their homework. Be responsible for your own chores. Make your own bed, hang up your own clothes, keep your things picked up if you expect your children to do likewise. When you have a church or community responsibility, be someone others can count on. Children notice when you shrug your shoulders and say, "I'm sure the leader can find someone else to set up for the sale." If you are responsible, they probably will be too.

2. Give children real responsibilities. Start when they are very young. With your help, Miss Three can pick up her toys. She can be responsible for putting her pajamas away in the morning. Mr. Four can be learning to brush his teeth every day without being told. Older children can be responsible for taking out the garbage, mowing the lawn, washing the dishes or the car, putting away the groceries, taking care of the baby while Mom or Dad cooks supper, or cooking supper themselves. They can be real members of the family firm with real responsibilities. They can also be responsible for their outside job—school—by doing their homework promptly, turning it in on time, budgeting their time so they get big projects done, studying for tests, keeping up with assignments, getting to practices and lessons on time.

3. Notice and compliment responsible actions. Children like to know they are doing well. When children are learning to be responsible, compliment every evidence of responsibility. Then fade the compliments to once in a while, instead of all the time. Be especially careful to notice any unusual display of responsibility and good judgment. Mom had asked Kailey, age 10, to take care of Jill, her 2-year-old sister, while she went grocery shopping. The girls were having fun splashing in the pond in their yard when Jill accidentally stepped on a piece of glass and cut her foot. Kailey comforted her, took her inside the house, washed the foot well, put pressure on it until the bleeding stopped, put on a disinfectant, and covered the cut with a sterile bandage. When Mom got home, she complimented Kailey on her quick action and good judgment.

4. Use Grandma's rule rather than tangible rewards as much as possible. Grandma always said "work before play" and "spinach before dessert." Encourage children to be responsible by doing their work first. Playtime comes after worktime. Children are more likely to do their responsibilities if they have something to look forward to. Grandma was pretty smart about kids, after all. Stickers, stars, and check marks on a chart are helpful for getting children to remember their responsibilities. Paying them for everything they do—good grades, household chores—produces irresponsible children who will do something only if they're going to get paid. They are working for the money, rather than the good feeling of being a responsible person others can count on.

5. Don't rescue children from the consequences of their behavior. Learning to be responsible includes accepting the consequences of irresponsible behavior. If Diana reads a book for two hours when she should have been doing her social studies project, don't rush in to help her get it done on time. Let her struggle with the consequences of her irresponsible behavior. She will learn responsibility by suffering the consequences of a poor grade. Natural consequences are a wonderful real-life teaching tool. Don't deprive your children of their best learning experiences by rescuing them whenever they're in a jam. Naturally, when the jam isn't their fault, a family-wide rescue operation is definitely in order.

6. Dialogue about short-term and long-term consequences of behavior. Try to get your children to begin seeing ahead to what might happen—looking down the road and around the corner, if you please. If you forget your assignments . . . If you forget to put the milk in the refrigerator . . . If you play video games instead of doing your schoolwork . . . If you don't feed the dog . . . If you tease your brother . . .

Play the game of What will happen if . . . ? Don't rush in to supply the answers. Wait for their thinkers to wake up.

7. Establish consequences for irresponsible behavior. Consequences can be very effective deterrents to irresponsible behavior. If your kid knows he will lose significant privileges if he acts irresponsibly, he will think carefully about his behavior and probably will come down on the side of responsibility. Be sure the consequences suit the kid's age. Don't treat Miss Thirteen like you treat Miss Three. But do establish clear consequences for irresponsible behavior.

8. Teach that responsibility has two sides: avoiding wrong and doing right. "I didn't do anything wrong" doesn't mean the child acted responsibly. Maybe she should have taken positive action. Responsibility includes both sides—avoiding wrong and doing right. Some children have a hard time learning this, but don't give up. In time the idea will click. You did something wrong or you didn't do something right are two sides of the same coin. Either way you acted irresponsibly.

9. Help children own their behavior: admit their mistake, tell the truth, apologize, make restoration, and commit to more responsible actions in the future. Admitting a misdeed opens the door for learning. Your child will not profit from his mistake unless he first admits he made one. Be patient and persistent. Use questions instead of yelling (see chapter 4). Don't proceed to the next step until your child has admitted his mistake. Talk about what needs to happen next, and help him follow through to make things right. Go with your son when he returns the candy bar he stole from the store. Show your support, but don't return the candy bar for him. He needs to apologize and make restoration. Be sure to get his commitment to act more responsibly in the future. Sometimes a written contract for future behavior can be very helpful.

10. Encourage responsibility to God, as well as to family, friends, and community. We all have responsibilities to our family, our friends, the community, and to God. Most of all to God. Help children think about what each of these areas means. What responsibility do we have to God? to our family? to our friends? to the community? How do we act out these responsibilities?

FOCUSED GUIDELINES

I have chosen two important areas for focused guidelines: work and money. They are related, and yet different. Responsibility in these two areas goes a long way toward making life simpler and better. Obviously, responsibility includes many other things. Use similar guidelines for any specific area on which you want to focus.

Responsibility for Work

The child who has learned to take pride in a job well done, and who is self-motivated toward excellence, comes to adulthood with an enormous advantage. She has responsible work attitudes that will serve her well the rest of her life. She knows how to work hard, delay gratification until the job is done, be self-disciplined and persistent. Because work helps other people, she feels connected to her community. She probably will want to be involved in service activities—for her family, her church, and her community. Service will be an important part of her life.

Children begin to learn attitudes toward work and service when they are very young. These guidelines will help your family get a head start on the work and service pathway:

1. Start with easy jobs and gradually increase the difficulty. Miss Two can help carry Baby's bottle, Mr. Five can empty the wastebaskets, Miss Seven can set the table and clean it off after the meal, and Mr. Ten can mow the lawn.

2. Give specific instructions so your child will know how to do the job. Children need clear directions. When children can read, write the step-by-step instructions on a card. Whoever does that job can easily refer to the card. Keep the cards for all the home jobs together. Punch a hole in each and put them on a ring. Be clear about the final result you are looking for. One time I was working with a family with a 13-year-old boy. The parents' main concern was that he didn't do his jobs around the house well. When I asked for specifics, they were very hazy. I knew the child could never please them because they couldn't tell him what they wanted. It took us quite a while to work out exactly what kind of result would please them. The boy seemed very relieved to know just what was expected. Until a child knows exactly what you expect, he cannot earn your "well done."

3. Make it rewarding to work. Notice and compliment a job well done. Children need to know they have done well. Compliment the part that was done well. Be specific in your comments: "I like the way you left the sidewalks clean when you mowed today." Feedback encourages better work. Don't use work as a punishment. This can easily develop negative attitudes toward work. The only exception is work that is clearly related to the misdeed (working to restore something, such as scrubbing the kitchen floor the child has carelessly or intentionally dirtied or earning money to pay for a broken toy). Work with your child. Companionship makes any job easier and more fun. Besides, it provides some of that "quality time" we like to talk about. Talk comes more easily when the hands are occupied.

4. Develop responsible, positive attitudes toward work. Watch what you say about work. If you moan and groan over every chore, your kids will too. They probably will try it, even if you are cheerful, but eventually they'll catch your pleasant attitude. Notice how much the job contributes to the welfare of the family. Work together as a family to help an elderly neighbor rake leaves or wash windows. Help with the work bee at the church. Make work a social occasion. Sing a happy song as you work. Race to see who can finish a window first. Take pride in a job well done.

5. Encourage jobs outside the home. As your children grow older, encourage them to find jobs outside the home—mowing lawns, delivering newspapers, raking leaves or shoveling snow, baby-sitting. Be sure your child knows how to do the job and that it is reasonable for his age. Go over safety issues with him. Require your child to complete a formal training class before baby-sitting for pay. If none is available in your community, do one yourself with your child and her friends. When baby-sitting, your child should always know where you are in case of emergency. Working for other people helps children mature in their understanding of people and how to get along with many different types. Your daughter will not be so easily thrown by peer pressure because she's been out in the real world of work. She has had practice in thinking on her feet. She will become more responsible.

Responsibility for Money

Give your children a head start on their financial future by teaching them responsibility for money. How people spend their money shouts their values. In today's world, being able to handle money well—be it little or much—is a crucial skill. In God's view, handling money tests loyalty and commitment to Him. Give your children an advantage.

1. As soon as your child knows the names of the coins and their number value, start with a small allowance. Explain that, as a member of the family firm, your child has a responsibility to help with the jobs and she also has the privilege of sharing in the income. Make the amount in keeping with what you expect her to do with the money.

2. Teach your child how to set aside some of her allowance for giving to God and to other people. Help her count and set aside a tithe (one tenth) for giving. She could give this amount each week at church or she could save it for a bigger gift. Begin with giving when children are very young. Giving to others provides an antidote for selfishness.

3. Teach your child how to set aside some of her allowance for savings (another tenth). Get her an attractive see-through bank so she can see how much she has saved. Saving is an important habit to cultivate. Begin young. She could save toward buying something she wants.

4. As soon as your child can write numbers, help him set up a simple system for keeping track of his allowance and what he has spent. A small notebook works well. He can write the date and the amount at the top of the page. Expenditures go on the lines below. Keeping track of what he spends builds care in handling money. When your child has additional income, be sure to include it in the record keeping. When you give the next allowance, look over his accounting system. Compliment wise choices and careful records.

5. Discuss what your child is responsible for buying before you give the allowance. As he gets older, increase the allowance and the items he is responsible for buying. For example, by fourth or fifth grade he could be responsible for everything he needs for school (except textbooks, of course). That might include supplies, field trips, lunch, birthday gifts for friends, etc. Estimate what that will be for the year, and give him an appropriate allowance. Be sure he has enough money to cover expenses, giving, saving, and "fun money." But not too much "fun money"—he needs an incentive to earn.

6. Gradually increase her financial responsibilities, until she is buying all of her own clothes by the time she gets to high school. Decide on her clothing allowance for the year and give it to her in monthly installments. Encourage her to get a job outside the home so she can earn money for other expenses. If you need her at home (to care for a younger sibling, for example) so she does not have time to get an outside job, pay her as you would anyone else you might hire for the same job. Require some saving for college and other long-term projects during these years. Many teens want their own car, but most families cannot afford this luxury. Even if you can afford to give your child a car, it's usually not a good idea. Research surveys show that high school students who don't have a car get better grades and are more involved in extracurricular activities.

7. Before your children leave home, give them the experience of buying the family groceries and paying the household bills for three months. They can buy groceries from your shopping list, being careful to check for sales. Paying the household bills gives real-life experience in reading bills, paying on time, writing and mailing checks. Of course you must still sign the checks, since it is your account. Most teens are quite surprised to see how much money it takes just to pay the regular household bills. That's a useful bit of knowledge. The last year our son lived at home (a college senior), he chose the grocery shopping as his job for the year. He did it well, shopped sales, and learned how much money it takes to feed a family. A year later he was married.

8. Give your children some experience with loans and paying interest. If someone comes up with an unexpected expense and needs money, make it a formal loan. Decide on the amount and charge the same interest rate as major credit cards are currently charging. This is a good chance for your child to do some real-life math calculations. Decide on a payback schedule. Keep track of payments and interest paid. Your children will get the idea very quickly that it costs a lot more to buy on credit—a lesson they must learn in order to have a responsible financial future. Many adults have never learned that lesson—their credit cards are always maxed out. Of course it would be easier for you to just give your child the money, rather than go to the bother of payments and interest, but she needs the lesson in credit buying.

9. Do not pay your children for doing their regular chores. Everyone needs to help the family firm. That is one of their contributions. However, I think it is appropriate to pay for extra chores. For example, when my children were teenagers, I inquired what a cleaning service would charge for cleaning our windows. Then I offered them a chance to have the job. They grabbed because it paid well and they wanted the money. If you make your children responsible for their own expenses, then they have some incentive for working to earn money. If you just hand out money anytime they ask, they have no incentive for earning. They think money grows on trees—the Mom or Dad Money Tree. They haven't a clue how hard you work for that money. They need that clue.

10. If you have followed a carefully planned program for learning to handle money, by the time your children are in senior high school and college they should be quite responsible with those dollars. When our daughter left for dental school we were in a financial position to give her, up front, all the money we had to spend for her education (a loan without interest, I might say). When I tell this story at workshops, someone always asks, "How did you know she wouldn't go wild, buy herself a new sports car, spend it all, and then you'd have to bail her out with the school bills?"

Well, we knew her and didn't have any doubts. We were quite confident in her money-handling skills. After all, she'd been through a careful learning sequence. She invested the money and didn't have to touch the principal for living expenses until her junior year. Furthermore, she had $10,000 left at the end. Then she did buy herself a new car. She made faithful payments on that educational loan until she had her first baby.

Then we decided to cancel the rest and make it our gift to her education. Today she handles her family's money very carefully. When they applied for a recent mortgage, the company was shocked that they had no debts—not even credit card debts. I know another young couple whose credit cards—and they have several—are always at their limit and they pay hundreds of dollars a year in interest. Naturally, they cannot seem to get ahead financially. Unfortunately, they also learned their financial management habits at home when they were growing up—habits that did not teach them to delay gratification, habits that are not helping them now. Be sure your child has learned responsibility for money.

TROUBLE WITH RESPONSIBILITY?

Some children are naturally more responsible than others. They seem to be born that way, or at least they learn much more easily. Responsibility seems to fit their personality. Oldest children seem to fit this pattern most often, but not always. Their parents pride themselves on how well they have taught responsibility to these kids—until a sibling comes along who is a happy-go-lucky kid merrily whistling his way through life without a thought for tomorrow or even today, for that matter. Then they wonder where they went wrong. The throw of the genes dice gave them a kid who doesn't much care about being responsible. And he doesn't want to learn. He will be a challenge in the responsibility game.

Other kids are irresponsible, never complete school assignments or work, don't keep promises, and can't be counted on to remember anything. But it isn't their personality. They have simply learned bad habits, habits of irresponsibility for work, money, promises—you name it. They've never had a chance because their family didn't insist they learn to be responsible.

Either way—learned or inborn—these kids need to learn to be responsible. Begin at the beginning. Go back over the previous guidelines. Figure out where you went wrong with this child. Pick one or two areas in which you want to develop responsibility. Develop a contract with your older child or teen. Spell out exactly what type of behavior you expect and the consequences for failure to follow the guidelines. Be sure your child has input into this contract. Do everything possible to engage him in this process. If he won't be engaged, use your parental authority to tell your child what you expect. Follow Grandma's rule without fail—work before play. Make it rewarding to be responsible. Compliment efforts and improvement. Gradually work toward the time when your child takes pride in being responsible.

Tell a younger child clearly what is expected: "We expect you to pick up your pajamas every morning. We will remind you only once. If you do it you can put a smiley face on your chart. If you don't do it, then there will be a consequence you won't like." Then follow through. Younger children usually respond to incentives—stars or smiley faces on a chart of work responsibilities and a hug for a job well done. However, consequences for ignoring the plan need to be clearly in place.

Usually a child is irresponsible because parents or caregivers have not insisted that she be responsible. Many parents tell me they have tried charts and consequences, and nothing seems to make a difference. But when I push for details of what they have tried, it usually turns out they themselves have not been responsible. Sometimes they followed through, but the next time they were tired or hurried and the child did what she wanted. That is the surest way in the world of developing irresponsible behavior in your children.

Children are quick to pick up that you don't always mean what you say. They always hope this is the time you won't say or do anything. They will test every time. If sometimes you do and sometimes you don't, they will continue testing and never develop consistently responsible behavior. We call this random reinforcement. It is very powerful. The behavior continues because you never can tell when you will get a reward. Fishing and gambling are very popular activities. Need I say more?

If the consequences are consistent and predictable, eventually kids will get tired of knocking their heads against the wall and will learn to do what is required of them. An especially self-willed child will check in once in a while to see if the wall still holds. If it does, he will back off and continue the responsible way. The happy-go-lucky kid will always have more of a struggle with responsibility, but he can learn.

Correcting irresponsible behavior won't happen overnight. Be consistent and don't give up. Eventually your child will respond, although things probably will get worse before they get better. Why? Because the kid is used to doing what she wants most of the time and tolerating your occasional upsets when you make her be responsible for her actions. She will try to push against the wall every time, until she learns it simply doesn't give. Then things will get much, much better. It's worth hanging in there.

Joey had always gotten good grades and done his school assignments on time. Suddenly, in the eighth grade, his grades plummeted and he developed an I-don't-care-about-anything attitude toward school and work. His parents talked with the teachers, talked with him, tried the usual incentives and consequences. Nothing made any difference. Joey, previously responsible, had become seriously irresponsible. Time for serious action. Joey could easily develop a habit of irresponsibility that would not serve him well during his teens and later. Joey's parents decided to pull out the big guns and let Joey know they were very serious about this matter.

Big guns mean **"We are really serious about this!"** Joey's parents locked his room where all his electronic toys were kept, and told him he would have access to his room when his grades came back to normal. He slept on the sofa in the family room. He had access to his room only to get his clothes. He could not visit with friends after school or on weekends. He was required to sit at the table in the family room, under an adult's supervision, and do his school assignments. He was not allowed to watch television, either. He was required to do his home chores. In other words, his life became pretty sterile of the "fun" things he had previously enjoyed.

Six weeks went by, and there was no improvement in his grades. In fact, he did the assignments and then "forgot" to turn them in to the teacher. But his parents did not relent. "It's your problem, son," they told him. "You hold the key to the 'fun' things in your life." And they kept on with the established contract. Finally, it dawned on Joey that they meant business. They really weren't going to let him visit his friends, watch TV, go in his room, or play computer games until his grades improved. Suddenly, in three weeks his grades shot up to what they'd been before and stayed there.

Whenever there was a slight inclination toward irresponsibility in the future, his parents only had to say "Remember the eighth grade?" and Joey suddenly found it very desirable to be responsible. As a young adult Joey laughs about "the eighth-grade" experience and acknowledges it was exactly what he needed.

It takes time and effort to follow through to be sure your child is learning. You may have to pare down your own responsibilities to give more time to helping this child learn. Pray for insights and for strength to act. Irresponsibility can be corrected.

FAMILY ACTIVITIES

Responsibility Ball: Be sure each family member understands what responsibility means—doing what you said you would do, for example—before beginning this activity. Have everyone sit on the floor in a circle, square, or triangle, depending on how many are playing. Toss or roll a ball to someone and chant, "Responsibility ball coming your way! Tell us what you did today!" The person who catches the ball tells about a time when he or she was responsible that day ("Made my bed!"), then tosses the ball to another person. The faster the plays go, the more fun it is. Even young children catch on fairly quickly. The game can be adapted for different ages by allowing the younger children to repeat something, but older kids and adults must think of something new each time. If a person can't think of anything, other family members could offer suggestions. If your children need more activity, act out rather than tell what happened. This is a great way to focus on the positives.

Best Buys: Take a family trip to the mall to learn how to shop. Beforehand agree on one shopping goal—something your child wants to buy with money he has saved. Help him figure out ahead of time what qualities are important. Go to every store that stocks the desired item to compare prices. Take along a clipboard on which your kids can write the name of the store and the amount. Complete the shopping trip by purchasing the item at the best price, and give everyone a treat. Children need lots of experiences looking for the "best buys." Compare shopping ads for groceries. Show your adolescents how you comparison shop for a car or other major item. Show them how to check consumer magazines or Internet sites for quality evaluations. Look at the ads for used items. Make it a family game to look for "best buys."

QUOTABLE WISDOM

What did your parents say about responsibility, work, and money when you were growing up? If it was valuable, pass it on to your children or pick from the following wisdom quotes:

"Hold yourself responsible for a higher standard than anyone else expects of you. Never excuse yourself."

—*Henry Ward Beecher*

"Excellence is never an accident."

"A stitch in time saves nine."

—*Traditional proverb*

"There's no traffic jam on the extra mile."

"When you invite trouble, it's usually quick to accept."

"When you sow wild oats you can expect a bumper crop."

—*Traditional proverb*

"Promise only what you can deliver. Then deliver more than you promised."

"Dreams come true for those who work while they dream."

"A penny saved is a penny earned."

—*Traditional proverb*

NATURE TRAILS TO RESPONSIBILITY

God speaks to us through nature. Keep your eyes and ears open for nature trails to responsibility.

Ants: Set some crumbs on the deck or sidewalk near your house. Watch as the ants gather to carry the food home (or buy an ant farm to watch, or go see one at a nature preserve). See the long line and how they cooperate. Ants work together to gather food for the winter and to protect their tunnels and food supply. They are clean and honest and hardworking. No one shirks. Each ant is responsible for its part and together they get the job done. The Bible even gives ants as an illustration of hard workers (Prov. 6:6-8).

Beavers: Go for a ride in a woods to see if you can find a beaver dam. Notice the trees the beavers have cut down, the dam they have built, and their houses. If there are no beavers where you live, borrow a video or book on beavers from the library. Notice how hardworking and responsible beavers are. They build the best possible lake and house, and work hard gathering food to store for the winter. **Squirrels** also work very hard gathering and storing food for the winter.

Earthworms: Just after a rain look for earthworms on the sidewalk, driveway, or lawn. Earthworms are indispensable to farmers and gardeners. They process the earth so plants will grow. On an acre of land, earthworms pass 10 tons of dirt through their bodies. They are nature's hardworking rototillers.

EVERYDAY TRAILS TO RESPONSIBILITY

The following check-up list focuses on everyday ways to be responsible. Each item can be adapted for younger children or adolescents. Talk about the ways you are proud of your children's growing sense of responsibility or ways in which they could improve. Encourage comments about each item, examples, and maybe ideas for other areas in which responsibility really shows in real life. Maybe they will suggest areas in which you could improve! Make a plan for improvement. Always compliment progress.

CHECKUP ON RESPONSIBILITY

	Rarely				Always
I get my homework done on time.	1	2	3	4	5
I try to do my chores well	1	2	3	4	5
I keep my promises.	1	2	3	4	5
You can count on me to finish any job I start.	1	2	3	4	5
I am proud of my grades because I do my best.	1	2	3	4	5
I help my family every day. I'm part of the family team.	1	2	3	4	5
I give fair value when I work for money.	1	2	3	4	5
I keep track of my money, spend carefully, and save.	1	2	3	4	5

KEYS TO RESPONSIBILITY

1. Model responsibility in your own life.

2. Give children real responsibilities.

3. Notice and compliment responsible actions.

4. Use Grandma's rule rather than tangible rewards as much as possible.

5. Don't rescue children from the consequences of their behavior.

6. Dialogue about short-term and long-term consequences of behavior.

7. Establish consequences for irresponsible behavior.

8. Teach that responsibility has two sides: avoiding wrong and doing right.

9. Help children own their behavior.

10. Encourage responsibility to God, as well as to family, friends, and community.

CHAPTER 13

Self-control and Moderation

But the fruit of the Spirit is . . . self-control.
Gal. 5:22, 23.

Many people today are ruled by their feelings. Our local newspaper and the national news media have highlighted the dangers of "road rage," angry drivers with trigger-point tempers. *Look my direction, and I'll get even with you. What right do you have to be on the road? I want it all to myself! You're in my way.* And they vent their anger, sometimes at gunpoint. I suspect they didn't learn self-control when they were toddlers.

Wow! Did you see the new secretary? And one thing leads to another—and a family no longer exists. Every package carries the warning: This can be dangerous to your health. But people still smoke, and do drugs, and do alcohol. Almost every magazine I pick up extols the health advantages of exercising every day. Do I do it? Well, sometimes . . . but certainly not every day. I can't seem to find time in my schedule. But the real problem is that I'm not self-disciplined enough to follow through with my good intentions.

Kevin loves to read. He'd rather read than do anything else. Chores . . . *What are those? Was I supposed to feed the cat?* Schoolwork . . . *Not to worry. I'll get it done sometime.* Practice the clarinet? *Let me finish this chapter first.* Time to eat? *Why can't I read at the table? I can read and eat at the same time.* Socialize? *Why do I háve to play with those kids just because their family came over?* And Kevin disappears into his bedroom to read. *Why do I have to learn to write? It's such a pain. I'll have a secretary someday, and she can do the writing for me.* Kevin has a hard time with self-control and moderation. He's a very smart kid and manages to get good grades in most subjects because schoolwork is so easy for him, but unless he learns to be more self-disciplined his smartness won't be worth much in the real world of work.

Moderation is the other side of the self-control coin. Like twins, they go together. They produce a happier and more productive life. How can we help our children incorporate self-control and moderation into their characters?

Let's see what self-control and moderation look like in real life.

WHEN I AM SELF-CONTROLLED AND MODERATE . . .

I am in control of my feelings. I don't have to yell and shout or be angry when someone crosses me. I can control the situation calmly.

I eat what's good for me. I don't stuff myself with junk food every day. I don't put harmful substances in my body, such as drugs, alcohol, and tobacco.

Self-discipline
Organization
Order
Self-denial
Temperance
Moderation
Restraint
Abstinence

I work on keeping my life organized and scheduled so I can get things done. I try not to procrastinate, but to plan ahead.

I can wait for something I want when I know it's better to wait.

I follow the training rules for my sports team, even though it's tough sometimes.

I don't have to buy everything I see at the mall on the spot. I think about whether I need it and whether I can afford it before I part with my money.

I am determined to remain a virgin until I get married. It's tough, but I know I can do it. I respect my dates and don't get us in compromising situations. I want to give myself to my future spouse morally pure.

I think even good things can be done to extreme. If all the TV programs were good ones, would I watch all of them? Of course not. I have to choose what is the very best. I can't do everything that pops into my head. That's what self-control is all about. It means turning off the TV or the computer game when I need to study. It means doing my chores before reading a book or playing ball. It means watching what I say and do.

GOD'S VIEW OF SELF-CONTROL AND MODERATION

God made us with the ability to think and to feel. Although both are important in life, feelings can be difficult to manage at times. They often try to persuade us to take the easy way—to be lazy and undisciplined about our lives, do whatever we feel like at the moment. God gave us the ability to think so we can decide what is best or right and, with His help, do it. The right thing is not always the easy thing.

Self-control is a character trait God wants for us. He wants to help us be self-controlled so we can live upright and godly lives, not controlled by our passions, but by our commitment to live God's way. He is right beside us helping us every day.

Bible People

The real-life biographies of the Bible show the positive influence of self-control and the opposite negative effect. Check these out with your children: Daniel and his three friends in the Babylonian court (Dan. 1); Uriah the Hittite and King David (2 Sam. 11); Ahab and Jezebel (1 Kings 21:1-

Do not be deceived: God cannot be mocked. A man reaps what he sows.
Gal. 6:7.

But the fruit of the Spirit is . . . self-control.
Gal. 5:22, 23.

A person who does not control himself is like a city whose walls have been broken down.
Prov. 25:28, ICB.

Add . . . to knowledge, self-control; and to self-control, perseverance.
2 Peter 1:5, 6.

For the grace of God that brings salvation has appeared to all men. It teaches us to say "No" to ungodliness and worldly passions, and to live self-controlled, upright and godly lives in this present age, while we wait for the blessed hope.
Titus 2:11-13.

So whether you eat or drink or whatever you do, do it all for the glory of God.
1 Cor. 10:31.

24); Joseph and his master's wife (Gen. 39); Joseph's reunion with his brothers (Gen. 42-45); Hophni and Phineas and Eli, their father (1 Sam. 4:11-22); Nadab and Abihu (Num. 3:2-4); Jesus (Matt. 4:1-11; 27:32-66); King Herod and Salome (Matt. 14:1-12); King Belshazzar (Dan. 5); Peter tries to walk on water (Matt. 14:22-36); Peter in the Garden of Gethsemane (Matt. 26:36-45). The list goes on and on. Tell some of these stories to your children. Read them in the Bible. Encourage your children to make a skit, drawings, songs, mime, paper cutouts, clay objects—anything that comes to mind to make the Bible story and its lesson of self-control a part of their thinking.

HOW TO HELP CHILDREN DEVELOP SELF-CONTROL AND MODERATION

Self-control seems to come more easily for some children than for others. They seem to have a natural inclination toward being organized, keeping with a schedule, and resisting temptations that other children cave in to. As easy as it is for your little choleric or melancholy or as difficult as it is for your budding sanguine or phlegmatic, self-control is a character trait that is invaluable in all aspects of life. Self-control and moderation yield enormous rewards. Some children just need more time and training to catch on.

GUIDELINES FOR YOUNG CHILDREN

Eighteen-month-old Kara tentatively reached out a chubby hand to touch the plant on the coffee table, then turned her head to see what Mommy would do. Mommy had babyproofed the house, except for that one plant. She had decided that Kara needed to learn a little self-control and could certainly be taught to stay away from one thing.

Mommy responded quite predictably. She had said it before. "No, Kara. Don't touch!" And she carefully but firmly pulled Kara's hand away from the plant. "No, No," Mommy said, shaking her head. "Come into the kitchen with me. You can play with the big spoons."

Kara followed Mommy into the kitchen and gleefully banged the big spoons for a while. Suddenly the silence was overwhelming, and Mommy knew she'd better investigate. Where was Kara? One guess was enough. Kara had put her hand in the plant again and was sprinkling dirt on the coffee table. "No, Kara! No, No! Don't touch." This time Mommy gave Kara a smart little spank on her hand. Kara whimpered as if her feelings were hurt, but turned toward the plant again.

It took a couple days for Kara to catch on that Mommy really meant what she said. Kara was not to touch the plant. Every time she got near the plant, Mommy reacted very predictably. Kara and Mommy even sang a little song about touching, "This is Mommy's, I won't touch, for I love her very much!" Kara had taken her first step toward self-control. There would be many more steps to conquer, but she was proud of her achievement. When Daddy came home, Kara went to the living room, pointed toward the plant, and said, "Mommy. No, no!" But she didn't touch the plant. Daddy hugged her and said, "Good girl!"

Learning self-control during early childhood is an indispensable building block of self-concept, social development, character, and spirituality. Children who respect limits and have learned self-control are liked by other people and get many positive "strokes" every day. This, in turn, builds their own self-respect.

Children who have not learned self-control terrorize shop owners and homemakers and alienate their playmates. Of course, they get very few positive "strokes," and their self-respect suffers. Later on, the Christian life will seem restrictive. "Saying no" to drugs and peer pressure will be very hard. They prefer instant gratification of every whim and a "do it if it feels good" lifestyle.

Achieving self-control is a major developmental milestone for young children. Most children have it in place by 3 years—not that they are always self-controlled, but they know how to restrain their actions and tell themselves not to do certain things.

How can you help your young child develop self-control?

1. Concentrate on one or two important lessons at a time. A houseful of breakables is too much for a toddler, but she can learn not to touch one plant or vase. Don't try to teach too many self-control lessons all at once. Your youngster will be overwhelmed. But it is very important that she learn to restrain her actions when needed. If you say, "Oh, she's too little. Maybe when she's 3 or 4 she'll understand," you will have missed the critical time for teaching self-control. It will be much harder later on.

2. Make the limits very clear, and be very predictable in your response to testing the limits. Be sure your child knows exactly what behavior you expect ("you may not hit your brother"). Always—every single time—respond with a consequence that encourages self-control. You've lost the battle if you ignore the behavior sometimes and pounce on it other times. Your child will quickly learn to ignore limits, and will not develop self-control.

3. Be generous with your praise of self-control. Children need to hear again and again that they are pleasing you. This builds self-control and, in turn, positive feelings about themselves and their family.

GUIDELINES FOR OLDER CHILDREN

As children get older there are other steps you can take to encourage them to develop self-control.

1. Establish a daily schedule in your home with regular times for eating and sleeping, playing, working, and studying. When you have established consistent, predictable times to do certain things during the day, children feel more secure. They know what to expect, and they get themselves into a routine more easily. The atmosphere encourages self-control. Evening meal, brief family time, study time. No TV on school nights. No phone calls from friends until lessons are done. Lay out your clothes for tomorrow (in climates where the weather is somewhat predictable!), get ready for bed, snuggle and secrets time with Mom or Dad. The kids feel secure. And they are learning self-control. Yes, it takes effort. No, you can't be gone every evening. Yes, it will be worth it down the line.

2. Model self-control and moderation in your own life. Be careful about the other models your child sees. What can you expect when you are reading a novel while the breakfast dishes are still on the table, the bedrooms are in disarray, and the kids are running around yelling that they can't find their school assignments? Self-control and moderation begin with the adults in the family. This doesn't mean there is never a time for spontaneity, for abandoning everything to do something very special. "The bluebirds just got here, Mom. Come see them!" Of course, you'll leave whatever you're doing to admire the bluebirds settling in their nesting boxes. But all spontaneity can be disastrous and all self-control can be rigid. Can you balance self-control and moderation with spontaneity? That's the trick.

Be careful about other models in your child's life. Cartoons model unrestrained aggression and violence; many cartoon characters smoke tobacco and drink alcohol. Many of the sponsors for athletic events are cigarette and alcohol companies. Exercise some control over the amount of exposure your child experiences to negative models. Maybe you have a negative model in your home—a spouse or older sibling. Explain to your child that this person has made some wrong choices right now, choices that will do him harm. Your child can make good choices. She can be in control of her own life.

3. Help your children learn to manage themselves and their time. Children need to learn practical management skills: planning their time, keeping track of their school assignments, dividing a long assignment into manageable parts so it can be finished on time, taking care of their clothes, organizing their belongings, doing the important things first instead of procrastinating, setting goals and steps to accomplish the goals, doing their chores without being reminded, saving money to buy something special, practicing a musical instrument or a sport every day to attain mastery. These are skills that can be learned, but children need help learning them. They don't come naturally to most children. Don't count on the schools to teach them. You are your child's primary teacher.

4. Use reasoning when you discipline so children will understand why they must behave in a certain way. Avoid harsh, power assertive discipline. Children who grow up with harsh discipline tend to be very weak on self-control. Someone else has always controlled them so they have never learned to manage themselves. Be warm and communicative, along with the reasoning, and you will encourage your children to be self-disciplined.

5. Teach your children to step back and think before they act: What is the right thing to do? Without thinking they will simply do what they want to do, instead of doing the right thing. What is best for me and for others? What would God want me to do? Teach your children that they can choose how they will behave. They don't have to be overwhelmed by their feelings or impulses. They can be in control. It's a wonderful feeling of power to be in control of yourself.

Explain that it's a little like sitting back in the audience and watching yourself onstage. When you sit in the audience you can think better about what is the right thing to do. When you are onstage acting you are just sort of going through your lines, without thinking.

Explain that you, the child, are the director of this play. You tell the actor (yourself) what to do so the play will go well. You are in charge. Chapter 9 has some hints about dealing with peer pressure that could be helpful in teaching self-control.

Teach your children the "count to 10" strategy for managing angry feelings. Count to 10 slowly before you respond. You can practice it as a family. Any family member can count out loud when he or she is thinking about how to handle anger or other negative feelings. Your children will learn that even the adults have to "count to 10" sometimes to manage their feelings.

Remember, they are only children and they will make mistakes, just as we adults do. A mistake is not the end of the world. A mistake is a step to better things.

6. Don't give your children too much too soon and too easily. Waiting for your first pair of panty hose or bra until they are really needed, waiting to date until you are old enough to be responsible, waiting to drive the car until you have passed driver's education and are old enough to get a license, waiting for your first car until you're old enough to take care of it and pay for the insurance, waiting for grown-up clothes until you are grown up, waiting for a credit card until you can pay the bills, waiting for sex until you are ready to deal with the consequences—and the list goes on. Children and teenagers are always begging for the next step. They want to become adults before they are ready emotionally to cope with the experiences of adulthood. You will do them a *big* favor by insisting that they wait until the appropriate time. They will also be learning valuable lessons in self-control. They need to be children as long as possible. When children take on adulthood too early, many times they regress back to childhood later on. Childhood precedes adulthood for very good developmental reasons.

GUIDELINES FOR TEENAGERS

To the above guidelines, add a few specific to the teen years:

1. With your teenagers develop specific guidelines for key areas. These might include driving and use of the family car, dating, sexuality, use of money, drugs, alcohol, and tobacco, and personal appearance, or whatever your child needs.

Make a date for a sit-down conference with your child to develop the guidelines for a specific area. Let your teenager suggest guidelines first. Write them out. If there are areas in which you feel additional guidelines are needed, bring them up along with your reasons. Be willing to negotiate. When you have agreed on the guidelines, print them as a formal contract to be signed by the teen and the responsible adult/adults. This contract should also spell out the consequences for ignoring the guidelines. Give a copy to the adolescent, keep a copy for yourself, and post a copy conspicuously on the refrigerator or wherever you post important notices. If you have more than one teenager in your family, the same guidelines might work for all, or you might need to develop a separate contract for the younger and older ones.

Contracts can save lots of headaches and hassles during the teen years. Teenagers like to be very clear about what is expected of them. Clear contracts have helped a lot of the families I have worked with who were having difficulties with their teenagers. The parents of one 13-year-old complained that he didn't do his home chores well. But when I tried to get them to specify what "well" meant to them, they didn't know. So we had to negotiate then and there what they were expecting. They said he didn't make his bed right. So I asked what would satisfy them—did the top of the bed need to look like the military, or would a few wrinkles be OK? They said his music was too loud. But they couldn't explain what "too loud" meant, so the boy suggested that when they got home he would put on some of his favorite CDs and try different levels of volume. When the volume was OK with the parents, he would place a marker on the volume control at that spot. Sounds picky, doesn't it? But it worked very well for that family because the boy now knew exactly what was expected of him.

On the other hand, your teenager may not need a contract for most of the above areas. There may be only one or two areas that are giving trouble and in which a contract would be helpful. Preventive contracts can be very helpful. They keep trouble from happening.

Our single, young adult daughter was with us at a workshop I was giving on parenting skills and listened while I explained about contracts and their helpfulness with teenagers. I used the illustration of a contract for using the family car. Later in the day she said to me, "I would have been insulted by a contract for the car!" I replied, "That is exactly why I didn't make any formal contracts with you and your brother. You were respectful of the rest of the family and we got along fine without writing it all down on a piece of paper. But not every family gets along that well, and some teenagers are more difficult than others. That's why contracts can be very helpful."

We had two cars, one for the exclusive use of my pediatrician husband, and the other for the children and me to share. But we lived only one mile from school and work, so by using bikes and sharing rides we all got along fine with the one car. No one monopolized the car, and we consulted with each other about specific times when we needed the car. No contract was needed.

Think carefully about your family situation. If your teenagers are responsible, don't insult them with contracts. Your verbal agreements will probably be enough. But if you are having trouble communicating with your teenagers, contracts can be a really helpful way of getting around the impasse and smoothing some of the bumps on the rough ride through adolescence.

2. Communicate your desire to help your teenager move toward independence. Make your child's thirteenth birthday a very special event. Perhaps take her to a restaurant where you can linger over a good meal. Explain that, since she is entering her teens, you want to talk about moving toward independence. Together, come up with a list of the skills she will need to be independent by the time she graduates from high school.

For starters, you might include money-handling skills (checkbook use, paying bills, buying groceries, saving, taxes, etc.) and people relationship skills (how to make new friends, how to select good friends, how to say "No," how to handle people who are smothery or too aggressive, how to handle a date who demands too much or gets abusive, etc.). Write these in a blank book, allowing space to write progress notes on each skill. Then decide which skills would be appropriate for this year. Plan how she can work on those skills. Have a "check-up on skills" conference once every three or six months. On her next birthday, review the year and decide on goals for the next year. Gradually she will be moving toward self-control and independent living.

This plan places you squarely on her side—helping her to achieve independence. Most adolescents fear that their parents are never going to let them be independent. Making a plan for independence reassures your teenager that you will not keep her "a baby" forever. It also removes quite a bit of the wind out of the sails of rebellion. There is no need for rebellion when you are working together toward the goal of independence.

When your teenager leaves home for college or a job, you will know he is well prepared because you have planned carefully for this new step.

FOCUSED GUIDELINES

I have chosen two areas for focused guidelines: drugs and dating. Both are key areas in which self-control plays a major role.

Drugs

We know a lot more than we did just a few years ago about who is likely to abuse chemical substances and why some children and adolescents become involved in smoking, drinking, and drug use. While research has not provided all the answers yet, we do know enough to give some excellent guidelines for prevention of substance abuse:

1. A strong family relationship is the best protection your children can have. This includes lots of love and affection, open communication and expression of feelings, respect for each family member, and reasonable rules enforced with love and firmness. Your religious commitment and community are important factors, also. Your church should have the same characteristics as a strong family. Together your family and church community can provide a large measure of protection.

2. Make your family's position on the use of alcohol, tobacco, and drugs very clear. Do you want your children to say, "No, never" or "No more" or "No, not today"? Many times parents who don't use any of these substances assume their example will be enough and never make their position explicitly clear or do any drug education. Remember, your children will probably see other role models who may influence them toward alcohol or other drugs. Make your family position very clear. Express your positive expectations for your children.

3. Practice what you preach about substance abuse. Children from homes in which there is drinking, drugs, and smoking are much more likely to indulge as well.

4. Do everything possible to help your children develop strong self-respect. Encourage their individuality, respect their viewpoints, provide support and affirmation, especially during the preteen and early teen years. Males are more vulnerable to substance abuse. Find a positive male role model for both girls and boys. Chapter 7 has ideas for helping children develop self-respect.

5. Teach responsible social problem-solving skills and behavior. A surprising number of young people say they drink to "get away from my problems" or to "deal with anger and frustration." They are at special risk for long-term use and substance abuse. Don't rescue your child from every difficulty or make life too easy. Don't make excuses or overprotect. Children need to confront difficulties so they can grow strong. They need to feel responsible for their lives and in control. They need to know how to solve their problems. A substantial body of research points out that they need to overcome social problems early, otherwise they will become teenagers with significant behavioral and psychiatric problems, including substance abuse.

6. Educate yourself about drugs and addictions so you can provide accurate information to your children. Give your child important information about any family history of chemical dependency. Eighty percent of all alcoholics have a heredity of chemical dependency in their parents or their grandparents. Your children need to know that they might be especially vulnerable and how to take charge of their future. Remember to make your propaganda early, before children become defensive.

7. Teach decision-making skills and strategies for dealing with peer pressure. Peer pressure is one of the reasons young people try chemical substances. Help them learn how to make friends and evaluate friendships. See chapters 8 and 9 for ideas for dealing with decisions and peer pressure.

8. Help your children achieve academic success. From the very beginning, children need to be involved in learning, and they need to feel successful. This is an important component of self-respect and self-esteem. If children do not feel successful in school by age 11, they will most likely abandon trying in favor of other forms of success, usually negative and involving substance abuse. Do whatever you have to do to help your children learn.

9. Provide many opportunities for your children to develop critical thinking skills. Children need many opportunities to talk about values, moral issues, and everyday life. They need to think and evaluate. This dialogue needs to begin at home. It can be a protection against substance abuse.

Dating

Prepare your children well for the dating scene. It is fraught with pitfalls as well as joy and pleasure. Preparation helps avoid the pitfalls.

1. Begin early to prepare for dating experiences. Teach social skills and how to make friends and judge friendships. Teach boys how to respect girls and how to show them a good time without getting involved with sex. Teach girls how to dress attractively without being sexually provocative. Teach both boys and girls to respect the parents of their date. Boys should never sit in the car and just honk for the girl to show up. Boys worth dating always go in and greet the family. Girls worth dating usually have parents who want to meet their girl's date.

2. Decide on an appropriate age for your child to begin dating. Do this long before the hormones surge. You might want to make a difference between ages for dating in a group, such as going to a banquet where adults are present, and single dating (one boy and one girl going somewhere together in his car). Discuss this age with your child and look forward to the time when she will begin dating. Be positive about this rite of passage. "When you are 16 [or whatever age you have selected] and you begin dating . . ." If you are hoping your child will get a college education, postpone single dating as long as possible. Give your child a chance to develop some career goals and mature emotionally before confronting the insecurities and pressures of dating.

3. Develop clear guidelines for appropriate dating activities. Develop these with your child. An adolescent who has a list of possible dating activities in the back of his mind can forestall some real difficulties.

4. Communicate clear rules for dating behavior that help prevent overwhelming temptations for sexual activity or alcohol or drug use. Insist that at least one adult chaperon be present at all parties and that your child does *not* go to a party where drugs or alcohol is available. Be very clear that your child should not be alone with a friend of the opposite sex at your home or anyone else's home. According to national surveys in the United States, at least three fourths of teenage sex takes place in one of their homes when their parents are not present. Having to share the family car, instead of having their own, during high school prevents a lot of problems.

Don't think it can't happen to your child. It can and does happen to "very nice kids." Just look at the teenage pregnancy rate. Be sure your kids have earned your trust before you believe everything they say about where they are going and with whom. Sex is an extremely powerful drive, especially in young males.

5. Be sure your adolescent knows she can always call on you for a rescue operation. When she leaves on a date be sure she has enough money to call home and to get home, if necessary. Cellular phones and beepers can be very helpful. Be sure she knows she can call anytime and you will pick her up, no questions asked. She needs that security.

6. Teach your preadolescent how to handle other kids or adults who invade their private space in offensive ways. Your child needs to know how to handle the person who tries to be too intimate, becomes aggressive or abusive. Unfortunately, these days not everyone can be trusted. Both he and she need to know how to handle difficult people.

7. Make your home an attractive place for your child's friends to gather. Keep the cookie jar and the snack shelf full. With your child, select games and music that are attractive to kids and yet pass your standards. Be friendly, but not overly intrusive. I always figured that if the kids were at our house, I knew what they were doing. Many young people today don't really have much contact with the adults who are supposed to be part of their lives. They will naturally be drawn to a home with warm and friendly adults.

8. Encourage group activities for preteens and early teens. Group activities help children learn social skills and prepare them for later dating. Get together with other parents and plan activities. Don't expect other people to baby-sit your kids all the time. Be part of the action yourself. Someone has to get it started. I was always grateful that there were a lot of group social activities in the crowd our children ran around with in high school. There was individual dating, but most of their socializing involved the whole group. You can encourage that with your children's friends by helping to organize activities.

TROUBLE WITH SELF-CONTROL?

Temper tantrums often are the first major trouble spot many parents confront with teaching self-control. Every child will try to pull off temper tantrums or maybe breath-holding spells. It's easy to say that if the tantrum doesn't get the child what he wants, he will give up on tantrums. But usually it isn't quite that easy.

Tantrums usually start almost as a natural reaction brought on by fatigue or pain or frustration because something won't happen right. Baby is building a block tower and it falls down. Grandma wants baby to stop playing and take a nap. She loves playing and hates to be interrupted for naps. Frustration and rage emerge as a tantrum. Some children have very short trigger points and are easily frustrated, while others can endure more disappointment before erupting. Fatigue creates a short fuse that makes a tantrum more likely. It doesn't actually cause tantrums.

Young children who are completely out of control because of tiredness and an obviously difficult time over something need the comfort and security of an adult who can physically restrain them until they quiet down. Discipline won't do any good. These children need to be held firmly and gently soothed until they are calmer. Then there can be talking and reasoning.

When you realize the child is throwing a fit just to get attention, do not give her the attention she seeks. Ignore her. Take her to a safe place— her bed or a blanket on the floor or a playpen—and tell her you cannot talk with her until she calms down. Leave. Don't look back. Just leave.

Nothing gets a parent's attention quicker than a tantrum. It can actually be scary, especially if the child is a breath holder. (Usually nature will take over rather quickly and restore breath.) Some children cry so hard and go into such a big rage that they vomit. *Never* give your child what he wants because he threw a tantrum. Resist giving him any attention, and be sure no one else gives him attention, either. Once he catches on that this is the perfect way to get attention or what he wants, you will be a long time dealing with the tantrums. Don't let them get started as a pattern of behavior.

Many children will stop the tantrums when they realize there is no benefit.

But there are some children who are more difficult. They came with very volatile emotions. They have no patience from day one. They get angry at the least provocation, will throw themselves on the floor, kick and scream, and bang their heads. They are just plain difficult to handle. Try the calming routine to see if it works. Otherwise, take the child to a quiet place and leave. Tell the child you will come back when he is calmer.

For a 2- or 3-year-old who is still throwing tantrums, sending the child to her room and emphasizing that she may come back when she has herself under control may work. Gradually, not immediately, if you are perfectly consistent. But if you only ignore most of the time, but occasionally the child gets what she wants, you will reinforce the behavior and it will never stop without heroic efforts on your part.

Children with volatile tempers have a hard battle ahead of them. They need all the help they can get to control their emotions. If they don't learn to control their feelings, they become the adults who throw plates, break windows, physically abuse their spouse and children, and pull guns on the highway. Control is imperative. A 7- or 8-year-old who still throws himself on the floor in a fit of rage needs strong medicine to convince him to make the effort to control himself.

Some children will learn to control themselves in situations in which it is demanded of them, such as school, but continue to throw tantrums at home because the parents allow it. They mistakenly think the child will outgrow this behavior. Take the situation in hand. Explain the seriousness of the issue to the child. Explain what you will do if he throws a tantrum. Let him know you mean business. And do it. He will test you out because he has a very bad habit that will be hard to break. Don't go soft. Be tough and help him break the habit. That's the best you can do for his future. Tough love is definitely needed. It will work.

FAMILY ACTIVITIES

Food Choices: Show your children the food pyramid. If you do not have one, they can make one from magazine pictures. The sections, from bottom to top, are Grains and Pasta, Vegetables, Fruits, Proteins, Fats, and Sweets. Have fun finding pictures of different kinds of food for each section. Ask each person to pretend to be a food and tell everyone why they should eat that food. Find pictures of unhealthy food choices. Talk about why they are unhealthy.

Simon Says: Children love to play this game. The leader says, "Simon says to . . . [raise your hands, for example]." If Simon says to do it, the players are supposed to follow. Occasionally the leader inserts a command without the Simon says, to try to catch the children. Keep it snappy, especially for older children. This game demands careful listening and self-restraint.

Animal Statue: This is a great game for learning self-control and most children like to play it. Mark a starting line and a finish line. The leader stands on the finish line with his or her back to the group of people playing. The players stand on a starting line. The leader, without looking back at the players, calls out the animal and the kind of walk: (two elephant steps, for example) and counts slowly to 10. Everyone playing does the two elephant steps, mimicking the walk of an elephant. When the leader finishes counting and turns around, everyone is supposed to be standing as still as a statue, looking like an elephant walking. If the leader catches anyone moving, the player has to go back the steps just taken. Playing continues with another call from the leader: three rabbit hops, for example. The first person to reach the finish line becomes the next leader. This is a great game for learning body control.

QUOTABLE WISDOM

"The man who loses his head is usually the last one to miss it."

"He overcomes a strong enemy who overcomes his own anger."

"So long as a man is angry he cannot be in the right."

> —*Chinese proverb*

"It is easier to swallow angry words than to have to eat them."

"The best answer to anger is silence."

> —*German proverb*

"Anger is only one letter short of danger."

"He who reigns within himself, and rules passions, desires, and fears, is more than a king."

"Hot words make cool friendships."

NATURE TRAILS TO SELF-CONTROL AND MODERATION

Gerbil: Jean Mayer, professor of nutrition at Harvard University, told this story at a seminar my husband attended. His boy frequently heard Mayer talk about scientific experiments and the research he was doing. One day he told his dad that he wanted to do an experiment too. So they designed an experiment to see how much food his pet gerbil would eat. The first day the boy gave the gerbil 15 sunflower seeds. The gerbil ate them all. Each day the boy added one more sunflower seed to the gerbil's diet. On day two the gerbil got 16 seeds, on day three 17 seeds, and so forth. The gerbil ate all the seeds it got until it reached 33. Even though the boy gave his pet one additional seed each day, the gerbil would not eat more than 33 seeds. It carefully hid the extra sunflower seeds. It never overate.

But the day the gerbil received 100 seeds, it added one more to its diet. It ate 34 seeds every day after that. Mayer concluded that the gerbil was using enough energy hiding the extra seeds that it needed a bit of extra nourishment. The gerbil showed marvelous self-control by never eating more than it needed. It also provided well for its future by working hard to hide the extra seeds.

Sharks: Sharks have a reputation for being ferocious people attackers. My husband had an experience diving at Cocos Island in the Pacific Ocean, near Costa Rica, that taught him that sharks are not always attackers. When they aren't hungry they will leave people completely alone. The six divers in his party swam peacefully among a large school of hammerhead sharks who paid no attention to the divers. There were plenty of fish for the sharks to eat, and they were well fed. They weren't hungry. Animals seem to do better than people with self-control and food. They will eat only as much as their bodies need, no more. People many times eat a lot more than they need for the health of their bodies.

Lilies and Roses: Jesus used the beautiful lilies of the field as an example of God's care. White lilies and white roses symbolize purity. Try to find a white rose or lily for your daughter to wear as a reminder of the purity God wants her to maintain.

EVERYDAY TRAILS TO SELF-CONTROL AND MODERATION

Whenever your child is involved in a real-life situation from which he can learn about self-control and moderation, stop whatever you are both doing and talk. Be sure the conversation suits your child's age. Let your child do most of the talking, with some guidance from you. One of the following stories might serve to get you started on the topic.

Early Childhood: Rachel and the Candy

Rachel had been working hard to learn the ABCs. Finally she said them perfectly. The teacher was very pleased and said, "Rachel, you have worked very hard learning the ABCs. I am proud of you. I have a candy jar in my desk. You may get yourself a candy to celebrate."

Rachel went to the desk and found the candy jar. When the teacher wasn't looking, she took a whole handful of candies. One of the other kids saw what she had done and went to tell the teacher. What do you think the teacher will do? Was Rachel using self-control? What can Rachel do now to make things right with the teacher? How can the teacher help Rachel learn self-control?

Late Childhood: Broken Nose

Milton accidentally stepped on James's toe while rushing out to recess. James angrily punched Milton on his face and broke his nose. Blood came rushing down Milton's tender nose. His face transformed from pale to purple as he cried in pain. The teacher observed the whole incident, but couldn't stop James, because it all happened so fast. Did Milton purposely step on James's toe? Why do you suppose James punched Milton? James thought Milton had stepped on his toe on purpose. What should he have done to check it out? What can be said or done at this point? What can the teacher do to help James develop self-control? How can James learn to be self-controlled?

Adolescence: Pizza Party

Jackie invited her friend Steve to a pizza party at her house. He arrived a few minutes early and started eating before everyone else. Before long, Steve's appetite approved his inclination to eat a whole pizza. As he got ready to attack another box of pizza, Jane felt she had to get him to stop because some of her other friends hadn't had any pizza yet. She really couldn't afford to order more. What should Jane do or say? How could she utilize this delicate moment to explain kindly the necessity and need of having self-control to Steve without embarrassing him or hurting his feelings?

KEYS TO SELF-CONTROL AND MODERATION

For younger children

1. Concentrate on one or two important lessons at a time.

2. Make the limits very clear and be very predictable in your response to testing the limits.

3. Be generous with your praise of self-control.

For older children

1. Establish a daily schedule with regular times for eating, sleeping, playing, working, and studying.

2. Model self-control and moderation in your own life. Be careful about other models your child sees.

3. Help your children learn to manage themselves and their time.

4. Use reasoning when you discipline.

5. Teach your children to step back and think before they act.

6. Don't give children too much too soon and too easily.

For adolescents

7. With your teenager, develop specific guidelines for key areas: driving, dating, sexuality, money, drugs, alcohol and tobacco, personal appearance.

8. Communicate your desire to help your teenager move toward independence.

CHAPTER 14

HONESTY AND INTEGRITY

Deliver my soul, O Lord. Ps. 120:2, NKJV.

Our local newspaper carried the story of a seventh-grade girl who became angry at her substitute teacher because he insisted she obey the classroom rules. To get even, she accused him of sexually abusing her and got several of her classmates to corroborate her fictitious story. By the time law-enforcement officers and social workers had sorted out the mess and the girls had confessed to lying, the teacher's reputation was ruined. No school would hire him, even though he was innocent.

Recently I read an article in an educational journal about a professor at a major university who watched many students blatantly cheating while he was proctoring a final examination. When he spoke to them, the students brashly denied cheating, even though he had seen them copying from their crib sheets and they knew it. A number of students wrote him notes saying that if he reported them they would accuse him of harassment and would see that he lost his job. Although he reported the problem to top academic administration—certainly the path of integrity—nothing was ever done about it. The students were never disciplined, or even spoken to.

I have had a number of similar experiences, even while teaching in a Christian university—students handing in work that others had done and claiming it as their own; cheating on major comprehensive examinations; cheating on field work or internship records. The list could go on and on. That's cheating at the graduate level, but cheating begins in grade school. Ask any elementary teacher.

Whatever happened to honesty and integrity?

Yes, indeed, honesty and integrity are rare qualities in this day of weak character and "do whatever will get you ahead." We see its lack in top government officials, nationally acclaimed television evangelists, and in our own everyday lives. How can you teach your children to be honest? What do honesty and integrity look like in real life?

WHEN I AM HONEST AND A PERSON OF INTEGRITY . . .

I tell the truth, even when it is very difficult.

I do not cheat on my school assignments. I do my own work and get the grades I deserve.

I play the best I can in sports. I play by the rules.

I don't gossip about other people.

When I work, I don't fool around and waste time.

I keep my promises. I do what I say I am going to do. People can trust me.

> Principle
> Truth
> Character
> Sincerity
> Genuineness
> Decency
> Honor

I will always do what is honest and right, even though it might hurt me. I want people to know that I am a person of integrity. I want my word to mean something.

GOD'S VIEW OF HONESTY

God has plenty to say about dishonesty, lying lips and actions, and dishonest business practices. Dishonesty is an abomination to Him. God's character includes absolute, transparent honesty and integrity. We can trust His promises. He never lies.

Lying originated in the heart of Lucifer, the fallen angel. He used it very successfully in the perfection of

> *Keep your tongue from evil and your lips from speaking lies.*
> *Ps. 34:13.*
>
> *I hate every false way.*
> *Ps. 119:128, NKJV.*
>
> *The Lord abhors dishonest scales.*
> *Prov. 11:1, NIV.*
>
> *Providing for honest things, not only in the sight of the Lord, but also in the sight of men.*
> *2 Cor. 8:21, KJV.*

*You should do
that which is honest.
2 Cor. 13:7, KJV.*

*Finally, brethren,
whatsoever things are . . . honest
. . . think on these things.
Phil. 4:8, KJV.*

*No lie was found in their mouths.
Rev. 14:5, NIV.*

*May integrity and uprightness
protect me.
Ps. 25:21, NIV.*

Eden. "You will not die if you eat of the fruit of this tree." Eve fell for the deception, and we all know the results in misery and broken lives.

God wants us to be honest in every aspect of our lives. He wants us to be persons of sterling integrity. He wants us to shine like polished gold in a dishonest world. He wants to be with us every day helping us to be honest. He wants our honesty and integrity to flow from our love for Him.

Bible People

Because the Bible records real life—not some glorified PR version—there are biographies of many Bible people who had difficulty with honesty and integrity: Achan (Joshua 7), Ananias and Sapphira (Acts 5:1-11), Peter at Jesus' trial (Matt. 26:69-75), Rebecca and Jacob (Gen. 27:1-17), and Joseph's brothers (Gen. 37), among others.

The Bible writers also recorded scenes of sterling integrity: Daniel did not hide his devotion to his God (Dan. 6:10-12). Shadrach, Meshach, and Abednego stood up for their beliefs (Dan. 3:16-18). Joseph refused the temptation to be dishonest with his employer (Gen. 39:6-19). John identified with Jesus at His trial (John 18:15).

Help your children understand that honesty and integrity do not always lead to an easy way out. Sometimes the way of integrity is difficult and full of detours, but the end result shines brightly. Along the way a clear conscience brings freedom and joy.

The lives of each of these Bible people contain important lessons for your children. Take the time to really get to know each one. There is a modern equivalent for each temptation to be dishonest. See if your children can think of how this temptation would really feel in their own lives.

HOW TO HELP CHILDREN DEVELOP HONESTY AND INTEGRITY

Children learn how to live from watching us live, no matter how much we tell them to live differently. Nowhere is that statement more applicable than to honesty and integrity.

1. Model honesty and integrity in your own life. Your children will not be more honest than you are. What price would your character and integrity bring in the marketplace? Would it sell on the bargain counter with last season's leftovers? Or would it be displayed with the highest quality merchandise in the store, sought after by discerning people? Do your acquaintances say, "He can be trusted—he's a man of integrity"? "You can count on her. She's honest to the penny"?

Children pick up the informal lessons of everyday living faster than deliberate attempts to teach them. Every day provides opportunities for informal lessons on integrity and honesty.

You check the charge tape at the grocery store. The clerk undercharged you for an item, or gave you too much change. How do you deal with a mistake in your favor? What if it were in the store's favor? Splendid informal lesson for your kids. Believe me, it's a lesson they will get an A+ on. They will know exactly how to act in a similar circumstance in the future.

The library books or videos are due today. You're in a hurry. Do you take them back, or do you say, "It doesn't matter. I can usually talk the librarian out of a fine"? No mention of other people who might be waiting for the video or book, just the implicit lesson that if you're smart you can usually find a way around the rules.

"We're running late for your swimming lesson. We'll just watch the radar. We can fool the police any day!" said with a laugh and a bit of bragging. Implicit lesson: It's OK to be sneaky and "above" the rules. Think of how many times your children can use that lesson!

"Looks like we're out of paper clips and Scotch tape. I'll bring some home from the office tomorrow. Anything else we need?" Sammie Six pipes up, "But isn't that stealing?" "Oh, no, darling. Everyone does it!" Implicit lessons: It's OK to steal from someone who's richer than you are.

Honesty on the job isn't that important, anyway. It's OK to be as dishonest as the next guy.

What informal lessons are your children learning from watching you live during an ordinary day? They are very apt students, quick to learn and quick to apply. Don't be surprised if you see the same scenarios repeated in their lives. The real question is Will you recognize the lesson junior learned? Or will you wring your hands and moan, "How could junior be so sneaky? We always taught him to be honest"?

Maybe you almost put this book down in disgust after the first couple examples. *How unreal! Nobody lives that way today!* But something kept you reading. Now the light is beginning to dawn. There is a commandment that says "Thou shalt not steal" and another that reads "Thou shalt not bear false witness." *Wait a minute, maybe I've been following the crowd.* All those everyday lessons in dishonesty have piled up. *What can I do now?*

Take heart. You can do something now. The next time one of those situations comes up, you can be honest with your kids and say something like this: "I don't think I've always been very honest. Now I realize I need to be honest. I'm not bringing any more supplies home from the office. We'll buy our supplies at the office supply store. I have already paid my office for the supplies I stole [hard word, isn't it?] before, as best I could figure out how much it was [or intend to do so]. Please forgive me for showing you a dishonest way to live. Will you help me be more honest in the future?"

Your children will be shocked, but they won't forget the new lesson, either. It may prick their own consciences into restoring some things they have taken. As a family you can move ahead, helping each other live more honestly. God's Word provides a standard of honesty most of us are still aspiring to. Share it with your children and move ahead together.

When you have done the above, you can move on to the rest of these suggestions. But if you are regularly teaching dishonesty by your everyday actions, all the rest of the guidelines come across as hypocritical. It's a "Do what I say, not what I do" sort of thing. Children will always learn the "I do" way of living, and they will not respect you for teaching one thing and living another. Integrity is the name of this game. The plays are obvious—even very young children understand. Teach what you live.

2. Look for real-life models of honesty and dishonesty to share with your children. Teach them what honesty and dishonesty mean by real-life examples. Stories of famous people (you can find examples of honesty, even though the dishonest ones seem quite overwhelming), clippings from your local paper, and real-life situations you or your children observe can all provide models of either honesty or dishonesty. Talk about what happened and the consequences of both. Get the children to think about the effects of acting honestly or dishonestly. Try to help children grasp the real-life consequences of honest or dishonest behavior. Their understanding will depend on their age.

Honesty often saves time and makes everyone feel more comfortable. For example, a telemarketer calls. Instead of listening, when you know you don't want the merchandise, simply say "I'm sorry, but I am not interested in what you are selling. Please do not call me again." Hang up. Be polite but firm. Honesty saves everyone's time. Honesty builds trust. Don't say "It won't hurt" to your child before a dentist visit when you know it will. Be honest about the hurting, but provide reassurance and comfort.

Honesty saves a lot of maneuvering. One lie is seldom enough to cover one's tracks. One lie leads to another until there is a string of them and there seems to be no way out. And then there's the problem of remembering what was said. Pretty soon the lies contradict each other. The best memory is a honest one.

3. Notice and compliment honest actions. Reinforcing good behavior is always appropriate. Notice honest actions, even small ones. Compliment. "I noticed you were honest about who ate the cookies. Thank you for your honesty." Most of the time we notice only the dishonest actions. They are more glaring, and we are in a mind-set for correcting errors. Children like to be noticed. Complimenting honest actions will lead to more of the same, and the dishonest actions will begin to be less frequent as they are replaced with honesty.

4. Provide consequences for dishonest actions, but give children an opportunity to start over again. Don't keep reminding them of the times they were dishonest. Make a clean slate where they can write a new story. Show them a small chalkboard, write the lie they told on it, and then erase it completely. White boards and magic slates don't work as well for this illustration, as they tend to leave a bit of color or a dent in the black backing that clever children will be sure to point out. The chalkboard works best. You can even wash it completely clean to illustrate forgiveness, if the eraser is less than effective.

Children need to learn the seriousness of telling lies or other dishonest actions. Your message needs to be very clear and firm: Lying is totally unacceptable. Stealing is never acceptable. Help your child return a stolen item to the store. Don't make the confession for her, but accompany her to provide courage and support. Copying from another child on a test or for a project is both stealing and lying.

When a child deliberately lies and refuses to acknowledge that he did so, you need to make your message clear with a consequence that won't be forgotten soon. When your child admits to telling a lie or being dishonest in some way, deal with the situation differently. Compliment the confession. "That took courage to admit you lied." Then deal with the aftereffects of the lie. Perhaps someone was hurt or something was broken and restitution is needed. Confession doesn't eliminate restitution. Make the honesty message clear.

If your child lies frequently and then easily confesses, he is learning a bad habit. He is lying for convenience and then depending on your good graces to let him "get away with it." He needs some consequences that will make your message very clear. Think carefully about the pattern of behavior that is developing and act accordingly.

5. Help your children learn to figure out how to deal with difficult situations. Sometimes a child—or teenager or adult— is dishonest because she can't figure out how to resolve the situation she is in. She needs to learn problem-solving skills so the situation will be easier to deal with the next time. She won't be so tempted to lie her way out.

"Lucinda," called Mommy. "Who made this terrible mess in Mommy's room?"

"I don't know," lied Lucinda. "The cat must have done it."

Mommy's perfume bottles and lotions were strewn all over her dresser, with some on the floor. Spilled hand cream dripped down the front of the dresser. It was a big mess.

"I don't remember seeing the cat in my room this morning. I was in here just a short while ago and nothing was spilled," responded Mommy.

"I saw the cat running down the hallway toward your room," lied Lucinda.

"Well, let's go find the cat," suggested Mommy. Lucinda blanched, but went with Mommy to find the cat, who was sleeping peacefully in the sunshine on the deck on the other side of the house.

Many tears later Lucinda finally admitted she had made the mess. When Mommy asked Lucinda how the bottles got spilled, she explained, "I was trying to get some hand cream for my hands, like you do . . . and I couldn't reach the bottle . . . and all the bottles fell over. Then I got scared and ran away. I was afraid to tell you."

"Lucinda, you did two things that were wrong. You took something that didn't belong to you and you lied about it," stated Mommy very clearly.

"Lucinda, when you want something that doesn't belong to you, how can you solve that problem?" Lucinda and Mommy talked about asking permission. Then Mommy said, "You had another problem. When you want something that is too high for you, what can you do about it?"

"I could get a chair and climb up," Lucinda suggested hesitantly.

"Anything else you could do?" continued Mommy.

"Well, I suppose I could ask you to get it for me," admitted Lucinda. "That would solve both problems, wouldn't it?"

It takes time to teach problem-solving skills, but it is time well spent.

6. Teach your children that honesty is never rude.
Some people use honesty as an excuse for rudeness and bad manners. They excuse their actions with "At least I'm honest." Honesty is always kind and loving. It should never be confused with rude, intrusive comments. I once read that if you love someone enough, you can tell them anything that needs telling. If you don't, you deserve what you get. Teach your children to tell the truth, when necessary, in the kindest way possible.

Being honest is a habit. All habits take time and persistence to develop. Help your children learn to live open, transparently honest lives. Don't give up too soon. Children are learners in the school of honesty.

TROUBLE WITH HONESTY AND INTEGRITY?

No child is honest all the time. Children must learn to be honest and eventually develop integrity, a process that takes many years of careful training. First, children must learn the difference between truth and lies. Between the ages of 3 and 4 is the best time to begin teaching the difference between truth and lying. By age 4 most children understand lying and have also made some deliberate attempts to deceive. They can tell the difference between fantasy and reality. While they are learning this difference, they need input from adults who will say, "Really? I didn't see a purple turtle in the yard. That was a funny made-up story, but it didn't really happen. Sometimes it's fun to make up stories." Children need to learn that concealing the truth is just as dishonest as actually telling a lie. It is a lie acted out.

Children deceive for many reasons. According to Paul Ekman, author of *Why Kids Lie*, the most common reason is to avoid punishment or adult anger. Sometimes they want to get something, preserve their privacy, protect their friends or themselves from harm, win the admiration of others, avoid embarrassment, or test or challenge authority. They may be naturally lazy and don't want to be held accountable for their actions. Some of these reasons are more characteristic of early childhood, while others happen more often during the preteen or early teen years. The most critical periods are from ages 3 to 4 and during early adolescence when peer pressure is strongest. Children who lie the most tend to have parents who lie more themselves. They have less parental supervision and experience more parental rejection.

While all children must be held accountable for occasional dishonesty, some children develop a pattern of continual deceit. These children usually have other behavioral problems as well. According to William Lee Carter, in his book *KidThink*, deceitful children are usually very insecure. They cover up their insecurity by manipulating people and circumstances. They do not want to accept responsibility for their actions. They also may have an unhealthy pride. They are very touchy about themselves and anything that might embarrass them. They get angry when you try to help them with their faults and claim they don't have any! They flaunt arrogance and wear their pride on their sleeves.

One of the most exasperating characteristics of deceitful children is their ability to be vague and unclear. Communication is a disaster area. They won't tell you how they really feel. You get the sense that what they are saying doesn't match with their feelings, but you can't quite pin them down on this. They won't tell you what really happened or why they lied or cheated. Your attempts to play detective end in frustration, with the child still in control. What can you do?

You need to work on two fronts at once: Deal with the behavior and work on the underlying reasons. First, **consider your priorities for this child.** Are your expectations too high, more than she is capable of? Maybe she isn't a straight-A student or he isn't a star athlete. The pressure to be what she cannot be sets the child up to be deceptive about what is happening in her life. It also makes her feel very insecure. Change your priorities to better match this child's natural gifts and abilities. Communicate this clearly. Compliment the child on his strengths. Communicate your love and concern in ways the child understands. Work on developing a stronger self-image. (See chapter 7 for ideas.) Gradually he will become more secure, and the need to deceive will lessen. However, it will probably not go away easily, as deceit has become a bad habit. Habits take effort to change. Deceit has provided some payoffs that will be hard to give up.

Be a parent who provides clear leadership. You don't have to understand every reason for your child's behavior. Act on the evidence you have. Act clearly. State your own honest emotions, but avoid anger, sarcasm, or any other negative reaction. Remember, *when you are out of control your child is in control.* Provide clear limits for behavior. The consequences should match the crime—not be overly strict or too lenient. Overly severe punishment encourages deceit. Leniency allows children to develop irresponsibility and get into a pattern of deception. Uphold your child's dignity, but don't let her get away with being irresponsible and not facing the results of her actions. Don't let her manipulate you into "giving up" in exasperation or avoiding confronting the problem. That's exactly what she wants.

Enlist the cooperation of other people. You need all the help you can get to help your child turn around. Communicate frequently with teachers and coaches. Enlist the help of other family members. The fewer opportunities the child has to manipulate and deceive, the sooner she will change.

Always encourage new beginnings. Show your child God's forgiveness. Pray together about the problem. Emphasize that God is always willing to forgive and help get rid of the bad habit. God's love surrounds and supports the child always.

FAMILY ACTIVITIES

True or False: This game can be adapted for all ages of children. When played with very young children, the object is to teach them what is meant by true or false. When played with older children and teenagers, the object is to nudge them to be more selective about what they believe or accept as truth.

For young children, begin by making some easy-to-identify statements, such as "There are four people in our family." Then ask: "Are there really four people? Was what I said true or false?"

Continue with anything you can make up. Humor helps make the game fun. Make some really crazy statements, as well as simple true ones. You can reverse the game by saying true or false and asking the children to make a statement that fits.

For older children, who already know what true and false mean, begin making rather simple statements, sometimes humorous, to get the game started. Then proceed to statements that require more thinking to decide if they are true or false. If you have teenagers, work with statements that require them to look up the answer. The children can take turns making the statements and trying to fool other people. This game can be as simple or as complicated as your family wants.

Sources: The object of this game is to help children learn to evaluate the sources of information they hear or read, to make them more discriminating in what they believe. Gather as many of the following means of communication as you can find: a newspaper, e-mail, encyclopedia, Bible, popular magazine, professional journal, a personal letter, note a child wrote in class, a historical novel, a romantic novel, an official biography, an unofficial biography, a movie video, a *National Geographic* informational video, etc. Ask each person to select one item and tell the others how good a source of information it is. Talk about each item. What makes you think it is a good or a bad source of information? Why? How can you decide for sure? Then arrange them on the floor in order of reliability of information. Whom can you really believe? Mom and Dad? Grandpa and Grandma? Cousins? Best friend? This activity could continue for several family nights.

The Law: Work together as a family to find out what the law says about people who lie to a policeman or in court. What are the consequences for stealing if the person is convicted? Investigate other dishonest practices as they come up in the news (plenty of examples available these days!). If possible, visit a courtroom. In most county courts the public are allowed as visitors at any trial. Or talk about a courtroom visit your children made with their class at school. Did the children think the lawyers were telling the truth? What made them think so? Whom can you really believe?

QUOTABLE WISDOM

"An honest countenance is the best passport."
>—*English proverb*

"Although dying of thirst, I drink not the water of a stolen fountain."
>—*Japanese proverb*

"Ill-gotten money does not remain with one."
>—*Japanese proverb*

"Lying lets you live one night, the truth makes you live forever."
>—*Tunisian proverb*

"A good liar needs a good memory."
>—*Arabic proverb*

"A liar is not believed when he speaks the truth."
>—*German proverb*

"A good conscience is a soft pillow."
>—*German proverb*

"Truth and oil always come to the surface."
>—*Spanish proverb*

"Honesty is the best policy."
>—*American proverb*

"Don't believe anything you hear and only half of what you see."
>—*American proverb*

NATURE TRAILS TO HONESTY

Yeast: Yeast provides a good nature lesson on honesty and integrity. When we put yeast in the bread dough, it permeates everything. It is impossible to pick out the yeast. Once the action of the yeast begins, the dough gets bigger and bigger. There is no way of stopping the action of the yeast and still save the bread. You can cool or freeze the dough to stop the yeast action, but as soon as you warm up the dough, the yeast will go on working.

Yeast is like lying—it permeates everything. Once you tell one lie, you often need to tell others to cover your tracks. The lies get bigger and bigger, just as the yeast does for the bread.

Yeast is also like integrity—it permeates everything you do. Everyone who knows you respects your integrity. You are a person of your word and you will do what is right, even if it is not convenient. People trust you because integrity permeates everything you do.

Jellyfish: When we lived in the Caribbean, going to the beach was our favorite recreation. The warm water and brilliant blue color attracted us and many other people. Some months of the year we had to be a little careful because jellyfish were more common. We didn't want to bump into one because they can have a nasty sting.

Jellyfish look like a transparent blob, shaped like an open umbrella on top with tentacles hanging down. They float in the water, usually washed about by the waves, waiting for their food to swim by so they can inject their venom. They don't pursue their food, but simply wait for something to swim by. Sometimes they get in trouble and bump into something because they can't swim well, but just float on the waves.

They remind me of boys and girls who just float along with what everybody else is doing. If it's convenient, they tell a lie; if it's convenient, they tell the truth. They just float along doing whatever seems convenient. After a while other kids avoid them, just as people avoid jellyfish. They don't want to get stung by their lies. They prefer to be with kids who can be counted on to support their friends—not just do what is convenient.

EVERYDAY TRAILS TO HONESTY AND INTEGRITY

Grab any real-life teachable moment to encourage honesty and integrity.

Early Childhood: Wal-Mart Toys.

Ruben enjoys going to Wal-Mart with his mother. Every time they go, he wants to go to the toy section. Today was no exception.

When they arrived home, Ruben immediately asked his mother if he could go play outside. Mother told him he had to eat his dinner first, but Ruben insisted that he wanted to go out and play right then. Mother began to suspect that there was a reason for his insistence. She noticed that

Ruben looked like he was holding something inside his jacket.

When Mother asked Ruben what he was holding inside his jacket, he hesitated, but finally told her that it was a toy from Wal-Mart. Mother knew she hadn't bought Ruben a toy at Wal-Mart. Ruben had stolen the toy from the store. What do you think Ruben should do? What should Mother do?

Late Childhood: The Math Test

"Well, class, study hard for your math test tomorrow," advised Mrs. White, "and I'm sure you will do just fine." These words kept going around and around in Samantha's head. She knew it was her own fault that she didn't know the answers to the test questions. She had watched her favorite TV program and then played a computer game instead of studying math the night before. She had even lied to her dad when he asked if she had homework.

Everyone else was busy writing, even her best friend, Ellen, who sat across from her. What was she going to do? If she failed the test she would get a bad grade in the class, her parents would be upset, and she would most definitely be grounded. The options kept going through her mind: she could cheat, ask the teacher if she could take it at a later date, turn it in blank, or guess her way through the questions.

Cheating would be simple, and it would get her a grade. It was easy to see Ellen's answers. The next day Samantha got her test back with an A on it. But deep down inside she felt ashamed of what she had done. Her parents had always taught her to be honest. What kind of ending would you give this story?

Adolescence: Bret and Harry

The school principal, Mr. Carter, had a tradition of giving sports champions a special invitation to his home for dinner. Bret and Harry were invited because they were the new football stars. During the evening both boys found themselves in Mr Carter's trophy room. They enjoyed looking at various trophies, medals, and other memorabilia. The gold, silver, bronze, and other precious materials really attracted Bret and Harry. They were alone in the room. What would it hurt if they took two small gold coins—really beautiful, shiny little pieces? No one would miss them from among this hoard of things.

Soon afterward they thanked Mr. Carter for the invitation and the wonderful evening. Then they left, each with a gold coin in his pocket. Several days passed. Mr. Carter didn't miss the coins—at least he didn't ask either boy if he knew anything about them. After a few days, however, that gold coin seemed to burn a hole in Harry's conscience. His parents had taught him to be honest and never to steal. He cringed when he said the word "steal"—it sounded like a criminal, but that is what he had done. He had stolen a coin from Mr. Carter. He felt nervous, tense, and jumpy.

How would you finish this story? What would you do if you were Harry? Should he say anything to Bret?

KEYS TO TEACHING HONESTY AND INTEGRITY

1. Model honesty and integrity in your own life.

2. Share real-life models of honesty and integrity with your children.

3. Notice and compliment honest actions.

4. Provide consequences for dishonest actions, but give children an opportunity to start over.

5. Help your children learn to figure out how to deal with difficult situations that test their honesty and integrity.

6. Teach your children that honesty is never rude.

7. Don't give up too soon. It takes time to develop the habit of honesty and integrity.

CHAPTER 15

Kindness and Compassion

Be kind and compassionate to one another,
forgiving each other, just as
in Christ God forgave you. Eph. 4:32.

We live in a world gone awry with violence and self-interest. "Me first" is the watchword, "Beat them up!" the rallying cry, and violence splashed across our TV screens and into our lives the end result of it all. Despite the fact that God's way is totally opposite, our children absorb these values from the world around them. His way—sharing, helping, comforting, forgiving, and serving others—is the central core of the Christian life.

The Valuegenesis study of 15,000 Christian youth ages 12 to 18, conducted by Search Institute, found that teenagers who valued service highly also showed a high level of faith maturity and commitment to their church. These same teens also came from families who worked together on helping projects. This shouldn't be surprising. After all, the Bible says, "Serve each other with love. . . . 'Love your neighbor as you love yourself'" (Gal. 5:13, 14, ICB).

Before children and teens can respond with love and caring to another person's distress, they must be able to empathize—put themselves in that person's shoes and look at life through his eyes and feelings. Sharing, helping, comforting, and cooperating are all part of the response to feelings of empathy and love. Children develop this ability gradually.

Many people think that young children are totally self-centered, but that isn't so. By the age of 1 year toddlers begin to show that they care about others and try to do nice things for others. Jodi, age 16 months, went to get her own blanket to cover her mother, who was resting on the sofa. If her generous, loving impulses are encouraged by the adults in her life, her feelings and expressions of compassion will grow.

Children who come from families and societies in which each family member must help in order to survive are more likely to develop a cooperative, altruistic attitude earlier in life. The competitiveness of Western societies discourages kindness and cooperation. In some studies children have been observed trying to lower a competitor's score in a game, even when there was no advantage to themselves. Competition discourages caring. Attitudes of competitiveness develop very young. Keep a watchful eye for what your child is developing—competition or compassion. Sometimes they are incompatible.

Adolescents have the ability to think about how others feel and express their compassion. However, in most studies caring and compassion seem to decrease during adolescence. Why? Religion seems to be the missing link. Teenagers who have an active religious life are more compassionate and caring than their peers. They are more willing to engage in service activities and help someone in distress.

How can you encourage a loving attitude of caring and service to others in your children? What do kindness and compassion look like in real life?

WHEN I AM KIND AND COMPASSIONATE . . .

I am helpful when I see a need.

I am understanding when something bad happens to a friend or someone in my family, or even someone I don't know. I try to comfort the person and help them.

Gentle

Thoughtful

Understanding

Helpful

Friendly

Loving

I am gentle to animals. I am never cruel to them.

I am friendly to people I meet. I smile and greet them cheerfully.

I am kind and friendly to kids who are picked on by other people, or who have disabilities.

I try to help people who are hungry or sick or live in places where there is war. Sometimes I help in a soup kitchen or take food to a needy family. I give my outgrown clothes to children who don't have enough clothes.

I show my love for people and animals by being kind and compassionate to them.

When someone is nasty to me, I ask God to help me be forgiving.

GOD'S VIEW OF KINDNESS AND COMPASSION

Compassion begins with God. His compassion for human beings brought salvation to this world. He encouraged His Son, Jesus, to come to be our Saviour from sin. God could have just wiped out the whole sinful world and forgotten about us. But He loved us too much. His heart is full of compassion and love for us.

When Jesus lived here He went everywhere helping people. He gave them food and healed their diseases. Jesus was full of compassion. He wants me to be kind to other people, too. He wants me to love people because "love is kind." When I don't feel like being kind to someone who hurt me, Jesus will fill my heart with His kind and forgiving thoughts if I ask Him. He wants me to help the hungry and the weak.

Bible People

The Bible has many stories

So in everything, do to others what you would have them do to you, for this sums up the Law and the Prophets. Matt. 7:12.

Finally, all of you, live in harmony with one another; be sympathetic, love as brothers, be compassionate and humble. Do not repay evil with evil or insult with insult, but with blessing, because to this you were called so that you may inherit a blessing. 1Peter 3:8, 9.

Love is kind. 1 Cor. 13:4.

Let us do good to all people. Gal. 6:10.

If your enemy is hungry, give him food to eat. . . . In doing this, you will heap burning coals on his head. Prov. 25:21, 22.

Cast your bread upon the waters, for after many days you will find it again. Eccl. 11:1.

about people who were kind and compassionate: Dorcas made clothes for poor people (Acts 9:36). David helped Mephibosheth, the grandson of his enemy Saul (2 Sam. 9). Jesus healed many, many people (John 4:43-54; Matt. 8:14-17; Mark 2:1-12). He gave them food when they were hungry (Matt. 14:13-21; Luke 9:10-17). Jesus told a story about the good Samaritan, a man who helped another man who had been injured by some robbers (Luke 10:25-37). Then there were Rahab (Joshua 2; 6:22-25), the Shunammite woman (2 Kings 4:8-10), and Joseph (Gen. 42-47), and many, many more.

Read about these people with your children. Center family night on one of the Bible people who especially lived kindness and compassion. Younger children could pantomime or make up a skit based on the story. Older children and teens could find interesting details of the story from a Bible commentary, encyclopedia, or source book. Everyone could be part of the creation of a mural about the person. When your family focuses in depth on a biblical person, he or she really comes to life and becomes a friend and a model for your whole family. If for a month your family nights center on Bible people who were especially kind and compassionate, the whole idea will begin to seep into your children's thinking and acting.

HOW TO HELP CHILDREN DEVELOP KINDNESS AND COMPASSION

The family plays the major role in helping children develop kindness and compassion. The early childhood years are the critical time for the family's input.

GENERAL GUIDELINES

1. Communicate deep disapproval of hurting people or animals. Don't be amused by your child's aggressive, hurting behavior. Place clear limits on hurting others. This communicates to your child that other people have feelings that must be respected. The child who is allowed to hurt people or animals is missing the first step in learning to be empathetic.

2. Help children understand how other people feel. Combine how the other child feels with explaining to your child what you think of his behavior. "You made Jon cry; it's not nice to bite." "Baby is happy because you played with her." As children grow older, try to get them to think about the effects of their actions on others. Ask the child how she thinks the other person felt. Some children empathize with others easily. They were born with greater ability to empathize.

One day when I was teaching a small group of toddlers 18 to 22 months old, I learned just how young some children can understand how other people feel. I was telling them how important it is to come quickly when Mom or Dad says "It's time to put on your shoes." We were going to practice coming quickly when I called each child's name. However, I had only one pair of toddler's shoes to distribute to the three children in the group. I gave a shoe to Joey and Melissa, and told Dennis, the oldest of the group, that he would have a turn later.

However, as soon as Joey, the youngest, got his shoe, he looked around at the other children. He saw that Dennis didn't have a shoe, so he immediately went to Dennis and gave him his own shoe, then looked at me with a big grin on his face. I hugged him and said, "Thank you for sharing with Dennis."

3. Set an example of how to be caring toward others. Adults who are warm and friendly, who model altruistic behavior, and who teach children how to be unselfish and helpful are the most effective in helping children grow up to be altruistic. "Mrs. Hernandez can't go out, because she broke her leg. I think she must be lonely. Let's go visit her and take her some goodies to eat." When your children do many of these kindnesses with you, they will eventually catch on and start coming up with ideas for helping others on their own.

4. Promote a positive view of people. Assume the best of others. Avoid criticisms and negative statements about people. Children are more likely to develop empathy and caring when they view people positively. Help your children develop friendships with children of different cultures and races. They will be much more likely to be helpful and friendly to everyone if they know people from many cultures.

5. Give children many opportunities to help. Children who grow up helping choose to be more helpful later on. Make helping a game. Overlook their childish mistakes—enjoying being helpful is the main idea.

6. Encourage children to think of themselves as helpful, caring people. Make this a part of their self-concept. "Thank you for being so kind and helpful today. Thank you for setting the table and entertaining the baby. You are a kind and helpful person." Comment often about kind and helpful behavior. Between the ages of 6 and 9 children are especially sensitive to what you say about them. They incorporate your ideas into their developing self-concept. Helping your children develop a positive sense of self-respect pays big dividends in many areas of their lives.

7. Counteract children's natural inclinations to selfishness. Selfishness and jealousy sent Satan hurtling from heaven. These traits are the opposite of love and service. Provide children with consistent lessons in sharing. Limit clothes and toys to reasonable numbers. Do everything you can to replace "give-me-its" with sharing and caring about others.

8. Get your family involved in helping projects on a regular basis. To really get the helper's high that comes from helping someone, your family must be personally involved with people in need. Have you ever felt on a real high after helping someone? Researchers have noted that such a strong good feeling probably comes from the release of endorphins, similar to those released by the well-known runner's high. Endorphins create a feeling of well-being and euphoria. You can get it from helping, just as well as from running! Choose a family project and get everyone involved. You'll be glad you did.

TROUBLE WITH KINDNESS AND COMPASSION?

Some children are naturally more kind and compassionate. They seem to be born that way. In fact, several researchers in child development have concluded just that: Some children are born more empathetic, and they show kindness to others when they are merely toddlers. Most children do not. These early empathizers will cry when others cry, pat their mothers when they appear distressed, or offer their own bottle to another crying baby.

Other children are, by nature, much less feelings-oriented. They will drive through life in the thinking lane, definitely not the feeling lane. Many children, although not early empathizers, learn to understand how others feel and grow up to be strong thinkers and compassionate human beings. Early childhood is the best time to learn about empathy. Children need to have empathetic feelings in place by the time they are 6 or 7.

But what about the children who seem to think only about themselves and don't have a sense for when to say or do something kind for another person? Some of these kids actually appear to lack the ability to express feelings and to understand how others feel. Can they be helped?

Jediah's mother expressed concern to me about his lack of feelings. He seems to be almost totally cognitive. He is very smart and loves facts about almost any subject. He can reason and analyze. But when she asks him how another person might feel, he has no idea, even though most 10-year-olds do identify with other children's feelings in some ways. She said he isn't disliked by other children, but is isolated from them. He doesn't do anything mean to other children, but neither does he do anything specifically kind or loving. He seems to prefer superficial relationships with other kids, and seems oblivious to the needs of others. His mother has been trying to teach him about kindness and compassion since he was a little tyke, but he seems to have absolutely no interest in learning. He doesn't think it is important to be kind to others.

I advised Jediah's mother to keep on trying and not give up yet. She should use every opportunity to help him think about how other people feel and what they might like or need. Point out how other children show kindness. They could play "Name the Feeling" and "Act the Feeling," using magazine pictures or miming a feeling. She could appeal to his sense of mastery and his career goals (he already has some) and try to get Jediah involved in activities in which he is directly helping others, so he will feel a bit of the joy that comes from helping. This may encourage him to begin to think about the needs of others. Jediah will need some measure of kindness and compassion in adult life, especially in a marriage relationship, even though he will probably always be more interested in thinking than feeling. His life will be very isolated and lacking in human relationships if he concentrates exclusively on his computer. I told his mother that it is definitely not too late to help Jediah become more involved in people relationships. He is a bright child, and he can learn what other children might do more naturally.

FAMILY ACTIVITIES
1. **Join a volunteer project** for a family vacation.
2. **Make good-cheer visits** to the elderly, sick, or shut-in. Take flowers, books, tapes, food, or pictures your children have made.

3. **Make scrapbooks** for children's hospital wards. Deliver, if possible.
4. **Make or buy toys** for hospital wards. Deliver, if possible.
5. **Make or buy toys** for a needy family. Deliver. Get to know the family.
6. **Share toys** with other families in need. Deliver. Get to know the families.
7. **Sort and give away outgrown clothes.** Help pack boxes for relief organizations.
8. **Invite a needy family** for Thanksgiving or New Year's dinner.
9. **Take a loaf of homemade bread** or jam to the people on your block.
10. **Collect canned goods** at Halloween and give to a needy family. Visit them.
11. **Help the elderly, the disabled or sick, or a single parent** in your neighborhood or church. Paint, rake leaves, shovel snow, mow grass, get the mail, get groceries, fix the roof, fix the fence, mend clothes. Accept no pay. This is a love gift.
12. **Correspond with a missionary.** Send things they need.
13. **Sacrifice candy for a month** and save money for one of the above projects.
14. **Help an isolated child** at school.
15. **Stand up for a classmate** who is being ridiculed or teased. Make this child your family's special project.
16. **Help with a local soup kitchen.**
17. **Collect food and clothes** for the homeless. Help distribute these items.

QUOTABLE WISDOM

"Two things stand like stone: Kindness in another's trouble, courage in your own."
—*Adam Lindsay Gordon*

"Always be a little kinder than is necessary."
—*Sir James Matthew Barrie*

"Have you had a kindness shown? Pass it on. Pass it on."
—*Henry Burton*

"Little deeds of kindness,
little words of love,
help to make earth happy
like the heaven above."
—*Julia A. Fletcher Carney*

"A kind face is a beautiful face."
—*M. Tupper*

"There are no boundaries to kindness."
—*Japanese proverb*

"The gentle heart does not grow old."
—*Tunisian proverb*

"No man's head aches while he comforts another."
—*Italian proverb*

"A word of kindness is better than a fat pie."
—*Russian proverb*

"Kindness is the sunshine in which virtue grows."

"Kindness consists in loving people more than they deserve."
—*Joubert*

"I expect to pass through life but once. If, therefore, there be any kindness I can show, or any good thing I can do to any fellow being, let me do it now, for I shall not pass this way again."
—*William Penn*

"The smallest act of kindness is worth more than the grandest intention."

NATURE TRAILS TO KINDNESS AND COMPASSION

Many times nature seems cruel. But nature also offers examples of kindness and compassion.

Geese: When geese are migrating they fly in a V formation. Leading the V takes a lot of strength because the leader takes the brunt of the wind. When the lead goose gets tired, it drops back in the formation and another goose takes its place. If one of the geese gets injured and cannot continue the flight, a companion always goes down with it until it is well, and then they resume the flight together. The geese demonstrate kindness and compassion to each other.

Dogs and Cats: Many times a nursing mother dog or cat will be willing to take in a baby from another mother and nurse and care for it like her own. Our local newspaper carried a story about a dog that had nursed nine piglets until they could feed themselves. God compares His love with the love of a nursing mother (Isa. 66:12, 13).

EVERYDAY TRAILS TO KINDNESS AND COMPASSION

Real kids, real places, real choices to make. Use your kids' real-life problems to help them learn to be kind and compassionate. For additional reinforcement, dialogue about one of these real-life scenarios.

Early Childhood: The Bug

Alabaster and Jeremy were playing in the park. Their grandma was watching them play on the swings. Soon they got tired of swinging and began to run around and around the playground. Panting, they flopped down on the ground near a bush.

"Oh, look, Jeremy! See that bug. It looks soft and squishy. I'm going to step on it and squish it. It might hurt us."

"No, let's call Grandma. She'll know what it is," Jeremy said. "Grandma, Grandma," he yelled. So Grandma came running to the kids. She thought that maybe they were hurt, but when she got there, no one was hurt.

"Grandma, look," pointed Jeremy. "Will it hurt us? Alabaster wants to squish it."

"Oh, no! Don't squish it! It's a caterpillar. It eats the leaves from the bush. If you leave it alone, someday it will turn into a beautiful butterfly," Grandma explained.

But Alabaster still wanted to squish it, or at least poke it with a stick. What should she do? How would the caterpillar feel if she poked it? What would happen if she squished it? Is it important to be kind to bugs? What do bugs do for us?

Late Childhood: What could you do?

Compassion means you feel bad because someone else is hurting and you want to help them. If you heard someone say the following things, how would you feel? How could you show compassion in these different situations?

Mom, coming in the door from work: "I'm so-o-o tired!"

"Wait up! I can't walk so fast with this cast."

"Class, I want you to meet Heinrich. His family just moved here from Austria."

"We just lost the game because of you!"

Your little brother: "I'm so scared! That bigger kid said he'll beat me up if I don't bring a $5 bill for him tomorrow. I don't have any money."

Adolescence: Janesta and Michelle

Janesta was the only African-American student at Lakeshore High School. Her parents had just moved into the district. Most of the other kids at the school had never had a friend who wasn't Caucasian. At first Janesta felt really isolated. No one spoke to her, and no one sat beside her at lunch. In fact, no one would even sit at her table. She had the feeling that the kids were talking about her, but everybody gave her the silent treatment if she came near a group of kids. This went on for the first two weeks.

Then one day Michelle decided to sit with Janesta at lunch. Michelle had attended a grade school with students from many different countries, so she was comfortable around people of different races. But there was the risk that her friends would abandon her if she was friendly to Janesta. No one else joined them for lunch. Finally, after another week or two, one of Michelle's friends came to sit with them at lunch. Gradually other kids joined them. By the end of the first semester Janesta had a few friends, but Michelle remained her best friend. Most of Michelle's friends didn't abandon her, but neither did they become Janesta's friends.

Janesta tried out for the cheering squad, but didn't make it. The rumor was that "they couldn't have someone who looked so different on the squad." Janesta felt bad, but kept her head up and remained friendly to everyone. Michelle encouraged her and stuck by her.

Their senior year Michelle decided to run for class treasurer. Unknown to her, Janesta also decided to run for a class office—vice president. Should they campaign together? Or would that hurt Michelle's chance for office? How would Janesta feel if Michelle didn't support her? There were still a lot of kids who resented Janesta and put her down any chance they got. Should

Michelle give up her campaign and concentrate on helping Janesta with hers? Or should she ignore Janesta's campaign and concentrate on her own?

Not all situations have easy answers. Let your family's discussion consider as many different angles as possible.

KEYS TO KINDNESS AND COMPASSION

1. Communicate deep disapproval of hurting people or animals.

2. Help children understand how other people feel.

3. Model how to be caring and forgiving toward your family and others.

4. Promote a positive view of people.

5. Give children many opportunities to help and to think of themselves as helpful, caring people.

6. Replace "give-me-its" with sharing and caring about others.

7. Get your family involved in helping projects.

CHAPTER 16

Contentment and Thankfulness

*I have learned to be content whatever
the circumstances. Phil. 4:11.*

Have you ever noticed that the more "things" kids have, the more they want and the less they appreciate what they have? Toys are thrown willy-nilly around the house and yard. Pieces are missing, and after only a few days (or hours) the toy doesn't run anymore and the kids have lost interest. And still we buy them more!

It's hard to resist the media blitz that makes us dissatisfied with our things. Before we know what hit us, we're sure Kristen won't be happy unless we buy her a playhouse with electric lights and period style furniture. And Michael is positive he can't live without the latest rage in toys that all the other guys have.

Good parents, after all, give their children these important "educational opportunities," the advertisers tell us. What they don't admit is that they have only one goal—to make money from our media-induced dissatisfaction.

God tells us something completely different—be content with what you have (Heb. 13:5). God's way is one of satisfaction, not dissatisfaction; thankfulness, not demanding self-indulgence. How can we turn things around? Dissatisfaction is, after all, the devil's way, and he's going to make "having more" look very attractive! Contentment and thankfulness begin with controlling our urge to have more.

What do contentment and thankfulness look like in real life?

Happy

Satisfied

Serene

Fulfilled

Appreciative

Grateful

Content

WHEN I AM CONTENT AND THANKFUL . . .

I am happy with the playthings I have. I don't beg and whine for more every time my family goes to the shopping mall.

I always say "Thank you" when I receive a gift. I write thank you notes to people who do nice things for me.

I am thankful to God for the wonderful things He has made—for flowers and birds and plants and shells and dogs and cats.

I do something every week to take care of the world God made.

I love to give presents to my family and friends. I like giving them surprises.

Every day I say "Thank You" to God for the blessings He has given me that day.

I am happy with the clothes I have. When I have outgrown my clothes, I give them to someone else who needs them.

I don't envy other kids and the things they have. I take care of my things and am happy with what I have.

GOD'S VIEW OF CONTENTMENT AND THANKFULNESS

God is the ultimate giver. He never tires of giving to His earthly family. All He wants in return is our expression of appreciation for His wonderful gifts. God loves to give wonderful gifts to all the people on earth. His greatest joy is in giving. All through His Word God makes it very clear that He wants us to be content with what we have, and to be grateful at all times. Jealousy and covetousness

*Now godliness with contentment is great gain.
1 Tim. 6:6, NKJV.*

*Be content with your wages.
Luke 3:14, NKJV.*

*Keep your lives free from the love of money and be content with what you have, because God has said, "Never will I leave you; never will I forsake you."
Heb. 13:5.*

have no part in His way of living. He wants us to thank Him always, even when life is tough. He wants us to bring Him our requests with thanksgiving.

Bible People

What is the most famous Bible story about thanksgiving? Probably the story of the ten lepers who were healed by Jesus (Luke 17:12-19). Only one came back to thank Him. What can you learn about gratefulness and contentment in these Bible stories? The paralytic at the Pool of Bethesda (John 5:1-15), Abigail and David (1 Sam. 25), Simeon and Anna (Luke 2:25-38), Mary (John 12:1-8), the rich man who wanted to build a bigger barn (Luke 12:13-21), Zacchaeus (Luke 19:2-10), the prodigal son and his brother (Luke 15:11-32), Judas (Matt. 26:14-56), Achan (Joshua 7), Ananias and Sapphira (Acts 5:1-11), the firstfruits offering at the Temple (Ex. 23:16-19). These stories should keep your family going for many family nights. Each has an important message from God about contentment and thanksgiving.

> *Let us come before His presence with thanksgiving.*
> *Ps. 95:2, NKJV.*
>
> *Give thanks unto the Lord, for he is good.*
> *Ps. 107:1.*
>
> *The Lord has done great things for us, and we are filled with joy.*
> *Ps. 126:3.*
>
> *Rejoice in the Lord always. . . . Do not be anxious about anything, but in everything, by prayer and petition, with thanksgiving, present your requests to God.*
> *Phil. 4:4-6.*
>
> *In everything give thanks; for this is the will of God in Christ Jesus for you.*
> *1 Thess. 5:18, NKJV.*

HOW TO HELP CHILDREN BE CONTENT AND THANKFUL

Thankfulness and contentment are a way of looking at life, a way that leads to happiness. How can you help your family develop an attitude of contentment?

1. Ask God to change your own attitude. There are many reasons you sometimes buy too many things for your children or yourself. It might unconsciously be to make up for what you didn't have as a child or to impress other people. You might do it because you feel guilty about the little amount of time you spend with your kids. Maybe you are impulsive, or an unconscious puppet of the advertisers. Or weary from work and worry, you simply get tired of hearing the kids' begging in the store, and give in!

God can help you change.

2. Take a hard look at what's happening in your home. Are your children's closets stuffed, their toy boxes running over? Are you stepping on toys everywhere you go? Are your children careless with their belongings? Do they have an attitude of "oh, well, we can get more "? Do they have a bad case of "give-me-its"?

Are your own closets stuffed and you can't find space to put the new kitchen gadget you just bought? Do you have a case of "give-me-its" too? Can you control your own spending? Are your credit cards maxed out? Do you wistfully say to your spouse, "Did you notice that Mary and Jon just bought a new ATV?" Are you constantly comparing what you have with what your friends have?

If so, it's time for a total family attitude readjustment! Any time of the year will do, but Thanksgiving is a perfect time for a new start. That's what it's all about—being grateful for what we have.

3. Take inventory with your children and your spouse. Help your children sort their toys and clothes. Encourage them to set aside things they don't use to give to a needy family or a local charity. After sorting, put half of their toys away. You'll be amazed at how much more interesting the remaining half will become. In a couple of months trade some of the current toys with the stored ones. Every time your children get a new toy, encourage them to give away an old one (not a bad idea for our own overstuffed wardrobes). Take some time with your spouse to do the same with your own "things." I have noticed that some women's magazines have at least one article in every issue on how to get organized. All the articles advise sorting and reducing as the first step to getting organized. It must be a national problem. At least it's comforting to know we aren't alone.

4. Check up on the importance of the media in your child's life. One of the main messages of the media is "the more things you have, the happier you will be." It's a message children—and adults, I might add—embrace quickly. We easily buy into a false set of values. The main goal of television is to make money for the program producers and for the advertisers. Children are exposed to many "gimme, gimme" messages every day. Contentment with what you have is definitely not a byproduct of these messages. Check up on the messages your children are receiving. Do something about them. Cut back on TV time. Watch out for sales messages on the internet, advertising in magazines and other places. Discuss with your older children what the advertisers are trying to accomplish. Demystify the process. Eliminate the exposure for younger children.

5. Begin to emphasize relationships over things. Encourage grandparents and other relatives to emphasize their relationship with your child by bringing "themselves" or something personal (such as themselves on tape reading a bedtime story), or spend time with the child doing something together. If you travel, don't bring a gift every time you come home. Instead, bring "yourself" and some time to be together. Hug or compliment your child for a job well done instead of giving money or other material rewards every time. The most rewarding thing you have to offer your child is yourself—your time and your relationship. Don't cheat your child by giving him things instead of yourself. If your family has been very "things" oriented, it will take time to make this transition to relationships. But eventually you will all be very happy you did.

6. Resist the impulse to buy more toys or clothes or "things." Ask yourself, Does he really need this? Will it encourage attitudes of contentment and gratefulness? Or will it foster pride, selfishness, and "give-me-its"? Even if your family has plenty of money to spend for Christmas, decide on a limit before beginning your Christmas shopping. Use the rest to buy clothes, food, and toys for families who won't have any Christmas. Deliver your Christmas packages personally to needy families. Let the whole family share in the joy of giving. Have everyone make a Christmas gift for other family members. No purchased gifts allowed. Or have each family member get only one major gift, with maybe one or two smaller ones. You'll be surprised how much more meaning the gifts will have.

7. Encourage expressions of thankfulness. Be sure each

child writes (or dictates) a thank-you note for each gift he or she receives at any time during the year. Yes, to grandparents, too. Make this a habit. Teach your children to receive gifts graciously, with a smile and an appropriate comment. "Oh, Grandma! How nice. Thank you," accompanied by a hug, will do the trick. Teach your children to be polite and never, never say disparaging things about a gift. Even if they are disappointed, consideration of the other person's feelings is more important than their own disenchantment. Rehearse how to receive a gift graciously. Remember, the gift giver invested time, effort, and goodwill in this gift. Everyone loves a gracious child. Time invested in teaching your child to be gracious and polite will pay big dividends down the road in increased self-confidence and many friendships.

8. Encourage an attitude of giving. Giving to others is a great antidote for "give-me-it's." Don't give children offering money—let them give to God from their own money. When your church or community collects gifts for needy families, let your children help select the gifts from your family, wrap them, and take them to the collection point. If possible, be part of the team that distributes the gifts. Give your children the responsibility of buying birthday gifts for friends from their own money (be sure their allowance is large enough to cover this expense) and wrapping the present (with your help, if needed). Take a small expression of friendship when you are invited out—a small bouquet of flowers or a special bit of food. Get your children involved in selecting the gift.

Encourage giving of self—gifts that don't cost money. "Mama, I want to give you an hour for a nap. I'll take care of Baby for an hour while you nap." What mama wouldn't love to receive that gift? Give your children a model of this kind of giving. "Josie, I see you are really stressed out with that school project. I don't have a lot of time right now, but I can give you 15 minutes to help you find material on the Internet." Phrase the things you do for your children in terms of giving. Encourage them to do the same. Thank them for their giving.

9. Encourage thankfulness and praise to God for His daily blessings. Praise and thankfulness to God can brighten our lives in surprising ways. It is one of the best medicines for discouragement and depression. During a particularly difficult period in my life, I fell into the habit of noticing only the disappointments or "bad" things that happened each day, an easy thing for me to do. This attitude soon led to feelings of depression and discouragement.

One day while I was reading an article from *Guideposts* magazine, the Lord spoke to me, and I decided to follow the suggestion of the author— begin a Blessings Diary in which I would write about the blessings God sent each day.

At first it was difficult to find "blessings," and there were quite a few days in which I resorted to noting the sunshine (it doesn't shine every day where I live), the summer flowers, or other general blessings. Gradually I was able to begin focusing on personal events, and my Blessings Diary became a real source of encouragement as I reviewed how God was leading and really helping with many small, as well as large, problems in my life.

Start a Blessings Diary for your family, and you will experience the same result. Your family, including your children, will begin to focus on the good things rather than the bad events, and the spirit of thankfulness will prevail. Anxieties will fade in the glow of what God has done for you. And you will notice something strange—God will begin to pour out blessings on your family, and everyone will notice. Your children will begin to lay the foundation stone of contentment and thankfulness in their character structure.

TROUBLE WITH CONTENTMENT AND THANKFULNESS?

Some children have great difficulty with contentment. They are anxious or pessimistic by nature or they are consumed by the green-eyed monster of jealousy. Contentment definitely doesn't come naturally. What can you do to help your jealous child get past these negative feelings?

Most firstborns feel at least a twinge of jealousy with the arrival of a new baby. Mommy seems to be totally occupied with the new arrival, and they miss being the center of attention. Mommy was sitting on the sofa nursing Baby Zach when 2-year-old Leah climbed up beside her. For a while she twirled a piece of Mommy's hair and watched the baby nurse. Then she stated firmly, with a meaningful look at the baby, "There are too many people on this sofa!" It was quite clear who was extra. Eventually Leah got over her feelings of being displaced, and today she and her brother are quite close. But similar scenes don't always have such a happy ending.

At 10 Paula is consumed with jealousy of her 7-year-old sister. When her baby sister first arrived, she acted quite civilized toward the baby, but vented her rage on her mother. Why did she have to bring this "thing" home? A child who talked freely and expressed herself with a large vocabulary, she suddenly started to stutter badly. I advised the family to ride it out, to ignore the stuttering and to treat Paula with much love and attention, and get her involved in caring for the baby. I felt the stuttering was definitely related to the new baby. But a year later she was still stuttering. It was hard to hang in there and believe this would disappear in time. But it did. Fourteen months after the arrival of the baby, Paula quit stuttering from one day to the next. She had figured out something in her little mind, but it soon became evident that she had not mastered her feelings of jealousy. They were now expressed directly toward the baby.

Most children manage to contain their jealousy and adjust to the new arrival in a year or two or three, but Paula never adjusted. At 10 her feelings of jealousy have turned to resentment and an anger that possesses her completely. She is always on the alert for any demonstration of what she considers "special favor" toward her sister, quick to defend her own rights. She reminds me of a lion crouched on a ledge, muscles tense, always ready for attack. She is certainly not a happy and contented child.

Grace Ketterman, a Christian psychiatrist, has an excellent discussion of jealousy in her book *You and Your Child's Problems*. She believes that jealousy rests on the belief that one is not as good as the other person. The jealous person is constantly plagued by feelings of uncertainty, doubt, and suspicion, that can ripen into anger and even hatred. This child privately compares herself with others. Jealous children tend to be sensitive and perceptive. They can easily see the good in others and may even exaggerate it. However, since they are insecure, they do not see their own good points clearly.

Another reason for jealousy may be an unconscious partiality on the part of the parents. All parents have dreams for their children, and one child may fulfill their dreams more than another. They love all their children, but they may give more of their approval to the ones who best fulfill their dreams. Relatives sometimes add to the feelings of disapproval by comparing the children. The one who feels left out—not approved—will develop jealousy. Some children in a family are more popular with peers than others. This can lead to jealousy of the more popular child. Some children receive more attention from parents because they have special needs. The "normal" child can feel jealous of the attention he is missing.

Back to Paula. On the surface, she has no reason to be jealous. She is better-looking than her sister, very intelligent, a straight-A student, and good at sports. As a young child she was very pretty, and adults adored her and showered her with attention. On the other hand, her baby sister was colicky all day for the first seven months. Consequently, her mom held her almost constantly. Baby sister had a very volatile disposition and was prone to major temper tantrums anytime something didn't go her way. Paula, however, had been even-tempered and had an easy disposition. Baby sister also had a very short attention span and was extremely active. When she started school, it became obvious she had a learning disability. Because of her special needs, she had probably received much more attention from the parents than Paula had. So, while Paula had many of the advantages, she was still jealous of the child who had received mega amounts of parental attention and made no effort to understand her sister's special needs.

What can Paula's parents do at this point? First of all, they can examine their way of relating to the girls to see if they are really impartial. Whenever a parent says to me "I can't think of anything good about that child!" I think there is probably partiality in the family. Every child can be complimented about something. Probably they are not aware of the extra attention they have showered on baby sister and how that affected Paula. They have always thought of her as the good child who didn't have any problems.

Next, they should talk with Paula about this, explaining that they don't love sister more than her. They had to give her more attention because she had some problems and needed extra help. Paula probably knows what those problems are. They should explain that they love Paula very much and are very proud of her. They didn't realize how much they were hurting Paula. Can she help them figure out a way to avoid making her feel left out when sister needs so much help? Listen to what Paula has to say. She probably will have some good ideas.

Then they can set up a plan for change. They will need to remind themselves frequently to act in the new ways. Discipline for both girls should be very fair. The family rules and expectations should be clear so both children can follow them. Include the girls in deciding on these rules and include them anytime a change is needed. Consistently follow through with both girls.

Last, they need to help Paula become more self-confident. Help her learn social skills. Help her develop empathy so she can avoid hurting others and make more friends. Help her learn to listen to others' concerns, not just talk about her own. Invite her friends to the home. Be sure Paula has something to share with her friends. Don't require that her younger sister always tag along. Paula needs a life of her own.

Sometimes a child is jealous of a sibling who truly is better-looking, has more friends, is smarter, or in some way is definitely more attractive and gets more attention from everyone. This child's parents will need to work hard to reinforce his assets and help him build confidence and give him more attention.

There will be times when Paula's parents will need to be very firm about stopping the jealousy habit. They need to encourage Paula to ask God for help in overcoming this bad habit in her life. She will be much happier and contented when she leaves jealousy behind.

FAMILY ACTIVITIES

Blessings Today: If our children don't hear about God's blessings from us, who will tell them? Start a family tradition for the evening meal in which each member of the family, even the preschoolers, tells about something special God did that day. It might be a special blessing for you personally, an answered prayer, or how God helped someone you know.

Thank You, God, Scrapbook: Make a Thank You, God, scrapbook with your children. This is a great family night activity. Make it as a traditional scrapbook, a computerized version, or a combination. Younger children could search for magazine pictures that tell about the special blessings of God for your family during the past week. Older children could write a short story about something they are thankful for, including computer clip or original art. Younger children could draw pictures, and you could write a story to go with the pictures. Each week select a special story from the scrapbook for retelling. In this way you will build a family tradition of the many ways God has led your family.

God in Our Family History: Tell your children about special times God blessed your family in the past. Family stories are the best ones;

they hold the most meaning. Family stories belong to your family, and no one else can claim them. For starters, How did you meet your spouse? Where did you live when you were first married? Where did you live when you were a child? What did you do? Even if you did not know God when you were a child, He was still present in your life, blessing you. Add these stories to the Thank You, God, scrapbook or record them on an audiotape as you tell them. Gradually you will build a cassette library of personal experiences. What a wonderful way to remember God's leading in your life and to pass His blessings along to your children!

Flowers: Observe wildflowers with your children. Learn to identify the different varieties. Take along a camera that your children can operate. They will love taking pictures of flowers. Remember with your children how Jesus used the flowers to teach us to be content. We should never worry about tomorrow because God promises to always take care of us. Grow some flowers. You can grow flowers in a pot, even in a high-rise apartment in the middle of a large city. Sow some wildflower seeds. Make the earth a little greener because you appreciate the natural world God has given you. Express your thankfulness for the flowers that brighten our lives and make our days happier.

Birds: Learn to recognize different birds in your area. Listen to their songs. Buy a CD of birdsongs and learn to recognize the different birds by their sounds. Listen to a CD of birdsongs for relaxation. Some wonderful relaxing music with birdsongs is available. Make the planet a better place by helping God take care of the birds. Make or purchase a bird feeder, and be sure to keep it filled year round. Provide a container for birds to bathe in. Remember with your children how Jesus used the birds to teach us not to worry about anything because God promises to always take care of us. Express your thankfulness for the beautiful birds that enrich our lives.

Green Activities: Gratefulness for the natural world God has provided for humans leads us to want to help Him take care of it. You and your children can do many "Green Activities" to express your thanks: Recycle trash, pick up trash along the road by your home, feed the birds, plant trees and other green plants, work to protect endangered species of natural life, develop a compost pile to use for fertilizer. Pick one or two activities that fit with your lifestyle. Get involved with your children. Be sure to make the connection between gratitude and your actions.

QUOTABLE WISDOM

"He who goes out of his house in search of happiness runs after a shadow."
—*Chinese proverb*

"The secret of happy living is not to do what you like but to like what you do."

"He that's content has enough. He that complains has too much."

"Contentment consists not in great wealth, but in few wants."

"Every person lives in one of two tents: conTENT or disconTENT. In which do you live?"

"Hope for the best, get ready for the worst, and then take what God chooses to send."
—*Matthew Henry*

"He who is not satisfied at his father's table will never be satisfied."
—*Lebanese proverb*

"The neighbor's cooking always smells better."
—*Maltese proverb*

"The grass is always greener on the other side of the fence. When you get there you discover it is plastic."
—*Adaptation of traditional American proverb*

"Those who know when they have enough are rich."
—*Chinese proverb*

"Never let your happiness depend on other people."

"A happy face can turn something ordinary into something special."

"He who is content can never be ruined."
—*Chinese proverb*

"Since we have loaves, let us not look for cakes."
—*Spanish proverb*

NATURE TRAILS TO CONTENTMENT AND THANKFULNESS

Birds: Although they have many enemies and face many dangers, birds seem happy most of the time. They always have a song, sing any time of the day, and chatter to each other. Even barnyard fowl do this. People should be thankful for the birds. Without them we could not live on earth very long. They do many things that are beneficial to people. They eat the seeds of harmful plants and help the farmer by eating harmful insects.

Robins eat worms that destroy plant roots and ruin crops. Owls eat gophers, mice, and rats. Birds drop fruit seeds over the land and seagulls act as scavengers. Birdsongs help us feel happy and rested. The birds that stay all winter brighten the landscape with their beautiful colors and cheer us when they come to the bird feeders. Returning birds are often the first sign that spring is just around the corner.

Flowers: In the Sermon on the Mount Jesus used birds and flowers as illustrations of His Father's care for nature and for people. "Be like the birds and the flowers," He said. Don't worry about tomorrow—God will take care of you. No need to be anxious. God takes care of the birds and the flowers. Why do we worry about what we will eat and what we will wear when God promises to take care of us? The flowers provide a constant reminder of God's blessing. Their beauty surrounds us, and they add joy to our lives. Stop and admire that gorgeous carpet of beauty beside the road.

EVERYDAY TRAILS TO CONTENTMENT AND THANKFULNESS

Everyday experiences are the best way to teach values. Grab them. Maybe one of the following stories can help your children learn about thankfulness and contentment.

Early Childhood: Lunch

Lunch is served, and Johnny is whining about the options available, refusing to eat and demanding junk food. Mother tells him that he can leave the table unless he wants to eat what is served. There will be no more food until the next meal. He whines some more and grudgingly eats a few bites.

Thanksgiving is approaching. The next day the family is preparing a grocery bag of food to take to the homeless shelter. Will there be children at the homeless shelter? How will they feel about the food in the bag? Will they be happy to eat it or will they whine and complain and ask for junk food? Have you ever been so hungry your stomach hurt and there was no food to eat?

Late Childhood: The Girl With Everything

Kari ran into the house eager to tell her mom what she had seen at Crystal's house. "Mom, you should see Crystal's house! Wow! It's so

KEYS TO CONTENTMENT AND THANKFULNESS

1. Ask God to change your own attitude about "things."

2. Take a hard look at the "things" in your home.

3. Take inventory with your family. Get rid of excesses. Resist the impulse to buy more toys or clothes or things.

4. Check up on the media messages your child is absorbing.

5. Begin to emphasize relationships over things.

6. Encourage expressions of thankfulness.

7. Encourage an attitude of giving.

8. Encourage thankfulness and praise to God for His daily blessings.

large you can almost get lost in it. Everyone has their own room and their own TV and computer and boom box and tons of CDs and videos. You should see Crystal's clothes. She has a huge walk-in closet full of clothes. It looks almost like a store. I've never seen so many clothes! She's having a birthday party next week, and she said she'd invite me. What on earth will I take to someone who has *everything*? I don't have any clothes, compared to Crystal. And we have only one TV for the whole family."

"Do you suppose Crystal is happier than you are?" Mom asked.

"I don't know. Her folks are gone on a trip to Europe, and only her nanny and the housekeeper were there. She said she loved everything about our house when she was here last week. I wonder why. It sure isn't as nice as hers."

Can things make you happy? How many things does it take to make a person happy? Can you be happy without lots of things? What is most important for happiness?

Adolescence: Deformities

Maria refuses to wear skirts because she thinks her legs are funny-looking. Her family keeps saying her legs are normal, but Maria refuses to believe them. She is always looking in the mirror and finding what she calls "deformities." Every day she complains about her "deformities." One day a new student arrives in her class. The girl is Maria's age, but is in a wheelchair. Staring at the wheelchair, Maria notices a dark-haired girl with a pretty face and a nice smile, but very deformed legs. Suddenly Maria remembers her own complaints about her "deformed" legs and blushes. What do you suppose Maria is thinking? What can she do to make the girl in the wheelchair feel comfortable at school?

CHAPTER 17

Patience and Perseverance

Rest in the Lord, and wait patiently for him.
Ps. 37:7, KJV.

Ruben was my student in the seventh grade. At the time I was teaching Spanish as a second language at an English school in Puerto Rico. Ruben was an ordinary student, getting a collection of B's and C's, maybe an occasional A. The class was small, and many of the students were very bright. Grades came easily for them. But Ruben was persistent. Day after day his mother encouraged him to do his assignments and keep at it. And he did.

As a young teacher I hadn't yet learned that persistence predicts success better than brilliance. I would never have predicted a brilliant future for Ruben. Yet today he is a very successful university professor in an extremely difficult field. He is recognized as an expert, sought by colleagues, and wooed for administrative positions.

Joel wanted to be a physical therapist. Learning was slow and difficult because of dyslexia. He repeated anatomy and physiology three times before he got the grade he needed to be admitted to professional school. Today he is a successful physical therapist with many people working for him—a modern entrepreneur in the medical field.

Jeanne was a successful school psychologist and doctoral student when she was stricken with multiple sclerosis. She decided not to give up her dreams of completing the Ph.D. degree. One class at a time. Plenty of time for rest. Extra time for exams. An internship completed in three years instead of one. A dissertation research project studying families with a parent with multiple sclerosis. Finally, 17 years after starting, Jeanne struggled to the platform on crutches to receive the coveted Ph.D. The audience broke out in spontaneous applause.

As a much wiser teacher, I now tell prospective doctoral students, "Doctoral degrees are *sometimes* awarded to the brilliant, but *always* to the persistent."

Patience and persistence are the magic ingredients that make the difference between mediocrity and brilliance. Between giving up and conquering in the Christian life. Between successful and failed marriages. Between having an idea for a book and actually writing one. (Wonder why I thought of that one?) Between wanting to win the pennant and really doing it. Between heaven and hell, actually. Hanging in there when everything is dark. Believing that God is hanging in there with us.

Let's get on the road to patience and persistence with our kids. First, What do patience and persistence look like in real life?

WHEN I AM PATIENT AND PERSISTENT . . .

I don't fly off the handle when I am irritated or someone crosses my path. I count to 10 and think, *I can handle this problem. What choices do I have?* Then I try to respond reasonably.

Longsuffering

Tolerance

Stick-to-it-ive-ness

Composure

Endurance

Calmness

I try to wait patiently when I can't have what I want. I know I can't have everything right *now*. Maybe there are some things I can never have. I have to accept disappointments and move on.

I don't interrupt people when they are talking. I wait for my turn.

I stick by a job until it is done. I don't run off to play when it gets boring or hard.

I try to think carefully about my choices and make a good decision. I try not to be impulsive and in too much of a hurry to think.

When I get stuck on a project and don't know what to do next, I don't give up. I try to find help and figure out what to do.

When I'm doing a big project, I try to plan little goals so I will finish by the deadline.

I try to be patient with people who are slow or who don't catch on as quickly as I do.

Love never gives up, so if I love someone I don't give up on them, no matter what.

GOD'S VIEW OF PATIENCE AND PERSEVERANCE

In God's view patience and perseverance are one and the same thing, it seems. Different Bible translations use one or the other word for the same passage. God knows how difficult it is to persist. Giving up when the going gets tough is the natural human tendency. So in His instructions to us He emphasizes how important it is to be patient and persevering to the end. He also promises to be right beside us until the end, through whatever difficulties and trials pop up in the middle of the road. Patience is definitely the Godlike way. Patience with people, patience with circumstances, patience with delays, patience when the end cannot even be imagined. Patience until the end. Love is patient, and it always perseveres.

He who stands firm to the end will be saved.
Matt. 24:13.

Hold fast till I come.
Rev. 2:25, KJV.

Patience is better than pride.
Eccl. 7:8, NIV.

Love is patient, . . . it is not proud. . . . It . . . always perseveres.
2 Cor. 13:4-7.

Let us run with perseverance the race marked out for us.
Heb. 12:1.

Add to . . . temperance patience; and to patience godliness.
2 Peter 1:5, 6, KJV.

Bible People

Bible biographies include the patient and the impatient, the persevering and the disheartened. Use some of these Bible biographies to help your children learn the consequences of patience and perseverance. Noah preached and built the ark for 120 years (Gen. 6:9-22). Moses started out impetuous and impatient. He killed a man. Then he fled to the desert where God taught him patience for 40 years (Ex. 2-4).

Joshua went forward patiently and persistently to conquer Canaan (Joshua 1-12). Jesus endured many difficult temptations and trials with utmost patience (Matt.4:1-11; 26:27-36; 27). David patiently waited many years to become king (1 Sam. 16:1-13; 2 Sam. 2:1-11; 5:1-4). Joseph waited patiently in prison, unjustly accused, with no hope of release (Gen. 39-41). Paul, impatient and headstrong at first, waited patiently in Rome as he neared the end of his life (Acts 28).

Challenge your children to find their favorite Bible biography about patience and persistence. Read it, retell it, act it, draw it, sculpture it, write it, engrave it on their minds until that person becomes their personal hero.

HOW TO HELP CHILDREN DEVELOP PATIENCE AND PERSEVERANCE

When the nurses brought newborn Danny to his mother for feeding, they always commented, "He's a real impatient one. The minute he opens his eyes he wants food!" Their observations were predictive. Sure enough, Danny has had lots of trouble in the patience arena. But he is learning— and his parents are too.

Not all children are like Danny. With guidance, most children, in the natural course of growing up in a family that models patience and persistence, will learn to be patient and persistent enough to deal with life on an everyday basis. A few general guidelines may be helpful as you guide your children.

1. Gradually teach young children how to wait for something they want. Very young children possess very little patience, but sometimes they show huge amounts of persistence. Just watch a baby trying to learn to crawl. But the most persistent crawler will need to learn patience. Expect your children to learn to be patient at appropriate times. Mom is talking on the phone. She cannot be interrupted except for an emergency. Insist on following this rule, but *help* your child learn to wait. Provide paper and crayons or an interesting book near the phone so the child has something to do while waiting for the conversation to end. Then be reasonable yourself. If you see the call is going to be long, ask for a small break and talk with your child.

Don't give in to whining or your efforts to teach patience will be lost. Make it very clear that you expect patience. Don't feel you have to jump instantly to give your little one everything he yells for. Soon he will be a little tyrant ruling your home. Insist on patience, but gauge the patience level by the child's age. Thirty seconds is an eternity to a 1-year-old and two minutes an eternity to a 4-year-old.

Explain that patience is waiting calmly. Mom, Dad, and Grandma love you and will provide whatever is needed in due time. "Dad cannot stop stirring the cream sauce to get you a toy. The sauce would burn. But he will help you get it when the sauce is done. If you whine and fuss, he will not get it for you."

An hourglass timer can be very helpful. Chrissy can watch the sand trickling through and know when her wait is almost over. And there is no way to hurry the sand through faster. For very young children use a 30-second or one-minute timer. As children get older, change to a two- or three-minute timer.

2. Engage your children in activities that cannot be finished immediately. Deliberately plan activities that will take more than one session to finish. Leave a jigsaw puzzle on a card table for the family to work on as anyone has time. Build a birdhouse or model airplane together. Sew doll clothes or real clothes with your child. These activities provide wonderful practice in learning to keep at it until the project is finished. The most effective learning comes when parent and child do the project together. Music lessons and sports practice are excellent persistence builders, too.

3. Help children learn how to deal with frustrations. Many adults have not learned this skill. It begins in childhood. Don't be caught by the trap that says "She's only a kid. She can't be expected to tolerate much frustration." If she doesn't begin to learn when she is young, she will never learn frustration tolerance.

Miss Ten threw a fit because her parents said they could not buy her the designer jeans she claimed she needed (interpret wanted). Even after the tantrum subsided, she refused to listen to reason and kept on yelling, "You don't like me! You never get me what I need!" So her parents decided to leave her alone until her head cooled. They walked away without further comment.

When she came to supper, still pouting but at least not yelling, they decided to try again. "Since we can't buy the designer jeans you want, how do you think you might get them?" It took several tries to get her to really think about the question. Finally they said, "We can buy you the regular jeans or we can give you what we would have paid for a pair of regular jeans and you can earn the money for the more expensive pair. Maybe you should think about it for a while before deciding what you will do."

Miss Ten thought about it and discussed the choice with her parents several times over the next few days. Finally she decided to earn the money to buy the more expensive jeans. But, amazingly, when she had enough money she decided not to buy them. She now knew how much effort it took to earn the money and decided she'd rather do something else with those hard-earned dollars. It was a wonderful lesson in frustration tolerance, perseverance, with the value of money thrown in for extra.

All kids need these lessons. Help them learn to think around a frustration and figure out what to do. Remind them, also, that some things really can't be changed and simply must be lived with. "Your sister is your sister. She is very different from you, but she is your sister. We aren't going to give her away, and you need to learn to get along with her."

"Your parents are divorced. It's terrible, but it can't be changed. We can have a happy home, even though you don't get to see Dad every week." Post the serenity prayer prominently in your home and refer to it often: "Lord, help me to change the things I can, to accept what I cannot change, and to know the difference."

4. Teach your children that success and perseverance are closely related. Success and perseverance are partners. Success never happens without perseverance. Kids often have the notion that only the smartest people succeed. The fact is that many successful people are not brilliant, but they are always persistent. You've heard the old saying "Genius is 1 percent inspiration and 99 percent perspiration." Teach it to your children. Help them learn to act on it. Teach your children that many people succeed simply by refusing to give up. Setbacks are only stepping-stones to victory. Listen to your kid's dreams and then help him reach them step by persistent step. Stories of persistent athletes, statesmen, inventors, and others abound. Ask your local librarian to help you find some to read with your children. Inspire and then practice.

5. Teach your children that impatience and impulsiveness can have very real consequences. Younger children can lose things, get hurt, or lose a prize because they didn't want to wait. Impulsivity can cause older children to lose friends, ruin a school project, lose a game, or get sucked into using drugs or doing sex. Pair the consequences with the impatience or patience so your children get the idea clearly. Use plenty of positive examples, not just negative ones. "You waited patiently for me to finish practicing the piano with your sister; now we can play ball together." Encourage older children and adolescents not to make impulsive decisions that they may regret in the future. It takes patience and perseverance to find the right friends and to develop relationships. Impatience can have disastrous consequences, such as babies out of wedlock, hangovers, and crippling car accidents.

6. When a task seems overwhelming, help your child over the difficult spot. There are little things you can do to encourage a discouraged and frustrated child. Go over to the child, ask about the difficulty, and then try to make one suggestion to help her get going again. If that doesn't do the trick, work with her on the next step. Maybe two hands are needed to hold the parts together for gluing or maybe she doesn't know how to find the information she wants in the encyclopedia. Expressing that you understand how difficult it is will sometimes encourage the child to go on.

Help her make smaller goals that will add up to finishing the project. Make a goal that can be finished soon. Then help her decide on the next step. She is more likely to keep on when she knows what to do next. Make a game out of finishing the project, if it can be completed in a few steps.

If your child gets tired of working before he finishes his household chores and wants to quit, point out something pleasant to do when he is finished. Help him finish. "There were a lot of dishes today. I'll help you dry the last few; then you can play ball with Mike."

TROUBLE WITH PATIENCE AND PERSISTENCE?

Some children, like Danny, do have a lot of trouble with patience and persistence. Built into their temperament are high levels of impulsivity and persistence. When they want something, they want it right now—not later. And it is very hard to distract them from what they want. These kids are often called stubborn because they persist in what they are doing despite other people's attempts to distract them. Parents like this combination of traits when their child plays alone for long periods of time or his older sister cannot be distracted from finishing her homework. However, when the same child insists on wearing a certain outfit or going on a certain outing the parents don't like, that same persistence can be viewed negatively. It is, however, just a manifestation of the same temperament trait of persistence. The child is really being very consistent.

Danny is one of those kids labeled "stubborn and strong-willed" (interpret high level of persistence). He showed his true colors in the hospital nursery. And he has continued to show them. However, high persistence has a very positive side, not always noticed by parents. Danny showed it one day when he was the Bible boy at a wedding.

Blue-eyed and blond, Danny looked adorable in his tuxedo. He marched down the aisle at the wedding proudly carrying the Bible to the minister and turned around to put his feet on the X at the place where he was supposed to stand.

The bride came down the aisle, and the ceremony began. Soon Danny started swinging his arms back and forth. (This shows high distractibility.) He looked at the members of the bridal party, then at the audience, and continued swinging his arms and twisting from side to side. No matter how much he moved, however, one foot was always on the X. He had been told to stay on the X—and he did.

Soon he felt hot and began to rub his forehead. The warmer Danny got, the more he rubbed. His ears and cheeks turned bright red. Soon silent tears trickled down his face. He was obviously miserable, but he never left the X on the floor where he had been told to stand. Sensing how wretched he felt, several people in the audience, beckoned for him to come down, but he stayed on that X. Even when his daddy motioned for him to come down, Danny remained on the X. He was going to do his duty no matter what happened (high persistence). After a while his daddy went to the platform, gently picked him up, and carried him out of the auditorium, where he could cool off. At the reception, minus the hot tuxedo jacket, Danny was again charming and engaging.

His parents told me that from birth Danny had shown an unyielding determination and temper. His parents soon realized that Danny had very strong ideas about what he wanted, and patience was not part of his makeup. Once he decided he wanted something, nothing could distract him, and temper outbursts occurred many times a day. They had worked very hard to help him control his temper and be more patient. Improvement was slow, but they could see progress.

Yet he could be the most charming child anyone ever met. His wonderful engaging smile could win the heart of anyone as he flirted coquettishly. Frequently he'd throw his arms around his mother's neck and whisper, "I love you."

At the wedding Danny had shown a true-gold quality—he would stick it out, no matter what. He would do his duty even though he felt miserable. Many children would have given up. Not Danny. He did his job even though it was hard—he kept his foot on the X.

If you have a stubborn, highly persistent child, remember Danny and the good side—stick-to-it-ive-ness. Your child has an inborn trait that will help him conquer difficulties that other people buckle under. He can be a strong leader who persists through the tough times. But he will need your guidance to learn when he needs to yield his persistence and adapt.

Danny also showed a very high activity level—swinging his arms, turning around on the X, wiggling and jiggling. His high activity level and impulsivity have a downside and an upside, too. He is intense. He moves fast and does things very quickly. He is constantly on hyper alert. He notices everything going on around him. He's like a crouched tiger with one foot on base waiting to steal the next one. He's an aggressive soccer player. He's quick to tell you he loves you and to compliment his mom on the good food. That's the upside.

The downside is that all that activity and impulsiveness can be hard to live with, especially if the rest of the family is more laid back. Patience is hard to come by. Deliberateness almost unknown. Planning and organization. What's that? His room resembles the aftermath of a hurricane. Some people would call Danny "difficult" because of his particular combination of temperament traits. How can a family live with such an intense, highly active child? Remember, there's an upside and a downside. To deal with the downside, consider the following suggestions:

1. Keep eating, sleeping, and exercise routines the same. Regularity is very important.

2. Prepare your child ahead of time for changes or situations that

may be troubling. Security is very important. This child needs to know what is going to happen. No surprises!

3. Establish a few well-chosen rules and stick to these. Be patient, persistent, calm, and firm about these rules.

4. Limit activities that overly excite (such as scary TV programs or large groups of people or new situations).

5. Be happy with very small steps—don't expect enormous progress.

6. Demonstrate plenty of love. Be sure your child *feels* loved.

7. Look for strengths and positive qualities and encourage these. Don't let this child get the idea that he is a disappointment to you. This may become a self-fulfilling prophecy that is very hard to overcome.

8. Save the battles for the really important issues.

9. Give yourself a break. Get away, do something for yourself.

10. Pray for patience and understanding. Do not give up! This child has enormous potential.

FAMILY ACTIVITIES

Try some new family activities in which everyone is learning together. Or do an activity that is new to your children. Children do not learn patience and persistence alone. These must be family activities. The focus should be on having fun while learning patience and persistence, and experiencing the rewards of persistence. Chose activities that will work for your family or make up your own.

1. **Learn to make a kite** and fly it.

2. **Put together a 2,000-piece jigsaw puzzle** or one of those that are only one color.

3. **Make a Christmas decoration** for neighbors or members of your extended family.

4. **Make and decorate Christmas cookies** for all your aunts and uncles and cousins or for each child's class.

5. **Learn to do counted cross-stitch.** Simple patterns are available. It's easier than crocheting or knitting. You can't lose a stitch, and the cloth is always there when you want to pick it up again. Great concentration developer.

6. **Learn to identify the songs of 10 most common songbirds** of your area.

7. **Learn to identify all the countries of Africa.** Learn something about each country, like its geographical terrain, or the most important products, or something interesting about its people or history. Maybe correspond with someone who lives in one of the countries.

8. **Learn to play hopscotch.**

9. **Learn to jump rope.** Older children can learn complicated maneuvers and jumps.

10. **Learn to skateboard.**

11. **Learn to in-line skate** as a family. No excuses, Mom or Dad. Everyone included.

12. **Memorize a classic hymn.** Learn about when and why it was written. Learn all the verses. Learn what they mean.

13. **Learn some basic tumbling moves,** such as rollovers and standing on your head.

14. **Memorize a new Bible verse** every week until you have learned a complete chapter. Start with an easy and short chapter, such as Psalm 23.

15. **Make a quilt together.** The split-rail pattern is an easy one that children can do. It involves only cutting and machine sewing. Lap size is manageable and can be finished in a reasonable time. Or make a quilt with 12-inch squares of plain muslin. Each family member makes some squares, drawing designs with permanent markers. An older child can sew the squares together. Each square could picture a family vacation or an important event for a family member.

16. **Make a simple woodworking project together.**

17. **Learn to read a simple recipe and make it.** Instant reward—something good to eat.

18. **Plant a small garden.** Nothing develops patience like waiting for plants to sprout and grow. A container garden on the patio will do just as well as a large garden.

19. **Commit to keeping a section of highway clean of trash.** Maybe you will even get your family name on a marker beside the road.

20. **Make a model together**—airplane, car, dollhouse, etc.

QUOTABLE WISDOM

"Genius is 10 percent inspiration and 99 percent perspiration."
—*Thomas Edison*
"You may have lost the inning, but you can still win the game."
"Patience with others' impatience is perfect power."
"If there is a lid that does not fit there is a lid that does."
—*Japanese proverb*
"Patience will pierce even a rock."
—*Japanese proverb*
"There is good in every delay."
—*Moroccan proverb*
"Hold on to the dog's tail until you have crossed the river."
—*Arabic proverb*
"The journey of a thousand miles starts with a single step."
—*Chinese proverb*
"The longest day will have an end."
"A tree often transplanted is never loaded with fruit."
—*Italian proverb*
"The greatest accomplishment is not in falling but in rising again after you fall."
—*Vince Lombardi*
"Patience opens all doors."

NATURE TRAILS TO PATIENCE AND PERSEVERANCE

Nature rarely seems to be in a hurry. Challenge your kids to amass evidence that the natural world displays enormous quantities of patience and perseverance. The testimony is overwhelming. For starters:

Water, ice, and wind: Water, ice, and wind are among earth's most powerful forces. Sometimes they display their might suddenly with hurricanes, tornadoes, and tidal waves. Other times their actions are very, very slow. Drip by drip stalagmites are built over hundreds of years. Little by little rocks crumble and eventually become soil. Season after season water and ice dig a canyon. Glaciers move inch by inch and change the face of the earth. No hurry. Just relentless small actions.

Oysters: Deep in the ocean the oyster accidentally admits an irritating grain of sand and eventually covers it with pearl, a layer at a time, until it becomes a sought-after jewel glistening with rainbows of color. Patience and perseverance can make any setback into something to be proud of.

Seeds and plants: A young plant works its way around a rock and emerges in the light. A tree root splits asphalt and cement. Seeds from the tombs of the pharaohs of ancient Egypt sprout, their life intact after centuries. Persistence can win against great odds.

EVERYDAY TRAILS TO PATIENCE AND PERSISTENCE

Using your own child's experiences for learning provides the best learning, but stories about other children can be useful too.

Early Childhood: Block City

Andre is playing with blocks. He has worked very hard to make a big project, bigger than any he's ever made. His brother Luis rushes into the room where Andre is playing, trips over a rug, and falls into the block city Andre has built. The whole thing comes crashing down. Andre is heartbroken. He was so proud of his block city and wanted to show it to Dad when he came home. What should Andre do? Will it help to get mad at his brother? Was it an accident or was it on purpose? Should he start rebuilding the block city? What should Luis do?

Late Childhood: The Art Project

Alexis is working on an art project that requires painting a picture of a barn on a board. The project is due the next day, and Alexis is working furiously to finish on time. The teacher will lower her grade if the project is turned in late. She is concentrating hard on her painting when her baby brother, David, comes toddling into the room and bumps into a bottle of paint. The paint runs all over Alexis' painting, ruining it. Alexis lets out a long wail and wants to strangle her baby brother, but of course she doesn't. What can she do? How can she finish the art project on time? How can Alexis survive this test of her patience and perseverance?

Adolescence: The Play

Brett auditioned for a part in the annual high school play. He had always wanted to try out acting and was thrilled when chosen for the part. It wasn't a lead part, but it was a good start for a beginner. He started immediately to learn his lines. But no matter how much he practiced the lines, or how many times he said them, he couldn't seem to remember every word. The director was very strict about learning lines perfectly and reprimanded him at the last rehearsal because he stumbled two different times. Brett feels very disappointed and discouraged. *Maybe I'm not cut out to be an actor. Maybe I'm not smart enough. Everyone else seems to know their lines. Why can't I remember mine?* What should Brett do with his frustration and discouragement? Should he quit the play and give up acting? How will he feel if he quits? How will he feel if he persists?

KEYS TO PATIENCE AND PERSEVERANCE

1. Gradually teach young children how to wait for something they want.

2. Engage your children in activities that cannot be finished immediately.

3. Help children learn how to deal with frustrations.

4. Teach your children that success and perseverance are closely related.

5. Teach your children that impatience and impulsiveness can have very real consequences.

6. When a task seems overwhelming, help your child over the difficult spot.

CHAPTER 18

Peace and Humility

But the meek . . . shall delight themselves in the abundance of peace. Ps. 37:11, NKJV.

All the world is looking for peace—at least that's what they say. It seems an illusive dream. When every group is fighting for their rights, peace will be a long time coming. I hear young parents moaning, "Oh, just for a few minutes of peace and quiet!" No one quarreling. No one shouting. Someone saying, "It's OK. I forgive you."

The world is full of people whose actions shout "ME, ME, ME! I want the biggest piece, the most expensive car, the biggest home, the classiest clothes, the most powerful job, the best-looking wife and kids. I want everyone to look up to me. I want to be important. ME, ME, ME!"

But peace begins with humility, a word most people don't want to hear these days. It doesn't fit with the corporate image of power. But it *is* the image of the Galilean Teacher and Healer.

One of my favorite preachers, Benjamin Reaves, has said, "True humility is not the denial of our gifts, but the recognition of their source." I like that. Humility doesn't mean that I am a doormat for other people to walk on. It doesn't mean that I grovel in the mud of self-recrimination and criticism. I am a worthy person, created by God, with abilities I can use to help others. Humility doesn't mean I can't be a visionary leader or an accomplished artist. Humility doesn't mean I cannot be recognized as a world-class athlete or speaker or musician. It means that I recognize God as the source of my talents. I am not proud and boastful of my accomplishments.

Peace begins in our hearts and homes. As the Chinese proverb states: "If there is righteousness in the heart, there will be beauty in the character. If there be beauty in the character, there will be harmony in the home.

If there is harmony in the home, there will be order in the nation. When there is order in the nation, there will be peace in the world."

How can you help your children embrace a life of peace and humility when all around them *me* reigns supreme? What do peace and humility look like in real life?

WHEN I AM PEACEFUL AND HUMBLE . . .

I am cooperative. I try to avoid fighting, and resolve my problems peacefully.

I work hard to do my very best, but I don't brag about it.

I try to react calmly, instead of becoming agitated or angry over things that I don't like.

If someone is mean to me, I try to remember that it is really their problem. I try to be understanding.

I am a good team player. I work hard for my team.

I am learning how to negotiate in difficult situations.

> Calm
> Cooperative
> Modest
> Submissive
> Gentle
> Long-suffering
> Accommodating
> Courteous

If the other team wins, I congratulate them. I do not complain that the umpire was unfair and that's the reason they won. If someone on my team made a real goof that cost us the game, I quietly try to help the team member know that anyone could make a mistake and I still respect him and want him on our team. He'll do better next time.

When I win or receive a special honor, I accept the recognition in a spirit of humility. I give credit to others who helped me achieve. I am proud and happy about my accomplishments, but not boastful.

I try to be courteous and helpful to anyone I meet.

GOD'S VIEW OF PEACE AND HUMILITY

The human heart is full of selfishness and self-centeredness. *Self* is most important. Only God can give us a different perspective. We cannot change ourselves, but we can ask God to change our selfish hearts to loving ones. Love does not boast, is not proud or self-seeking. Love seeks the best for others. Humility helps us live in harmony with other people. It leads to true

> *Honor one another*
> *above yourselves.*
> *Rom. 12:10.*
>
> *Do you see a man wise in his*
> *own eyes? There is more hope*
> *for a fool than for him.*
> *Prov. 26:12, NKJV.*
>
> *Prides goes before destruction,*
> *a haughty spirit before a fall.*
> *Prov. 16:18.*
>
> *God is not the author of*
> *confusion, but of peace.*
> *1 Cor. 14:33, NKJV.*
>
> *You, Lord, give true peace.*
> *You give peace to those who*
> *depend on you. You give peace*
> *to those who trust you.*
> *Isa. 26:3, ICB.*

peace in our hearts and lives. It is God's way in a confused and self-centered world. God's way is possible only when we are connected to Him.

Bible People

Examples of peace and humility and their opposites abound in the Bible. The Bible calls Moses the meekest man who ever lived, but he wasn't always that way (Num. 12:3). Check out how he changed from proud to humble. When Samuel went looking for Saul to anoint him the first king of Israel, where did he find him (1 Sam. 9-10)? When Joseph and Daniel interpreted dreams for their kings, they were both very careful to give credit to God, not themselves, for the interpretations (Gen. 41:25-28; Dan. 2:27-28). David wanted to build a temple to honor God, but when God said, "No, your son will build my house," David submitted humbly to God's direction (1 Chron. 28). Jesus painted the perfect picture of peace and humility when He lived on earth. How many stories can you find from His life that illustrate peace and humility? Check out Abraham and Lot's relationship (Gen. 13:8, 9), Jacob and Esau when they met after many years (Gen. 33:4), the publican and the Pharisee in the Temple (Luke 18:10-13), the widow's mite (Mark 12:41-44), and Mary pouring perfume on Jesus' feet (John 12:1-7).

The Bible also contains examples of the opposite of peace and humility. For starters, look at Nebuchadnezzar (Dan. 4) and the disciples of Jesus quarreling over who was most important (Mark 10:35-45).

These Bible stories will provide many opportunities for discussion and really living the stories. Use the learning modes your children like the most—music, drama, writing, sculpture, fact-finding, scientific reasoning, personal insights.

HOW TO HELP CHILDREN DEVELOP PEACE AND HUMILITY

Peace and humility go together—humility leads to peace. They are the epitome of the Christian lifestyle, the absolute opposites of what we see around us—war, fighting, aggression, pride, selfishness, and "me first." According to the Iowa Index of Leading Cultural Indicators, the juvenile violent crime rate in the United States has increased 150 percent in the past 20 years, while the overall juvenile crime rate has increased only 5 percent. Peace and humility are not easy to teach because they are so different from what we see and hear every day, but we can nudge our children in that direction. God's grace can permeate our lives and spill over into our children's lives, bestowing peace and humility.

GENERAL GUIDELINES

1. Model peace and humility in your family relationships. Encourage family members to think of others' needs. Demonstrate peace and humility in your own life. Explain that meekness brings peace and happiness. Model connectedness to God, as in a branch connected to the Vine. When we are connected to God, every show is His show, every ability is His ability lent to us.

2. Encourage an atmosphere of sharing and cooperative play. Downplay possessions and possessiveness. Encourage sharing and cooperative games. Limit backyard fighting with strictly enforced limits. Consider a firm rule that anyone fighting must leave your yard. Teach children to recognize words and actions that incite violence, such as "I'm better than you are!" "Nerdy, nerdy!" "Fatty, fatty!" "Mama's baby," or whatever the current epithets are. When your children recognize the "fighting words," then they can learn to defuse their own emotions and walk away from the scene without getting into a fight. They can also learn to stay away from kids who incite fighting. (See chapter 9 on how to deal with peer pressure.)

3. Encourage a positive self-respect, but discourage bragging and boasting. Teach children not to praise themselves, but to let others compliment them for their achievements. Encourage children to be proud of their efforts and that they *did* their best, but not to brag that they *are* the best. Instead of giving out buttons that say "I'm the best," give ones that say "I did my best." Explain the mystery of humility—if you think you have it, you don't.

4. Help children experience forgiveness, both giving and receiving. Provide your own powerful, consistent example of forgiveness for every family member. Don't bring up past misdeeds. Concentrate on the present. Help children learn to forgive each other. Teach that forgiveness is not natural to humans—it comes from being connected to God. We want to hold a grudge forever—it feels so good to be mad at someone, to get even. But when we do that, we are cut off from God. Your children need to know the truth about forgiveness: An unforgiving spirit will destroy their happiness. Anger can make them physically sick and rob them of everything joyful in life.

5. Avoid excessive competition. Encourage respect for each person's strengths. Encourage competition with yourself, to excel your own past record, rather than competing against other people. Focus on each family member's strengths. The child who is not very athletic—a trait valued by peers—may be very kind and compassionate or artistic or musical or a leader. Respect and rejoice in each person's strengths. When a child moans, "I wish I could run like Nick," talk about the amount of practice it takes to run fast. Help your child look at his body build and then find a sport that would be a natural for him. Applaud Nick's running, but encourage your child to develop his own strengths through practice.

6. Encourage family members to help each other through difficulties. We're a team, and we're all in this together. If a team member needs special support, we'll all do what we can to help.

7. Encourage nonviolence and peace. Don't buy war toys or encourage violent games. Avoid entertainment that glorifies violence. Teach peaceful ways to resolve conflicts. Be a promoter of peace in your neighborhood.

8. Refuse to allow negative communications in your

home. Encourage positive communications. Design a family constitution, which everyone signs: I will speak kindly to all family members. "Word wars," name-calling, sarcasm, or belittling should be off limits. Build a vocabulary of uplifting words. Show children how to communicate their anger or annoyance in nonviolent ways.

9. Show children how to handle praise. Practice a smile and a gracious "Thank you," accompanied by the appropriate body language for your culture. Practice giving credit to other people who helped. Help children avoid downplaying their achievement or looking embarrassed. No statement is needed beyond "Thank you" and a smile.

10. Teach children negotiation and peaceful conflict resolution skills. At a neutral time, when everyone is feeling pretty much on top of things, begin to teach children how to go about resolving conflicts. Teach communication skills—how to listen, how to say clearly what happened without being provocative, how to negotiate back and forth. Have periodic practice sessions. If you have not mastered some of these skills yourself, many churches and communities offer adult education classes in communication skills or you can get a self-instruction book at your local bookstore. These are skills that can be learned.

11. Hold children responsible for their behavior. Provide undesirable consequences for hurting other people, physically or verbally. Make your position very clear and follow through with the consequences. Never condone violence or other negative behaviors. Be consistent with your position. Don't laugh at violent behavior one time and punish it the next.

12. Create a calm atmosphere in your home. Loud music with a throbbing beat and other noise create an underlying tension that affects kids and adults. Everyone becomes revved up and is more likely to explode rather than be calm. Be preventive. Play calming music. Avoid loud noises, confusion, and overly stimulating music. If a jackhammer pounds all day outside your apartment or the freeway noise overrides any sane thoughts, consider moving. Live as close to nature as possible. Blue sky, trees, grass, flowers, and birds singing have a calming effect on everyone.

13. Teach children how to deal with personal safety issues. Many children experience much anxiety because of bullies and other issues of personal safety. Develop a clear plan of action so your children will know exactly what to do in case their personal safety is threatened. Teach them how to recognize danger signs and what to do.

FOCUSED GUIDELINES

Often children can play peacefully with anyone except their siblings. They will be kind and compassionate to other children and adults, but not to each other. Their basic rivalry gets in the way. They'd rather die, they say, than be nice to their brother or sister. If you can minimize sibling rivalry, your children will gradually begin to live more peacefully together and learn to enjoy each other.

Sibling Rivalry

"Mommy, Mommy! Joel hit me!" cries Celeste. You think you have everyone quieted down when Joel screams, "Get Celeste out of here! She just spoiled my Legos truck!" It never seems to end. What can you do?

Sibling rivalry seems to be the worst between 6 and 9 years, although it usually appears earlier and may last a lot longer. Many family specialists assume it is a natural and normal part of growing up and will, in time, disappear or at least reduce to a livable level. To some extent that is true, but not entirely.

Have you ever gone home for a family reunion and suddenly felt like a little kid again? Your parents told you what to do, and you felt all the old sibling rivalries playing around the edges of everything that happened that weekend. How do you feel when your sister gets a promotion and you don't? Or your brother definitely earns more money than you do? Some families become embroiled in rivalries that never die.

Of course, as Christian parents we have loftier goals for our families. We want love and compassion to prevail at home, as well as outside. What can you do to help reduce sibling rivalry and let your children begin to experience the joy of love and kindness to family members?

The Philadelphia Child Guidance Center offers some excellent guidelines for reducing sibling rivalry in their book *Your Child's Emotional Health*. I have adapted some of their guidelines for this section.

1. Check the quarrel quotient of your home. In a general atmosphere of quarreling and rivalry, children are going to do the same. Do you speak to your children in a petulant voice most of the time?

Do you and your spouse quarrel a lot? Are you a very competitive family, with each person trying to outdo the others? Do you criticize your children and your spouse a lot? Can your children rarely do anything that satisfies you? If your answer is yes to most of the above questions, expect a lot of quarreling among your children. Modeling is the most powerful teaching tool in a family. It's time for a sit-down, we-have-a-problem, look at your family. Don't delay.

2. Try to give each child individual attention. Be sure that each of your older children has individual time with each parent every week, and that younger ones have it every day. Even 10 minutes alone with Dad will be very helpful for a young child. A lot of sibling rivalry is a bid for parental attention. Even small amounts of very focused, individual time with a child every day can make a big difference. Do what the child wants during "her time." Give your undivided, focused attention. You may be surprised at the results.

3. Give clear guidelines that promote respect for each family member. This includes each person's possessions, as well as his or her privileges and rights. Make these guidelines very clear. Discuss them as a family if your children are old enough to understand a discussion. If not, state very simple rules for young children. Write the rules on a chart to be posted on your family's bulletin board. Respect privacy and possessions. Older children have more privileges than younger ones. Mom and Dad have a right to privacy sometimes, too. No one should invade the space of another without permission. No borrowing without permission.

4. Never compare one child with another. Comparisons breed envy and rivalry. Respect each child for his or her individuality. Encourage individual activities and accomplishments. Justin and Jason don't have to both excel in football. Resist the impulse to dress two children alike. Cultivate their individual personalities and abilities. Other adults and children will compare your children. You can't control that, but don't add fuel to the rivalry fire by doing it yourself. You can downplay the comparisons of others by bringing up the good qualities of both children.

5. Give your children lots of good-times-together memories. Give your children lots of memories of good times together—playing games, flying kites, going to the beach, having a winter picnic in front of the fireplace, playing kickball with Dad or Mom.

Encourage your children to do little kindnesses for each other as surprises, maybe on the sly so the other child doesn't know who did it. The list of potential memories is endless. These positive memories will help your children learn to like each other. They will share a big basketful of memories that will bind them together in years to come.

6. As much as possible, allow your children to settle their own conflicts. Obviously you can't do this when Mr. Four is clobbering Miss Six Months. Mom, Dad, or Grandpa to the rescue! Unless you actually observed what happened, you are only guessing about who did what. You are playing referee without seeing the play. Some kids are really adept at starting a quarrel and appearing to be innocent. Watch out for their traps.

Children need practice in conflict resolution—that's real life. They also need lessons in conflict resolution skills.

For two children who are quarreling over what computer game to play or who gets the computer, you could simply say, "You have five minutes to settle what computer game you are going to play. If you haven't figured it out by then, peaceably, the computer will be turned off and neither of you can use it for one hour." Say this in a very neutral, but firm, voice and set your timer. Follow through. Eventually they will catch on, except for the kid whose rage at even having a brother is so all-consuming he will do anything to spoil his brother's fun, even if he spoils his own also. If he hasn't resolved this anger during the first three or four years after the sibling arrives, you would be wise to get skilled counseling for this child.

TROUBLE WITH PEACE AND HUMILITY?

Some children appear to have an overdose of humility, but are really just shy and withdrawn. They may or may not have an attitude of humility. In fact, the opposite may be true—they are constantly thinking of themselves and comparing themselves unfavorably with others. This child needs lots of confidence-building help and encouragement. Check out the ideas in chapter 7 for building self-respect and confidence.

Other children appear to have an overdose of confidence. They boast, brag, and seek attention all the time. We call them center-stage kids. They talk loudly and boisterously. For sure you know they are around! They seem the opposite of humility. However, many boasters are really very insecure.

Bragging is a cover-up for their deep-seated sense of insecurity and failure. They may not receive much affection at home. They may also need to learn better social skills and develop a healthier dose of confidence and self-respect.

Other attention-seekers are simply extreme extroverts who have never learned to moderate their natural behavior. Their parents were too lazy, uninvolved, or didn't know how to set and enforce clear limits so their behavior could be more socially acceptable.

Others may be kids whose parents have forced them into the center-stage role by constantly bragging about them and "showing off" their smart or talented kid. The kid has acquired an overinflated sense of self-importance—the opposite of humility—by expecting to be admired all the time.

Take your pick of reasons. Build confidence, if that is needed, by recognizing real achievements, positive attitudes, and proper actions. Give your child opportunities to work with others, as a leader and as a follower. Do role-playing to develop social skills. Teach very specific ways of responding to social situations. Give appropriate attention every day.

Give the braggart, overly extroverted kid quiet, calm, understanding help. Encourage him to look for good traits in other kids and learn to compliment them. Put her in situations in which she will have to be a follower and learn to get along with the group. Explain the negative effects of her behavior on other children. Always give appropriate recognition for real accomplishments. Give him quiet activities. Help him learn to take turns and wait his turn to talk. Show him how to compliment others on their achievements. Be sure she gets plenty of affection at home so she feels secure in your love.

FAMILY ACTIVITIES

Reporters: Play being reporters who observe peaceful or violent solutions to conflicts, humility, or pride. Jot down notes. At the evening meal, or another time set aside for this activity, give the reporters an opportunity to report what they have observed. Remember, reporters must be objective and report accurately what they have seen. You might have a reporters section on your bulletin board or refrigerator where the reports can be filed. Younger children can give oral reports. Discuss each report, the negative and positive aspects of this situation as reported. How would Jesus resolve this conflict?

Family All-star Team: Create a family all-star team by discovering each person's abilities. Post your all-star team on the refrigerator or bulletin board or other prominent place. Each family member must be on the team and his or her roles clearly identified: Organizer (management skills), reporter (observation skills), cheerleader (enthusiasm), etc. The first week send out scouts looking for talent for your all-star team. All family members become scouts for the team. When the scouts bring in their reports of talent discovered in other family members, brainstorm together to make up team positions for each talent discovered. Each family member could have several positions on the team. When the family needs someone with a particular ability to do something for the family team, check the all-star team list. Of course, new talent can be discovered anytime!

Pride in Your Culture: Leaf through magazines with your children, looking for ways your culture encourages selfish pride and arrogance. Discuss what you find. What does it means to be proud and arrogant? How does pride control their thinking? What is the difference between feeling justifiably proud of one's accomplishments and arrogantly, selfishly proud? Analyze TV commercials the same way.

QUOTABLE WISDOM

"The boughs that bear most hang lowest."
—*Garrick*

"Humility is the crown of manhood."
—*Medieval Arabic proverb*

"You're always in the wrong key when you start singing your own praises."

"Some people are like a toy balloon: a pinprick and there is nothing left of them."

"Where there is peace there is blessing."
—*Yiddish proverb*

"It takes two to quarrel. It also takes two to make up."
—*Traditional proverb*

"Falling hurts least those who fly low."
—*Chinese proverb*

"Lighthouses don't ring bells and fire cannon to call attention to their shining; they just shine on."

NATURE TRAILS TO PEACE AND HUMILITY

God will speak to your children through nature, His second book of instruction. Keep your eyes and ears open for nature trails to peace and humility.

Beaver: Beavers are peaceful animals, always ready to help other beavers. If the lake they have worked so hard to build is taken by another animal, they will not fight for their rights. They will just move and start building another dam to make another lake.

Doves: Doves are an easy bird to recognize. They are quite large and have a distinctive shape with a small head and large body. Often you can find doves (or pigeons) in the park of a large city. They are a common bird in the country and in suburban areas.

Doves are a symbol of peace and of the Holy Spirit. Perhaps the two are related—the Holy Spirit brings peace. In times past people kept pigeons (scientifically the same as doves) for their ability to carry messages. They were the long-distance communication system and often carried messages of great importance—victories or pleas for help during battles. Doves are considered gentle birds and in Bible times were used by the poor people for sacrifices when they could not afford a lamb. The people also considered them symbols of love because they often saw doves cooing to each other and courting.

Sheep: The Bible probably mentions sheep the most of any animal. They were a part of the religious services as a sacrifice for sin, symbolizing the coming sacrifice of Jesus. Sheep have a reputation as being calm, peaceful, and meek. They are not fighters. They will go where their leader takes them. They depend on the shepherd for food, shelter, and protection. Sheep are used in the Bible as a symbol for humility. Jesus was compared to a sheep (Isa. 53:7), and we are also described as sheep (verse 6).

EVERYDAY TRAILS TO PEACE AND HUMILITY

Everyday situations your child confronts are the best way to teach values. Use these little stories, or similar experiences, to open the door to your child's thinking.

Early Childhood: Mary's Drawing

The teacher asked the children in kindergarten to draw a picture of anything they wanted to draw. Eagerly the children began to draw. After everyone was done, the teacher walked around to look at all of the drawings. When she got to Mary's drawing, she said, "Good job. It looks good." Then all the other kids gathered around Mary and started to praise her. "You draw good. Yours is better than anyone's." "Will you show me how to draw a flower like yours?" Mary feels good that the teacher and the other kids like her drawing. What should Mary say to the other kids? How should she act? Should she share with another kid how to draw a flower like hers?

Late Childhood: Student of the Month

Every month Dyke Elementary School posts the picture and names of the Students of the Month in the halls of the school so everyone can see who has been honored. For the month of November one of the teachers told her class that most likely two students would be chosen for this honor: Henry and Mike. Both eagerly looked forward to seeing their pictures on the hall bulletin board. However, at the beginning of the month when the pictures were posted, Mike saw Henry's picture and name, but did not see his name. He went to Henry and asked him, "How come your name is up there? I am a better student than you." How should Henry respond to this accusation without being boastful or making Mike angry?

Adolescence: The Gym Scene

Sam and Jake work out at the same gym. They are not best friends, but they know each other really well. One evening Sam came to the gym to work out. Jake had been using the only available bench press for the past 45 minutes. Sam asked Jake if he had finished with the bench press because he wanted to use it and didn't have much time. Jake was already having a bad day. He got really angry and cursed Sam out. He was obviously ready to start a fight, but Sam quietly left and did not say a word. The next day when Jake arrived at the gym he saw Sam working out on the bench press. Sam looked upset with Jake and did not pay any attention to him. Jake immediately felt sorry for the way he had reacted toward Sam yesterday. What can he do to regain Sam's friendship? How can he make it up to Sam for the way he acted yesterday? How can he resolve this problem peacefully?

KEYS TO PEACE AND HUMILITY

1. Model peace and humility in your family relationships.

2. Encourage an atmosphere of sharing and cooperative play.

3. Encourage a positive self-respect, but discourage bragging and boasting.

4. Help children experience both giving and receiving forgiveness.

5. Avoid excessive competition. Encourage respect for each person's strengths.

6. Encourage family members to help each other through difficulties.

7. Encourage nonviolence and peace. Be sure children know how to deal with personal safety issues.

8. Refuse to allow negative communications in your home.

9. Show children how to handle praise.

10. Teach children negotiation and peaceful conflict resolution skills.

11. Create a calm atmosphere in your home.

CHAPTER 19

Loyalty and Commitment

I have set the Lord always before me;
because He is at my right hand
I shall not be moved. Ps. 16:8, NKJV.

M om! What shall I do? I'm in a real pickle!" Donita's crestfallen face spoke volumes about her distress.

"What's the problem, Dear?"

"Well, it's this way. You know the Valentine's banquet is next week. Last week Kevin asked me to go to the banquet with him, and I said I would. But today, Michael asked me! Michael is Mr. Popular and Mr. Jock all in one! I never dreamed he'd ask me for a date!"

"What did you tell him?" responded Mom.

"Well, you know, I really want to go with him, but I already said I'd go with Kevin. But I didn't want to say no. I'm afraid he'll never ask me again. So I said I'd think about it and let him know tomorrow. What shall I do?" wailed Donita.

Loyalty and commitment. Mr. Popular. Promises to keep. Kevin. Everyday choices about loyalty and commitment. Big choices, little choices. Important choices.

Loyalty and commitment have two sides. On the good side, they are very desirable and in very short supply. Marriages collapse all around us because of lack of commitment to see them through the tough times. Spouses gossip about the intimate problems of their marriage. Employees and bosses speak out of both sides of their mouths. Sometimes it's hard to tell what anyone means. Few people have the courage to display their loyalty to God.

On the bad side, loyalty can be misplaced. Read all about it in your newspaper. People lie to cover up for their boss, shoot innocent civilians, spy, kill or rob for the gang, use the loyalty excuse for almost anything questionable they have done.

To be the positive character trait we want for our children and ourselves, loyalty has to be paired with integrity. Commitment needs a worthy cause. That's why this is the last chapter in this book. Faith in God, responsibility, respect, self-control, honesty, and integrity all ensure that loyalty and commitment will not be misplaced. Real loyalty stands on the shoulders of love—God's love.

What do loyalty and commitment look like in real life?

WHEN I AM LOYAL . . .

I will stand by my family no matter what happens, because I love them. If someone teases or pesters my younger sister, I will defend her. We stick together.

Love
Dedication
Allegiance
Friendship
Devotion
Fidelity
Faithfulness
Courage

I keep my promises to my family and my friends. They can count on me. When I say I will do something for them, I mean it, even though I might have to sacrifice something else to keep my promise.

I will be loyal to what my parents have taught me about what is right and wrong because I love them.

I don't gossip about my friends, or anyone else. I want to guard their reputation. Gossip hurts people.

I love my country and what it stands for. I respect my country's flag. I do my part to be a good citizen. When I am older I will learn how the government is run and I will vote at elections. I will help defend my country, if needed.

I am careful to choose friends who will be loyal to me, because loyalty is two-way. I choose friends who believe in the values I do. Although I am friendly to everyone, I choose my close friends with great care.

I can keep a secret. That is one way I show my love and loyalty to friends and family.

I believe God wants me to have a happy home when I grow up. I know that it takes time to find the right person to marry. When I marry,

I will promise God to be loyal and committed to my spouse. I will always keep that promise. It is one of the most important promises I will ever make, so I will be very careful to ask God to help me find the right person to marry. I can be loyal to that person now by keeping myself a virgin until I marry.

I give my boss a full day's work. I do not shirk work or bad-mouth the boss or place I work. I do my very best.

I am enthusiastic and supportive of good causes. You can count on me for school spirit day and to support the class car wash to raise money for our class trip.

I will also keep my promise to be loyal to God. Sometimes that takes a lot of courage. He will help me when there is a tough decision to be made. Because God loves me and is loyal to me, my loyalty to God must come first.

GOD'S VIEW OF LOYALTY AND COMMITMENT

Loyalty and commitment are very important in God's scheme of things. Because of His great love for us, God is absolutely committed to our salvation. He will be loyal to us to the very end. He is always hopeful for our future. He expects us to be loyal to Him, too. He will keep His promises to us, and He expects us to keep our promises to Him.

God wants us to have this same kind of loyalty and commitment in our relationships with other people. Loyalty and commitment mean that we

Stand strong. Do not let anything change you.
1 Cor. 15:58, ICB.

I will go to the king, even though it is against the law. And if I die, I die.
Esther 4:16, ICB.

But the person who continues to be strong until the end will be saved.
Matt. 24:13, ICB.

God has joined the two people together. So no one should separate them.
Mark 10:9, ICB.

The Lord will keep his promises.
Ps. 145:13, ICB.

will not gossip about people or hurt them. We will stand by them through times of joy and sorrow. We will always be there to help, as God is always there to help us. God expects us to honor our promise to our marriage partner—to be loyal and committed until death.

God showed the ultimate love and loyalty when He sent His Son, Jesus, to die on the cross to save us. He could have abandoned this sinful world, but His love and loyalty would not let Him do that. Instead, God chose to love us. He wants us to be His friends forever.

Bible People

Loyalty and commitment sometimes demand great courage. Many Bible biographies demonstrate that kind of courage: Esther (Esther 3-8); David and Jonathan (1 Sam. 18:1-4; 19; 20; 23:16-18); Hosea (Hosea 1-3); Ruth (Ruth 1-4); Shadrach, Meshach, and Abednego in the fiery furnace (Dan. 3); Daniel in the lions' den (Dan. 6); Caleb and Joshua (Num. 13;14); Abraham and Isaac (Gen. 22); Noah building the ark (Gen. 6-8), and Joseph (Gen. 39). The Bible also records stories of people who were not loyal. For starters, look at Jonah (Jonah 1-4) and Absalom (2 Sam. 13-18).

> A friend loves at all times, and a brother is born for adversity.
> Prov. 17:17.
>
> There is a friend who sticks closer than a brother.
> Prov. 18:24.
>
> He who covers over an offense promotes love, but whoever repeats the matter separates close friends.
> Prov. 17:9.
>
> Greater love has no one than this, that one lay down his life for his friends.
> John 15:13, NIV.

Esther, Daniel, and Joseph are particular favorites of children and adolescents. They inspire to the same kind of loyalty and courage in the face of difficulty. Engrave them on your children's minds and hearts through art, music, drama, and stories until they become heroes to be admired all through life.

HOW TO HELP CHILDREN DEVELOP

LOYALTY AND COMMITMENT

In many ways loyalty is intangible, harder to pin down and explain than the other values we have discussed earlier. Yet it is the ultimate expression of our love for each other and for God. I believe loyalty must be experienced in order to be understood. The experiences that lead to an understanding of loyalty begin very young.

GENERAL GUIDELINES

1. Be sure your child feels loved by his or her family. Loyalty begins with the love attachment between mother and infant. The ability to love and be loved grows out of the early attachment between mother and infant. Trust is the outgrowth of that early love. (See chapter 10 for ideas on how to help children develop trust.) It provides the essential foundation for loyalty. If your child has difficulty with love, go back to the beginning and try to build the love bond between you and your child. Focus on love, cultivate love, express it in many ways, be sure your child *feels* loved by you and other family members. The more, the better. Warm love from an extended family encourages strong loyalty to the family.

2. Model and explain your own loyalty and commitment. Be a model of loyalty and commitment. Children learn what they see you live. But living it is not enough. Your children need to hear you say what you are doing and why. "I promised to help clean the church this morning. Yes, I'm tired and I'd like to stay home, but I made a commitment. I won't let them down." Your explanation makes your model much more effective. Can your children trust you? Do you do what you say you are going to do? Trust is indispensable to loyalty. No one can be loyal to someone they don't trust. Model trustworthiness. Don't criticize persons in authority, especially institutions you want your child to be loyal to. Criticism makes it very difficult for loyalty to flourish. Speak well of the minister, the teachers, your ex-spouse, and others for the sake of your children.

3. Build loyalty to your family. Emphasize that we are a family team, we work together for the good of all the family members. We support each other. We go to games and recitals to show our support and love. If a team member has an emergency, everyone gets off the bench to help. Develop family traditions, tell stories about your extended family and the traditions in your home as you were growing up. If extended family members live nearby, get together often so everyone feels part of a big family. Display pictures of family members, e-mail, phone, send gifts.

Don't ask children to take sides in family disputes, particularly in divorce. Your children deserve the right to be loyal to both parents. I know there are times when one parent doesn't seem to deserve that loyalty (especially in abuse situations), but the person is still your child's parent. When you down the parent, you down the child, especially if the child looks like the parent or is the same sex. Let your child make her own decisions.

4. Provide opportunities for your child to experience loyalty and commitment. Pets, especially dogs, are a wonderful way for a child to experience loyalty. Taking care of a pet is a serious commitment that develops loyalty. A dog will respond with intense loyalty to her owner. Children get to feel both sides of the loyalty issue. The support family members provide for each other—helping with chores, attending sporting events or concerts—gives children experience with both sides of loyalty. *Asking* children to obey, rather than commanding them to, provides an opportunity for them to display their loyalty to you and the family. Notice and comment about every evidence of loyalty you see in the family.

5. Provide opportunities to think about friendships and loyalties. Help your children think through questions like these: Whom should they be loyal to? When? Who is loyal to them?

Help your children learn how to choose friends. What are the most valuable qualities in friends? What kinds of friends do they want? What does it mean to be loyal to a friend?

Teach your children to be very cautious about friendships with people with serious character flaws. These friendships will tear them down and put at risk their loyalty to God, themselves, and their family. The old proverbs "Birds of a feather flock together" and "It takes only one bad apple to spoil the barrel" are still true. They will become like their friends. Help your children understand the difference between being friendly to help a person and becoming a "best friend." This is a crucial difference that children and adolescents need to understand.

Emphasize that loyalty to God comes before all other loyalties. Loyalty to principles comes before loyalty to someone who is doing something wrong.

Don't sacrifice right principles for a friendship. If your friend asks you to sacrifice your principles, eventually the friendship will drag you down to that same level. What if a friend asks your child to lie to protect him? What if a boyfriend says, "If you loved me, you would do it"? What is the difference between loyalty and "ratting" on a friend or acquaintance? What would a loyal friend really do in these circumstances? Probably try to get the person to admit the wrong and do something to change. The loyal friend has the person's ultimate good in mind, not just a temporary fix.

Emphasize that loyalty is unselfish. True loyalty never uses other people for selfish means or self-aggrandizement. Loyalty never steps on other people to climb up. It never uses someone as a doormat. Loyalty stands by through thick and thin.

6. Choose family commitments carefully. Be careful not to make commitments you cannot keep, as a family and as individuals. Most families today live overly committed lives with too many easily made promises that cannot be kept. Discuss commitments. Bring every new major commitment to family council. Check everyone's schedule. Teach your children some time management skills. Model how to handle commitments. What you commit to, follow through on as a family and individually.

7. Help your children understand what loyalty to God means. *Loyalty to God includes obedience to His commandments.* God's Word makes this very clear. Many times it isn't easy and demands great courage. God promises to provide the courage to obey His commandments, and He always keeps His promises.

Loyalty to God also includes using our talents to honor Him. If your child is musical or artistic, will she use this gift to honor God or self? With abilities come great responsibilities to honor God with these gifts that He has given. Your children need to understand that abilities are gifts from God. Using these abilities for God expresses their loyalty to Him.

Giving God His part of our money is also a test of our loyalty to Him. Begin teaching this principle very young, with your child's first money. If Grandpa and Grandma send $10 for a birthday gift, how much belongs to God? Teach your children what God's Word says about tithe and offerings.

8. Help your children sort out conflicting loyalties. Young children have a hard time understanding different roles, let alone conflicting loyalties. They think of only one role at a time. Three-year-old Caroline Kennedy was widely quoted when she said, "My daddy isn't president. He's my daddy." As they mature, the idea of more than one role and loyalty becomes easier to understand. But the situations with conflicting loyalties can be very difficult. Divorce. Friends. Right and wrong. Kindly, prayerfully, help your children sort these out. Encourage them to think and express their thoughts.

9. Help your children understand that true loyalty must be earned. Loyalty betrayed may not get a second chance. If you gossip about your best friend's private secret, you deserve what you get— rejection. Bribes and manipulations have no part in true loyalty. As Benjamin Franklin once said: "Promises may get you friends, but it's performance that keeps them." If you want someone to be loyal to you, you must show yourself trustworthy. Finding a person to really trust can be difficult. It is risky to give loyalty. If you betray that loyalty, you may not get a second chance. Betrayal hurts deeply. If you have been on the receiving end of betrayal, you know. Be alert for any personal experiences to help your children understand this principle.

10. Help your children cultivate positive self-respect and identity. What they think of themselves will powerfully influence their loyalties. Some kids think of themselves as a "gang member," and their primary loyalty is to the gang. Whom does your child identify with? Who does he think he is? A rebel? A nerd? A jock? A nobody? A child of God?

Once upon a time there was a boy who lived in a certain village in Africa. The boy's father was a king, but he died weeks before the boy was born. When the boy was old enough to understand, his mother explained to him that he was not just anybody. He was a child of a king. Every day she reminded him that he was a prince.

In school, while all the other boys were causing trouble, fighting and throwing things around and disregarding the teacher's instructions, this boy was obedient and obeyed all of the rules. One day one of the teachers asked him, "Why are you so different? You don't misbehave like the other boys."

The boy replied, "I am different because I am not like the other kids. I am special because my father was a king. I am a prince, and princes don't behave the way the other kids are behaving." His loyalty to his father's throne came from a knowledge of who he was.

TROUBLE WITH LOYALTY AND COMMITMENT?

Children from divorced families often have difficulty with loyalty and commitment. They have learned to avoid being loyal to either parent around the other parent. They have also learned not to trust. Their views of a safe and reliable world have been shattered forever. They have experienced deep feelings of rejection and a pervasive sense of loss. Who *can* be trusted? These feelings can follow them into adulthood and affect their own marriages and their relationship with God.

Divorce wasn't the way you planned your life and wasn't what you wanted, but here you are living with what can't be changed. Are your children doomed to have difficulty with loyalty and commitment all their lives? Of course not! You *can* do something to help them put the pieces of their shattered trust back together again.

Children need and deserve optimal parenting. This includes parents who have resolved their own psychological issues, have mature personalities, do not use the child to meet their own neurotic needs, see the child as a developing person, believe the adult is responsible for and nurtures the child, and see themselves as adults who do what is best for the child, even if it might be personally inconvenient. As you can see, most of these affect the child's development of trust. It pays big dividends in the end to be really serious about rebuilding trust.

First, if you sense that you still have many unresolved issues related to the divorce, that you are angry and vindictive, that you want to make your ex-spouse "pay" by avoiding any contact and making your children your "mail carriers," please get counseling for yourself. You deserve to get past these issues and begin to have a life. Above all, your children should not have to pay psychologically for your own unresolved issues.

Children are children. They need to feel that someone who can be trusted will take care of them. Even adolescents need this feeling. Many children worry that the custodial parent will disappear on them, too. You are the adult who cares for your children. They are not there to care for you. Do not make your children partners in your adult life. They should not be your confidant or be a listening ear for all your troubles. They will lap up the feeling of being "an adult" mommy talks to, but in the end it will threaten their normal development. Get yourself an adult friend who can be trusted to be your adviser and confidant. Let your children be children. That is what childhood is for—to be a child who is cared for by adults. Make sure you care for your children. Don't be so involved in your own issues, you forget their needs. This will go a long way toward rebuilding trust.

Answer your child's questions about the divorce honestly and openly. Tell the truth with kindness. Don't play the blame game. It never helps children get past their feelings of rejection and loss. If your children ask, assure them this was not a hasty decision. Explain what you did to try to save the marriage. Keep emphasizing that they are not responsible for the divorce. Be as specific as possible about what to expect—when they will see the noncustodial parent and relatives, where they will live, where they will go to school, etc.

Do your best to maintain as much stability as possible. Ideally, children would continue in the same school and home, but that is not always possible. If you must move, be sure the children take their favorite things with them. This provides continuity and a feeling of safety. Explain the move carefully ahead of time and try to make it as child-friendly as possible. Sometimes it helps to locate near extended family who can provide additional support for your children. Provide as much stability as possible at home—regular meals and bedtimes, clean clothes, a clean house, consistent discipline, help with homework, interest in the child's life.

Make every possible effort to be trustworthy. Keep your promises. Do what you say you will do. Be punctual when you pick up children from school and games. Be sure your children know they can count on you. Be punctual and responsible for visitation, if you are the noncustodial parent. Concentrate on your relationship with your children when they are visiting. To help your children rebuild trust, delay dating until your children's lives are stabilized. A succession of dates can be very disconcerting to children. Just when your child begins to feel comfortable around this new man, he disappears on her too. Your dating is also threatening to teenagers who are themselves dating. They can see themselves in competition with you. This does not help rebuild trust.

Introduce your children to God, the heavenly parent who never abandons or rejects. He will never do a disappearing act. He will always be there to comfort and be their Forever Friend. They can tell Him the secrets they don't dare tell anyone else. Children and adolescents can find great comfort in a growing relationship with Jesus and God. This relationship will go a long way toward rebuilding trust, and subsequently loyalty. They will learn that God can be depended on. He is always loyal and committed to their best interests. His love surrounds them always.

FAMILY ACTIVITIES

Family Spirit Day: Schools often have "School Spirit Day." Why not have a Family Spirit Day? Plan an exciting activity to do together as a family. The activity should take the family away from home. Make up something crazy for every family member to wear—like a decorated baseball cap. The kids will think up crazier and funnier things than you will. Let them do it. If other people ask about what you are wearing, let the children tell them about Family Spirit Day. Make it a family tradition.

Family History Photo Album: Work together as a family to assemble an Our Family History photo album. Start with a family tree. Your children may have to make some phone calls to get all the information needed, but that will give them an opportunity to talk with extended family. Grandparents can be great sources of information. They might even send some mementos or photos for the album. Some families have very strong traditions for occupations, names, religious background, and other aspects of life. This activity could be an extension of the family genealogy activity suggested in chapter 11.

Church Search: Work together as a family to learn about your church. Find out about its history, traditions, and beliefs. Find out about early pioneers of the church. Is this church a family tradition, or is it a new church affiliation? Why did your family change churches? Find out how your church is organized administratively.

City Search: Work together as a family to learn about your city or town or county. Find out all you can about the founding of the city. What are its traditions? What festivals are celebrated every year? Are there different ethnic neighborhoods? If you live in a large city such as Chicago, New York, or London, you might have to confine your search to a specific section of the city. Do something as a family to improve your part of the city—pick up trash, erase graffiti, plant flowers or trees. Help your children develop pride and commitment to their city.

QUOTABLE WISDOM

"Loyalty is the holiest good in the human heart."
—*Latin*
"Loyalty is the highest compliment."

"I will speak ill of no man, and speak all the good I know of everybody."
　　　—Ben Franklin
"One man with courage is a majority."
　　　—Andrew Jackson
"Memory is a falcon that cannot be held; loyalty is a sparrow's nest that cannot be repaired."
　　　—Turkish proverb
"Loyalty is worth more than money."
"Faithfulness is a sister of love."
"You cannot run with the hare and hunt with the hounds."
"Rats desert a sinking ship."
"God always gives His best to those who leave the choice with Him."
"God does not ask about our ability or our inability, but about our commitment."
"If you don't live it, you don't believe it."

NATURE TRAILS TO LOYALTY AND COMMITMENT

Loyalty and commitment are often seen in the natural world. While animals do not think in the way humans do, they do demonstrate some of these humanlike characteristics in their behavior. Help your children look for loyalty and commitment in nature.

Dogs: Pet dogs are known for their loyalty to their masters. They will serve them and protect them from any threat of harm. They eagerly greet them after an absence. They will sleep beside their owner's chair or even on the bed, if allowed. If their owner is sad, the dog will nudge up close and try to cheer him up. Dogs have been known to travel great distances to find their owners after they moved to another part of the country. Loyalty is one of the reasons dogs are such popular pets.

Beavers: The hardworking beaver is faithful to his or her mate for life. They will care for each other, rear a family each year, and always be faithful to each other. There are many other creatures in the natural world that mate for life.

Hornbill: The hornbill birds make nests in hollow trees in which to lay their eggs. When the pair is ready to incubate the eggs, the male hornbill closes the entrance to the nest to protect the female and her eggs. He leaves a small hole in the entrance to feed his mate. He works faithfully to feed her. Back and forth he goes, many times a day, bringing food to the nesting mother hornbill. The job is hard. By the time the babies hatch he is almost a skeleton, but he has lived his commitment to his family.

EVERYDAY TRAILS TO LOYALTY AND COMMITMENT

Everyday experiences of your children are the best way to teach loyalty and commitment. Struggle through their experiences with them, let them think about what to do, and support them as they discover what loyalty and commitment demand. Use the following vignettes as additional learning experiences.

EARLY CHILDHOOD: The Snowball Battle

Pablo and Magla are the parents of two little boys. Pablito is 3 years old, and Jorgito is 2. On Sunday afternoons they usually do activities with the entire family. On one particular Sunday there was much snow, a perfect day for snow activities. So the family dressed warmly and drove to the dunes by Lake Michigan. The boys were so excited they couldn't wait to get to the dunes. When they arrived, they decided to slide down the slopes.

Soon the boys decided it was time for a good snowball fight. Pablito decided to team up with Daddy, figuring that Daddy was bigger and could throw faster, while Jorgito decided he would team up with Mommy. Halfway through the battle, Pablito sensed that they were losing, so he yelled out to Mommy asking if he could come on her side.

Immediately Mommy stopped and said to him, "Pablito, you chose in the beginning to team up with your father, so you need to be loyal to your decision and to your team, no matter what happens. You see, Daddy fought hard because he was loyal to your team." Pablito fussed and fumed and still wanted to change teams. He didn't fight hard and just stood there pouting part of the time. What do you think happened in the end? Was it fair for Mommy to say Pablito couldn't change teams? What choices did Pablito have?

Late Childhood: The New School

Tom was in the fifth grade. He didn't know anyone at his new school, and he wanted badly to have friends. The first week of school was over, and he still didn't feel that he fit in. The following Monday during recess Bobby, a popular boy in the class, approached him and began to talk to him. Tom couldn't believe that Bobby was actually talking to him, but he was. By the time recess was finished, the two boys agreed to meet again in the lunchroom.

Later that day, at lunch, when the two sat down to eat, Bobby showed Tom a pack of cigarettes he had hidden in his pocket. Bobby invited Tom to smoke a few with him after school at a secret spot. Tom's heart sank. He knew that his parents had always told him that smoking was wrong, yet he desperately wanted to fit in. What would Bobby say if he said no to him? Would he still talk to him?

Stop the story here and ask your children: What do you think will happen next? What would you do if you were Tom? What choices does Tom have just now? What might be the result of each of these choices? *After discussing these questions, continue with the rest of the story.*

After several minutes of wrestling with the possible choices, he said to Bobby, "I'm sorry. I don't smoke." Bobby, seemingly taken by surprise, didn't know what to say. Finally he replied, "That's OK, Tom. I don't smoke either. The reason I asked you was because everyone wondered if you would smoke just to fit in."

"Really?" said Tom, very surprised. "Yeah, I still want to be friends."

"Me, too," said Bobby. Tom was glad that he remained loyal to his belief and what he was taught by his parents.

What if the story had had a different ending? How else might it have ended? Does loyalty have a price?

Adolescence: Marcia's Favorite Team

Marcia loved to support her school's volleyball team. She always did. Whenever her team played, Marcia could always be seen and heard loudly and enthusiastically cheering them on. She even made posters and wrote verses in praise of her favorite team and players.

Then one day Marcia's cousin, Anita, came to live at their home. Anita was really good in volleyball, so she began to teach Marcia some of her skills. They started to become really close because of all the time they were together.

There was a small problem, though. Anita went to a rival school, where she also played volleyball. When the championships came around, Marcia started to have difficulty remaining a loyal fan of her school's team. She was caught up in the middle of a decision between her school team and Anita's school team because of her relationship with Anita. It was really a dilemma for her, and she didn't quite know what to do. *Stop here and discuss what Marcia might do.* Should she remain loyal to her school's team? What about her friendship with Anita? How might that affect her loyalty? What if the two teams were in the same league?

Continue the story. Finally, Anita helped her by reminding Marcia that she was loyal to her school's team before her friendship with her. She should continue to be loyal to her school's team because it was her favorite team. She told Marcia that she didn't mind at all because she understood.

What if this story had had a different ending? What if Anita had threatened to not be her friend if she wasn't loyal to her team? Is it possible to be loyal to two teams, for different reasons? Does loyalty demand single-mindedness?

KEYS TO LOYALTY AND COMMITMENT

1. Be sure your child feels loved by his or her family.

2. Model and explain your own loyalty and commitment.

3. Build loyalty to your family.

4. Provide opportunities for your children to experience loyalty and commitment.

5. Provide opportunities to think about friendships and loyalties.

6. Choose family and individual commitments carefully.

7. Help your children understand what loyalty to God means.

8. Help your children sort out conflicting loyalties.

9. Help your children understand that true loyalty must be earned.

10. Help each child cultivate positive self-respect and identity.